Odoo 10 Development Essentials

Fast-track your development skills to build powerful Odoo 10 business applications

Daniel Reis

BIRMINGHAM - MUMBAI

Odoo 10 Development Essentials

Copyright © 2016 Packt Publishing

All rights reserved. No part of this book may be reproduced, stored in a retrieval system, or transmitted in any form or by any means, without the prior written permission of the publisher, except in the case of brief quotations embedded in critical articles or reviews.

Every effort has been made in the preparation of this book to ensure the accuracy of the information presented. However, the information contained in this book is sold without warranty, either express or implied. Neither the author, nor Packt Publishing, and its dealers and distributors will be held liable for any damages caused or alleged to be caused directly or indirectly by this book.

Packt Publishing has endeavored to provide trademark information about all of the companies and products mentioned in this book by the appropriate use of capitals. However, Packt Publishing cannot guarantee the accuracy of this information.

First published: November 2016

Production reference: 1241116

Published by Packt Publishing Ltd.
Livery Place
35 Livery Street
Birmingham
B3 2PB, UK.
ISBN 978-1-78588-488-7

www.packtpub.com

Credits

Author

Daniel Reis

Reviewers

Ray Carnes
Olivier Dony

Commissioning Editor

Veena Pagare

Acquisition Editors

Prachi Bisht
Subho Gupta

Content Development Editor

Mehvash Fatima

Technical Editors

Prashant Chaudhari
Bhagyashree Rai
Khushbu Sutar

Copy Editor

Tom Jacob

Project Coordinator

Shweta H Birwatkar

Proofreader

Safis Editing

Indexer

Pratik Shirodkar

Graphics

Kirk D'Penha

Production Coordinator

Deepika Naik

Foreword

When I joined Odoo in 2009, my first task was to deliver training courses for consultants, including technical sessions for new Odoo developers. Daniel's *Odoo 10 Development Essentials* is the realization of my wishes from these sessions; the companion book I wish I could have given to the participants, to kick-start their first contact with Odoo.

Chapter after chapter, he walks you through the creation of your first Odoo app, following best practices at every step. Starting with a solid development environment, you'll soon feel comfortable with your Odoo system, and quickly shape up your typical app. From the model groundwork upwards, you'll learn about each layer, including the latest website features and the integration mechanisms for third-party systems. Most importantly, your journey will include quick references for most important API areas, and before you know it, you will grasp the fundamental design properties of Odoo—minimalism, modularity, extensibility, and scalability. Understanding this will be an invaluable asset for any task you set out to accomplish, and is what sets apart good Odoo developers.

This updated edition is a great reference for more experienced developers as well, as it focuses on Odoo 9 and 10, introducing a smarter framework, modern conventions and tools, and the removal of the first Odoo API.

The book also includes a wealth of *pro* tips, acquired through years of experience, that should make a seasoned Odoo developer out of you in no time, without the extra gray hair!

Last but not least, Daniel has a natural talent for this, so I promise you'll truly enjoy the *Odoo 10 Development Essentials* ride!

-Olivier Dony

R&D Engineer, Odoo Belgium

About the Author

Daniel Reis has been an active contributor in the Odoo community and a speaker at Odoo and other tech events. He is a member of the Board at the Odoo Community Association (OCA) and partner and advisor at Odoo integrator ThinkOpen Solutions. Daniel has a degree in Applied Mathematics, a Master in Business Administration, IT consultancy background, and he currently works as applications manager at Securitas Portugal.

About the Reviewer

Olivier Dony is a Belgian Civil Engineer graduated from UCL in 2003. Specialized in network engineering, databases, and information security, he has developed a passion for open source software over the 10+ years he has spent in the IT industry.

A self-described caffeine-based lifeform, he has found an ideal environment at Odoo Belgium since 2009, where he wears many hats: Community Manager, Security Officer, Research and Development Engineer, to name a few. His first mission at Odoo was to deliver training courses to consultants and developers, as he loves to learn new things every day and to disseminate the knowledge.

Away from the keyboard, he is the proud dad of two adorable kids, an enthusiastic reader of all genres, and he nurtures a passion for astrophysics, vintage space technology, and of course, coffee!

www.PacktPub.com

For support files and downloads related to your book, please visit www.PacktPub.com.

Did you know that Packt offers eBook versions of every book published, with PDF and ePub files available? You can upgrade to the eBook version at www.PacktPub.com and as a print book customer, you are entitled to a discount on the eBook copy. Get in touch with us at service@packtpub.com for more details.

At www.PacktPub.com, you can also read a collection of free technical articles, sign up for a range of free newsletters and receive exclusive discounts and offers on Packt books and eBooks.

https://www.packtpub.com/mapt

Get the most in-demand software skills with Mapt. Mapt gives you full access to all Packt books and video courses, as well as industry-leading tools to help you plan your personal development and advance your career.

Why subscribe?

- Fully searchable across every book published by Packt
- Copy and paste, print, and bookmark content
- On demand and accessible via a web browser

Table of Contents

Preface

Odoo is a powerful open source platform for business applications. On top of it, a suite of closely integrated applications was built, covering all business areas from CRM and sales to stocks and accounting. Odoo has a dynamic and growing community around it, constantly adding features, connectors, and additional business apps.

Odoo 10 Development Essentials provides a step-by-step guide to Odoo development, allowing readers to quickly climb the learning curve and become productive in the Odoo application platform.

The first two chapters aim to get the reader comfortable with Odoo, learn the basic techniques to set up a development environment, and get familiar with the module development approach and workflow.

Each of the following chapters explains in detail the key development topics needed for Odoo addon module development, such as inheritance and extensions, data files, models, views, business logic, and so on.

Finally, the last chapter explains what to consider when deploying your Odoo instance for production use.

What this book covers

`Chapter 1`, *Getting Started with Odoo Development*, starts with the setup of a development environment, installing Odoo from source, and learning how to manage Odoo server instances.

`Chapter 2`, *Building Your First Odoo Application*, guides us through the creation of our first Odoo module, covering all the different layers involved: models, views, and business logic.

`Chapter 3`, *Inheritance – Extending Existing Applications*, explains the available inheritance mechanisms and how to use them to create extension modules that add or modify features on other existing modules.

`Chapter 4`, *Module Data*, covers the most commonly used Odoo data file formats (XML and CSV), the external identifier concept, and how to use data files in modules and data import/export.

`Chapter 5`, *Models – Structuring Application Data*, discusses the Model layer in detail, with the types of models and fields available, including relational and computed fields.

`Chapter 6`, *Views – Designing the User Interface*, covers the View layer, explaining in detail the several types of views and all the elements that can be used to create dynamic and intuitive user interfaces.

`Chapter 7`, *ORM Application Logic – Supporting Business Processes*, introduces programming business logic on the server side, explores the ORM concepts and features, and also explains how to use wizards for more sophisticated user interaction.

`Chapter 8`, *Writing Tests and Debugging Code*, discusses how to add automated tests to addon modules, and techniques to debug module business logic.

`Chapter 9`, *QWeb and Kanban Views*, goes over the Odoo QWeb templates, using it to create rich Kanban boards.

`Chapter 10`, *Creating QWeb Reports*, discusses using the QWeb based report engine, and everything needed to generate printer-friendly PDF reports.

`Chapter 11`, *Creating Website Frontend Features*, introduces Odoo website development, including web controller implementations and using QWeb templates to build frontend web pages.

`Chapter 12`, *External API – Integrating with Other Systems*, explains how to use Odoo server logic from external applications, and introduces a popular client programming library that can also be used as a command-line client.

`Chapter 13`, *Deployment Checklist – Going Live*, shows us how to prepare a server for production prime time, explaining what configuration should be taken care of and how to configure an Nginx reverse proxy for improved security and scalability.

What you need for this book

We will install our Odoo server on an Ubuntu or Debian system, but we expect you to use your operation system and programming tools of choice, be it Windows, Mac, or other.

We will provide some guidance on setting up a virtual machine with Ubuntu Server. You should choose a virtualization software to use, such as VirtualBox or VMWare Player; both are available for free. If you are using a Ubuntu or Debian workstation, no virtual machine will be needed.

As you already figured, our Odoo installation will be using Linux, so we will inevitably use the command line. However you should be able to follow the instructions given, even if not familiar with it.

A basic knowledge of the Python programming language is expected. If you're not comfortable with it, we advise you to follow a quick tutorial to get you started. We will also make use of XML, so it is desirable to be familiar with the markup syntax.

Who this book is for

This book is targeted at developers with experience developing business applications willing to quickly become productive with Odoo.

Readers are expected to have an understanding of MVC application design and knowledge of the Python programming language. Being familiar with web technologies, HTML, CSS, and JavaScript, will also be helpful.

Conventions

In this book, you will find a number of styles of text that distinguish between different kinds of information. Here are some examples of these styles, and an explanation of their meaning.

Code words in text, database table names, folder names, filenames, file extensions, pathnames, dummy URLs, user input, and Twitter handles are shown as follows: Code words in text are shown as follows: "To create a new database, use the `createdb` command."

A block of code is set as follows:

```
@api.multi
def do_toggle_done(self):
    for task in self:
        task.is_done = not task.is_done
    return True
```

When we wish to draw your attention to a particular part of a code block, the relevant lines or items are set in bold:

```
@api.multi
def do_toggle_done(self):
    for task in self:
        task.is_done = not task.is_done
    return True
```

Any command-line input or output is written as follows:

```
$ ~/odoo-dev/odoo/odoo-bin.py -d demo
```

New terms and **important words** are shown in bold. Words that you see on the screen, in menus or dialog boxes for example, appear in the text like this: "Upon login, you are presented with the **Apps** menu, displaying the available applications."

Warnings or important notes appear in a box like this.

Tips and tricks appear like this.

Reader feedback

Feedback from our readers is always welcome. Let us know what you think about this book-what you liked or disliked. Reader feedback is important for us as it helps us develop titles that you will really get the most out of. To send us general feedback, simply e-mail `feedback@packtpub.com`, and mention the book's title in the subject of your message. If there is a topic that you have expertise in and you are interested in either writing or contributing to a book, see our author guide at `www.packtpub.com/authors`.

Customer support

Now that you are the proud owner of a Packt book, we have a number of things to help you to get the most from your purchase.

Downloading the example code

You can download the example code files for this book from your account at `http://www.packtpub.com`. If you purchased this book elsewhere, you can visit `http://www.packtpub.com/support`and register to have the files e-mailed directly to you.

You can download the code files by following these steps:

1. Log in or register to our website using your e-mail address and password.
2. Hover the mouse pointer on the **SUPPORT** tab at the top.
3. Click on **Code Downloads & Errata**.
4. Enter the name of the book in the **Search** box.
5. Select the book for which you're looking to download the code files.
6. Choose from the drop-down menu where you purchased this book from.
7. Click on **Code Download**.

Once the file is downloaded, please make sure that you unzip or extract the folder using the latest version of:

- WinRAR / 7-Zip for Windows
- Zipeg / iZip / UnRarX for Mac
- 7-Zip / PeaZip for Linux

The code bundle for the book is also hosted on GitHub at `https://github.com/PacktPublishing/Odoo-10-Development-Essentials`. We also have other code bundles from our rich catalog of books and videos available at `https://github.com/PacktPublishing/`. Check them out!

Downloading the color images of this book

We also provide you with a PDF file that has color images of the screenshots/diagrams used in this book. The color images will help you better understand the changes in the output. You can download this file from `https://www.packtpub.com/sites/default/files/downloads/Odoo10DevelopmentEssentials_ColorImages.pdf`.

Errata

Although we have taken every care to ensure the accuracy of our content, mistakes do happen. If you find a mistake in one of our books-maybe a mistake in the text or the code-we would be grateful if you could report this to us. By doing so, you can save other readers from frustration and help us improve subsequent versions of this book. If you find any errata, please report them by visiting `http://www.packtpub.com/submit-errata`, selecting your book, clicking on the **Errata Submission Form** link, and entering the details of your errata. Once your errata are verified, your submission will be accepted and the errata will be uploaded to our website or added to any list of existing errata under the Errata section of that title.

To view the previously submitted errata, go to `https://www.packtpub.com/books/content/support`and enter the name of the book in the search field. The required information will appear under the **Errata** section.

Piracy

Piracy of copyrighted material on the Internet is an ongoing problem across all media. At Packt, we take the protection of our copyright and licenses very seriously. If you come across any illegal copies of our works in any form on the Internet, please provide us with the location address or website name immediately so that we can pursue a remedy.

Please contact us at `copyright@packtpub.com` with a link to the suspected pirated material.

We appreciate your help in protecting our authors and our ability to bring you valuable content.

Questions

If you have a problem with any aspect of this book, you can contact us at `questions@packtpub.com`, and we will do our best to address the problem.

1
Getting Started with Odoo Development

Before we dive into Odoo development, we need to set up our development environment and learn the basic administration tasks for it.

In this chapter, we will learn how to set up the work environment, where we will later build our Odoo applications. We will learn how to set up a Debian or Ubuntu system to host the development server instances and how to install Odoo from the GitHub source code. Then, we will learn how to set up file sharing with Samba, which will allow us to work on Odoo files from a workstation running Windows or any other operating system.

Odoo is built using the Python programming language, and it uses the PostgreSQL database for data storage; these are the two main requirements of an Odoo host. To run Odoo from the source, we will first need to install the Python libraries it depends on. The Odoo source code can then be downloaded from GitHub. While we can download a ZIP file or tarball, we will see that it's better if we get the sources using the Git version control application; it'll help us to have it installed on our Odoo host as well.

Setting up a host for the Odoo server

A Debian/Ubuntu system is recommended for the Odoo server. You will still be able to work from your favorite desktop system, be it Windows, Mac, or Linux.

Odoo can run on a variety of operating systems, so why pick Debian at the expense of other operating systems? Because Debian is considered the reference deployment platform by the Odoo team; it has the best support. It will be easier to find help and additional resources if we work with Debian/Ubuntu.

It's also the platform that the majority of developers work on and where most deployments are rolled out. So, inevitably, Odoo developers are expected to be comfortable with the Debian/Ubuntu platform. Even if you're from a Windows background, it will be important that you have some knowledge about it.

In this chapter, you will learn how to set up and work with Odoo hosted on a Debian-based system, using only the command line. For those at home with a Windows system, we will cover how to set up a virtual machine to host the Odoo server. As a bonus, the techniques you will learn here will also allow you to manage Odoo in cloud servers, where your only access will be through **Secure Shell** (**SSH**).

Keep in mind that these instructions are intended to set up a new system for development. If you want to try some of them in an existing system, always take a backup ahead of time in order to be able to restore it in case something goes wrong.

Provision for a Debian host

As explained earlier, we will need a Debian-based host for our Odoo server. If these are your first steps with Linux, you may like to note that Ubuntu is a Debian-based Linux distribution, so they are very similar.

Odoo is guaranteed to work with the current stable version of Debian or Ubuntu. At the time of writing, these are Debian 8 "Jessie" and Ubuntu 16.04.1 LTS (Xenial Xerus). Both ship with Python 2.7, which is necessary to run Odoo. It is worth saying that Odoo does not support Python 3 yet, so Python 2 is required.

If you are already running Ubuntu or another Debian-based distribution, you're set; this can also be used as a host for Odoo.

For the Windows and Mac operating systems, install Python, PostgreSQL, and all the dependencies; next, run Odoo from the source natively. However, this could prove to be a challenge, so our advice is to use a virtual machine running Debian or Ubuntu Server. You're welcome to choose your preferred virtualization software to get a working Debian system in a virtual machine.

In case you need some guidance, here is some advice regarding the virtualization software. There are several options, such as Microsoft Hyper-V (available in some versions of recent Windows systems), Oracle VirtualBox, and VMWare Workstation Player (VMWare Fusion for Mac). The VMWare Workstation Player is probably easier to use, and free-to-use downloads can be found at `https://my.vmware.com/web/vmware/downloads`.

Regarding the Linux image to use, it will be more user-friendly to install Ubuntu Server than Debian. If you're beginning with Linux, I would recommend that you try a ready-to-use image. TurnKey Linux provides easy-to-use preinstalled images in several formats, including ISO. The ISO format will work with any virtualization software you choose, even on a bare-metal machine you might have. A good option might be the LAPP image, which includes Python and PostgreSQL, and can be found at `http://www.turnkeylinux.org/lapp`.

Once installed and booted, you should be able to log in to a command-line shell.

Creating a user account for Odoo

If you are logging in using the superuser `root` account, your first task should be to create a normal user account to use for your work, since it's considered bad practice to work as `root`. In particular, the Odoo server will refuse to run if you start it as the `root`.

If you are using Ubuntu, you probably won't need this since the installation process must have already guided you through the creation of a user.

First, make sure `sudo` is installed. Our work user will need it. If logged in as the `root`, execute the following commands:

```
# apt-get update && apt-get upgrade  # Install system updates
# apt-get install sudo  # Make sure 'sudo' is installed
```

The next set of commands will create an `odoo` user:

```
# useradd -m -g sudo -s /bin/bash odoo  # Create an 'odoo' user with sudo
powers
# passwd odoo  # Ask and set a password for the new user
```

You can change `odoo` to whatever username you may want. The `-m` option ensures its home directory is created. The `-g sudo` option adds it to the *sudoers* list so it can run commands as the `root`. The `-s /bin/bash` option sets the default shell to `bash`, which is nicer to use than the default `sh`.

Now we can log in as the new user and set up Odoo.

Installing Odoo from the source

Ready-to-install Odoo packages can be found at `nightly.odoo.com`, available as Windows (`.exe`), Debian (`.deb`), CentOS (`.rpm`), and source code tarballs (`.tar.gz`).

As developers, we will prefer installing them directly from the GitHub repository. This will end up giving us more control over versions and updates.

To keep things tidy, let's work in a `/odoo-dev` directory inside our `home` directory.

Throughout the book, we will assume that `/odoo-dev` is the directory where your Odoo server is installed.

First, make sure you are logged in as the user we created now or during the installation process, not as the `root`. Assuming your user is `odoo`, confirm it with the following command:

```
$ whoami
odoo
$ echo $HOME
/home/odoo
```

Now we can use this script. It shows us how to install Odoo from the source into a Debian/Ubuntu system.

First, install the basic dependencies to get us started:

```
$ sudo apt-get update && sudo apt-get upgrade  #Install system updates
$ sudo apt-get install git  # Install Git
$ sudo apt-get install npm  # Install NodeJs and its package manager
$ sudo ln -s /usr/bin/nodejs /usr/bin/node  # call node runs nodejs
$ sudo npm install -g less less-plugin-clean-css  #Install less compiler
```

Starting from version 9.0, the Odoo web client requires the `less` CSS preprocessor to be installed in the system, in order for web pages to be rendered correctly. To install this, we need Node.js and npm.

Next, we need to get the Odoo source code and install all its dependencies. The Odoo source code includes an utility script, inside the `odoo/setup/` directory, to help us install the required dependencies in a Debian/Ubuntu system:

```
$ mkdir ~/odoo-dev  # Create a directory to work in
$ cd ~/odoo-dev  # Go into our work directory
$ git clone https://github.com/odoo/odoo.git -b 10.0 --depth=1  # Get Odoo
source code
$ ./odoo/setup/setup_dev.py setup_deps  # Installs Odoo system dependencies
$ ./odoo/setup/setup_dev.py setup_pg  # Installs PostgreSQL & db superuser
for unix user
```

At the end, Odoo should be ready to use. The ~ symbol is a shortcut for our `home` directory (for example, `/home/odoo`). The `git -b 10.0` option tells Git to explicitly download the 10.0 branch of Odoo. At the time of writing, this is redundant since 10.0 is the default branch; however, this may change, so it may make the script future-proof. The `--depth=1` option tells Git to download only the last revision, instead of the full change history, making the download smaller and faster.

To start an Odoo server instance, just run:

```
$ ~/odoo-dev/odoo/odoo-bin
```

In Odoo 10, the `odoo.py` script, used in previous versions to start the server, was replaced with `odoo-bin`.

By default, Odoo instances listen on port `8069`, so if we point a browser to `http://<server-address>:8069`, we will reach these instances. When we access it for the first time, it shows us an assistant to create a new database, as shown in the following screenshot:

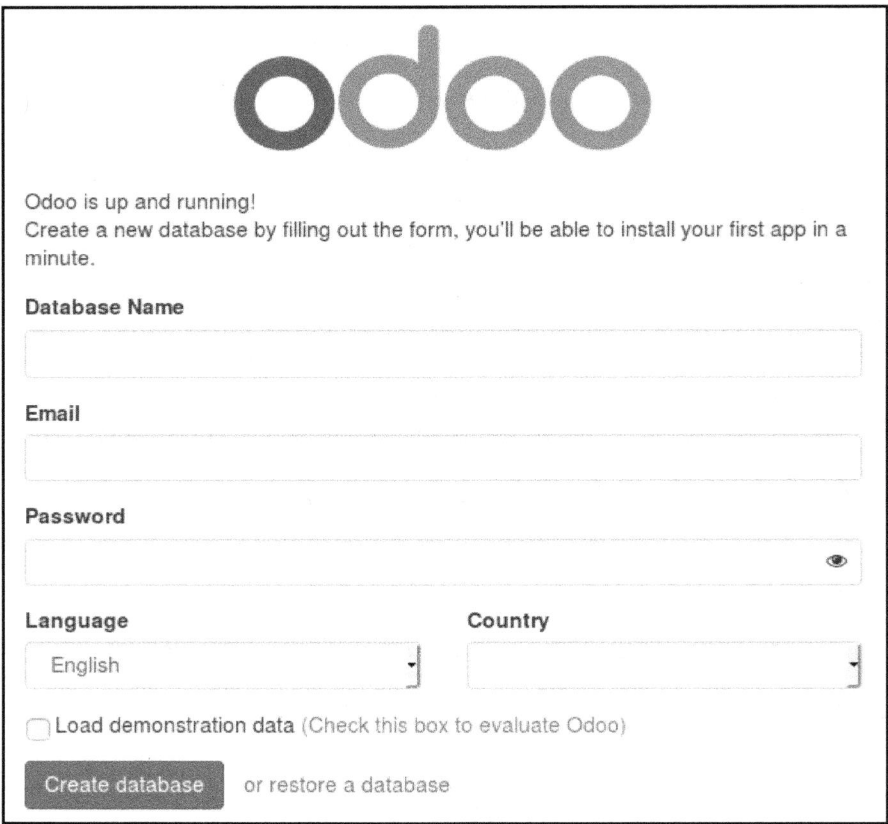

As a developer, we will need to work with several databases, so it's more convenient to create them from the command line, so we will learn how to do this. Now press *Ctrl* + *C* in the terminal to stop the Odoo server and get back to the command prompt.

Initializing a new Odoo database

To be able to create a new database, your user must be a PostgreSQL superuser. The following command creates a PostgreSQL superuser for the current Unix user:

```
$ sudo createuser --superuser $(whoami)
```

To create a new database, use the `createdb` command. Let's create a `demo` database:

```
$ createdb demo
```

To initialize this database with the Odoo data schema, we should run Odoo on the empty database using the `-d` option:

```
$ ~/odoo-dev/odoo/odoo-bin -d demo
```

This will take a couple of minutes to initialize a `demo` database, and it will end with an INFO log message, **Modules loaded**.

Note that it might not be the last log message, and it can be in the last three or four lines. With this, the server will be ready to listen to client requests.

By default, this will initialize the database with demonstration data, which is often useful for development databases. To initialize a database without demonstration data, add the `--without-demo-data=all` option to the command.

Now open `http://<server-name>:8069` with your browser to be presented with the login screen. If you don't know your server name, type the `hostname` command in the terminal in order to find it or the `ifconfig` command to find the IP address.

If you are hosting Odoo in a virtual machine, you might need to set some network configurations to be able to access it from your host system. The simplest solution is to change the virtual machine network type from NAT to Bridged. With this, instead of sharing the host IP address, the guest virtual machine will have its own IP address. It's also possible to use NAT, but that requires you to configure port forwarding so your system knows that some ports, such as `8069`, should be handled by the virtual machine. In case you're having trouble, hopefully these details will help you find relevant information in the documentation for your chosen virtualization software.

The default administrator account is `admin` with its password `admin`. Upon login, you are presented with the **Apps** menu, displaying the available applications:

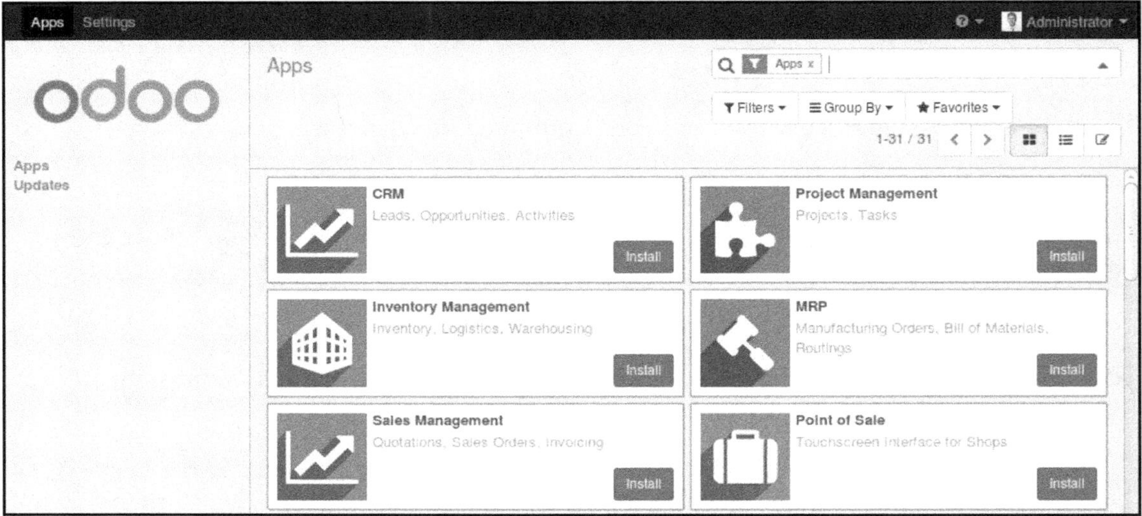

Whenever you want to stop the Odoo server instance and return to the command line, press *Ctrl* + *C* in the bash prompt. Pressing the up arrow key will bring you the previous shell command, so it's a quick way to start Odoo again with the same options. The *Ctrl* + *C* keys followed by the up arrow key and *Enter* is a frequently used combination to restart the Odoo server during development.

Managing your databases

We've seen how to create and initialize new Odoo databases from the command line. There are more commands worth knowing for managing databases.

We already know how to use the `createdb` command to create empty databases, but it can also create a new database by copying an existing one, using the `--template` option.

Make sure your Odoo instance is stopped and you have no other connection open on the `demo` database we just created, then run this:

```
$ createdb --template=demo demo-test
```

In fact, every time we create a database, a template is used. If none is specified, a predefined one called `template1` is used.

To list the existing databases in your system, use the PostgreSQL`psql` utility with the `-l` option:

```
$ psql -l
```

Running it will list the two databases we have created so far: `demo` and `demo-test`. The list will also display the encoding used in each database. The default is UTF-8, which is the encoding needed for Odoo databases.

To remove a database you no longer need (or want to recreate) to use the `dropdb` command:

```
$ dropdb demo-test
```

Now you know the basics to work with databases. To learn more about PostgreSQL, refer to the official documentation at `http://www.postgresql.org/docs/`.

WARNING:
The drop database command will irrevocably destroy your data. Be careful when using it and always keep backups of important databases before using this command.

A word about Odoo product versions

At the time of writing, Odoo's latest stable version is version 10, marked on GitHub as branch 10.0. This is the version we will work with throughout the book.

It's important to note that Odoo databases are incompatible between Odoo major versions. This means that if you run an Odoo 10 server against a database created for a previous major version of Odoo, it won't work. Non-trivial migration work is needed before a database can be used with a later version of the product.

The same is true for addon modules: as a general rule, an addon module developed for an Odoo major version will not work with other versions. When downloading a community module from the web, make sure it targets the Odoo version you are using.

On the other hand, major releases (9.0, 10.0) are expected to receive frequent updates, but these should be mostly bug fixes. They are assured to be “API stable”, meaning model data structures and view element identifiers will remain stable. This is important because it means there will be no risk of custom modules breaking due to incompatible changes in the upstream core modules.

Be warned that the version in the `master` branch will result in the next major stable version, but until then, it's not "API stable" and you should not use it to build custom modules. Doing so is like moving on quicksand: you can't be sure when some changes will be introduced that will break your custom module.

More server configuration options

The Odoo server supports quite a few other options. We can check all the available options with `--help`:

```
$ ./odoo-bin --help
```

We will review some of the most important options in the following sections. Let's start by looking at how the currently active options can be saved in a configuration file.

Odoo server configuration files

Most of the options can be saved in a configuration file. By default, Odoo will use the `.odoorc` file in your home directory. In Linux systems its default location is in the `home` directory (`$HOME`), and in the Windows distribution it is in the same directory as the executable used to launch Odoo.

In previous Odoo/OpenERP versions, the name for the default configuration file was `.openerp-serverrc`. For backward compatibility, Odoo 10 will still use this if it's present and no `.odoorc` file is found.

On a clean install, the `.odoorc` configuration file is not automatically created. We should use the `--save` option to create the default configuration file, if it doesn't exist yet, and store the current instance configuration into it:

```
$ ~/odoo-dev/odoo/odoo-bin --save --stop-after-init  #save configuration to
file
```

Here, we also used the `--stop-after-init` option to stop the server after it finishes its actions. This option is often used when running tests or asking to run a module upgrade to check whether it is installed correctly.

Now we can inspect what was saved in this default configuration file:

```
$ more ~/.odoorc  # show the configuration file
```

This will show all the configuration options available with their default values. Editing them will be effective the next time you start an Odoo instance. Type `q` to quit and go back to the prompt.

We can also choose to use a specific configuration file, using the `--conf=<filepath>` option. Configuration files don't need to have all those options you've just seen. Only the ones that actually change a default value need to be there.

Changing the listening port

The `--xmlrpc-port=<port>` command option allows us to change the listening port of a server instance from the default 8069. This can be used to run more than one instance at the same time, on the same machine.

Let's try this out. Open two terminal windows. On the first, run this:

```
$ ~/odoo-dev/odoo/odoo-bin --xmlrpc-port=8070
```

Run the following command on the second terminal:

```
$ ~/odoo-dev/odoo/odoo-bin --xmlrpc-port=8071
```

There you go: two Odoo instances on the same server listening on different ports! The two instances can use the same or different databases, depending on the configuration parameters used. And the two could be running the same or different versions of Odoo.

The database filter option

When developing with Odoo, it is frequent to work with several databases, and sometimes even with different Odoo versions. Stopping and starting different server instances on the same port, and switching between different databases, can cause web client sessions to behave improperly.

Accessing our instance using a browser window running in private mode can help avoiding some of these problems.

Another good practice is to enable a database filter on the server instance to ensure that it only allows requests for the database we want to work with, ignoring all others. This is done with the `--db-filter` option. It accepts a regular expression to be used as a filter for the valid database names. To match an exact name, the expression should begin with a `^` and end with `$`.

For example, to allow only the `demo` database we would use this command:

```
$ ~/odoo-dev/odoo/odoo-bin --db-filter=^demo$
```

Managing server log messages

The `--log-level` option allows us to set the log verbosity. This can be very useful to understand what is going on in the server. For example, to enable the debug log level, use `--log-level=debug` option.

The following log levels can be particularly interesting:

- `debug_sql` to inspect SQL queries generated by the server
- `debug_rpc` to detail the requests received by the server
- `debug_rpc_answer` to detail the responses sent by the server

By default, the log output is directed to standard output (your console screen), but it can be directed to a log file with the `--logfile=<filepath>` option.

Finally, the `--dev=all` option will bring up the Python debugger (`pdb`) when an exception is raised. It's useful to do a post-mortem analysis of a server error. Note that it doesn't have any effect on the logger verbosity. More details on the Python debugger commands can be found at `https://docs.python.org/2/library/pdb.html#debugger-commands`.

Developing from your workstation

You may be running Odoo with a Debian/Ubuntu system either in a local virtual machine or in a server over the network. But you may prefer to do the development work at your personal workstation, using your favorite text editor or IDE. This may frequently be the case for developers working from Windows workstations. But it also may be the case for Linux users who need to work on an Odoo server over the local network.

A solution for this is to enable file sharing in the Odoo host so that files are made easy for editing from our workstation. For Odoo server operations, such as a server restart, we can use an SSH shell (such as PuTTY on Windows) alongside our favorite editor.

Using a Linux text editor

Sooner or later, we will need to edit files from the shell command line. In many Debian systems, the default text editor is vi. If you're not comfortable with it, you probably could use a friendlier alternative. In Ubuntu systems, the default text editor is nano. You might prefer it since it's easier to use. In case it's not available in your server, it can be installed with:

```
$ sudo apt-get install nano
```

In the following sections, we will assume nano as the preferred editor. If you prefer any other editor, feel free to adapt the commands accordingly.

Installing and configuring Samba

The Samba service helps make Linux file-sharing services compatible with Microsoft Windows systems. We can install it on our Debian/Ubuntu server with this command:

```
$ sudo apt-get install samba samba-common-bin
```

The `samba` package installs the file-sharing services, and the `samba-common-bin` package is needed for the `smbpasswd` tool. By default, users allowed to access shared files need to be registered with it. We need to register our user, `odoo` for example, and set a password for its file share access:

```
$ sudo smbpasswd -a odoo
```

After this, we will be asked for a password to use to access the shared directory, and the `odoo` user will be able to access shared files for its home directory, although it will be read only. We want to have write access, so we need to edit the Samba configuration file to change it as follows:

```
$ sudo nano /etc/samba/smb.conf
```

In the configuration file, look for the [homes] section. Edit its configuration lines so that they match the settings as follows:

```
[homes]
    comment = Home Directories
    browseable = yes
    read only = no
    create mask = 0640
    directory mask = 0750
```

For the configuration changes to take effect, restart the service:

```
$ sudo /etc/init.d/smbd restart
```

Downloading the example code
You can download the example code files for all Packt books you have purchased from your account at http://www.packtpub.com. If you purchased this book from elsewhere, you can visit http://www.packtpub.com/supportand register to have the files e-mailed directly to you.

To access the files from Windows, we can map a network drive for the path \\<my-server-name>\odoo using the specific username and password defined with smbpasswd. When trying to log in with the odoo user, you might encounter trouble with Windows adding the computer's domain to the username (for example, MYPC\odoo). To avoid this, use an empty domain by prepending a \ character to the login (for example, \odoo):

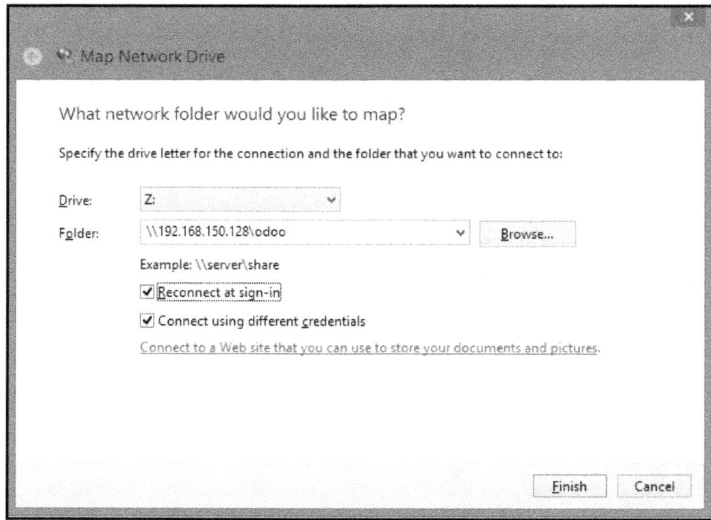

If we now open the mapped drive with Windows Explorer, we will be able to access and edit the contents of the `odoo` user's home directory:

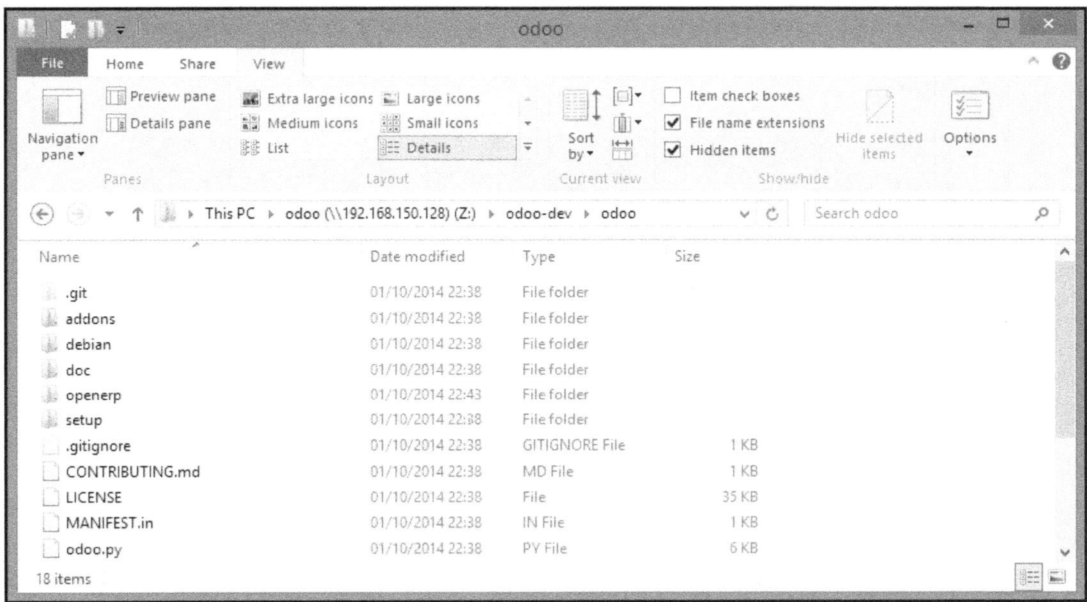

Odoo includes a couple of tools that are very helpful for developers, and we will make use of them throughout the book. They are technical features and the developer mode. These are disabled by default, so this is a good moment to learn how to enable them.

Activating the developer tools

The developer tools provide advanced server configuration and features. These include a debug menu in the top menu bar along with additional menu options in the **Settings** menu, in particular the **Technical** menu.

These tools come disabled by default, and to enable them, we need to log in as admin. In the top menu bar, select the **Settings** menu. At the bottom-right, below the Odoo version, you will find two options to enable the developer mode; any of them will enable the **Debug** and **Technical** menus. The second option, **Activate the developer mode (with assets)**, also disables the minification of JavaScript and CSS used by the web client, making it easier to debug client-side behavior:

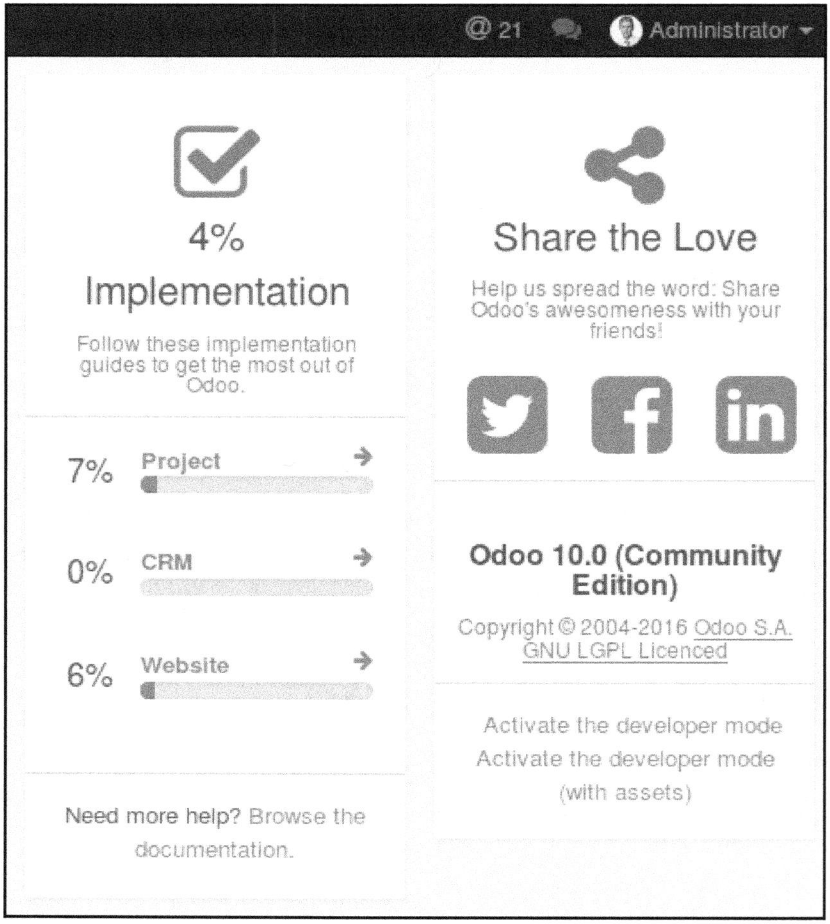

After that, the page is reloaded and you should see a bug icon in the top menu bar, just before the session user avatar and name providing the debug mode options. And in the **Settings** option in the top menu, we should see a new **Technical** menu section giving access to many Odoo instance internals:

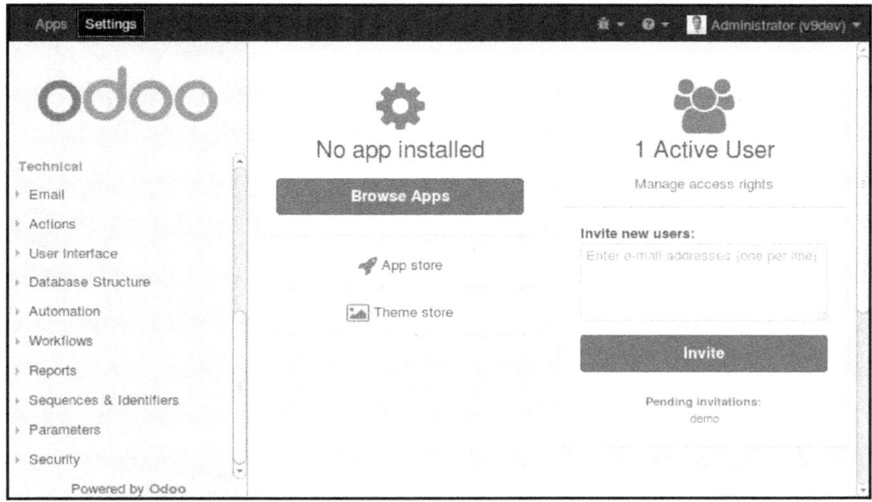

The **Technical** menu option allows us to inspect and edit all the Odoo configurations stored in the database, from user interface to security and other system parameters. You will be learning more about many of these throughout the book.

Installing third-party modules

Making new modules available in an Odoo instance so they can be installed is something that newcomers to Odoo frequently find confusing. But it doesn't have to be so, so let's demystify it.

Finding community modules

There are many Odoo modules available on the Internet. The Odoo apps store at `apps.odoo.com` is a catalogue of modules that can be downloaded and installed on your system. The **Odoo Community Association** (**OCA**) coordinates community contributions and maintains quite a few module repositories on GitHub at `https://github.com/OCA/`.

To add a module to an Odoo installation, we could just copy it into the `addons` directory alongside the official modules. In our case, the `addons` directory is at `~/odoo-dev/odoo/addons/`. This might not be the best option for us since our Odoo installation is based on a version-controlled code repository, and we will want to keep it synchronized with the GitHub repository.

Fortunately, we can use additional locations for modules so we can keep our custom modules in a different directory, without having them mixed with the official ones.

As an example, we will download the code from this book, available in GitHub, and make those addon modules available in our Odoo installation.

To get the source code from GitHub, run the following commands:

```
$ cd ~/odoo-dev
$ git clone https://github.com/dreispt/todo_app.git -b 10.0
```

We used the `-b` option to make sure we are downloading the modules for the 10.0 version.

After this, we will have a new `/todo_app` directory alongside the `/odoo` directory, containing the modules. Now we need to let Odoo know about this new module directory.

Configuring the addons path

The Odoo server has a configuration option called `addons_path` to set where the server should look for modules. By default, this points to the `/addons` directory, where the Odoo server is running.

We can provide not only one, but a list of directories where modules can be found. This allows us to keep our custom modules in a different directory, without having them mixed with the official addons.

Let's start the server with an addons path that includes our new module directory:

```
$ cd ~/odoo-dev/odoo
$ ./odoo-bin -d demo --addons-path="../todo_app,./addons"
```

If you look closer at the server log, you will notice a line reporting the addons path in use: `INFO? odoo: addons paths: [...]`. Confirm that it contains our `todo_app` directory.

Updating the apps list

We still need to ask Odoo to update its module list before these new modules are made available for installation.

For this, we need developer mode enabled, since it provides the **Update Apps List** menu option. It can be found in the **Apps** top menu.

After updating the modules list, we can confirm the new modules are available for installation. Use the **Apps** menu option to see the list of local modules. Search for `todo` and you should see the new modules made available.

Note that the second **App Store** menu option displays the module list from Odoo apps store instead of your local modules:

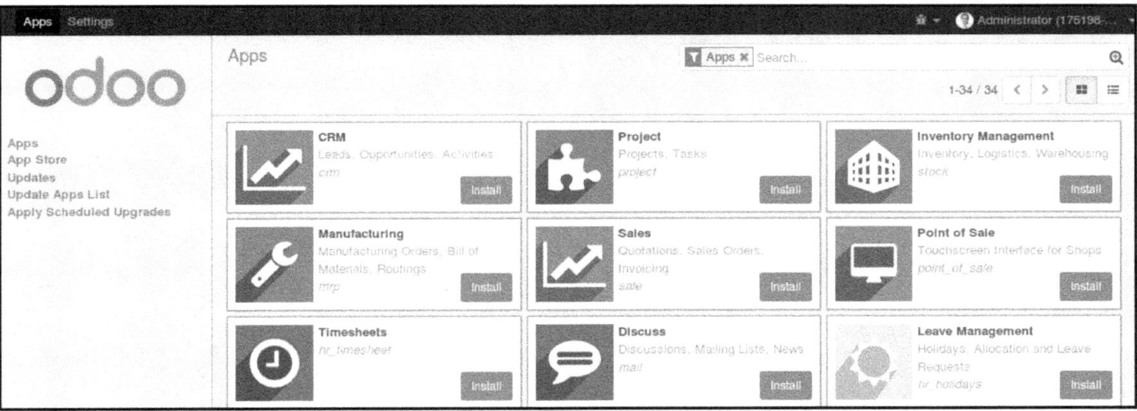

Summary

In this chapter, we learned how to set up a Debian system to host Odoo and install it from the GitHub source code. We also learned how to create Odoo databases and run Odoo instances. To allow developers to use their favorite tools in their personal workstation, we explained how to configure file sharing in the Odoo host.

We should now have a functioning Odoo environment to work with and be comfortable with managing databases and instances.

With this in place, we're ready to go straight into action. In the next chapter, we will create our first Odoo module from scratch and understand the main elements it involves.

So let's get started!

2
Building Your First Odoo Application

Developing in Odoo most of the time means creating our own modules. In this chapter, we will create our first Odoo application and learn the steps needed to make it available to Odoo and install it.

Inspired by the notable `http://todomvc.com/` project, we will build a simple To-Do application. It should allow us to add new tasks, mark them as completed, and finally clear the task list of all the already completed tasks.

We will get started by learning the basics of a development workflow: set up a new instance for your work, create and install a new module, and update it to apply the changes you make along with the development iterations.

Odoo follows an MVC-like architecture, and we will go through the layers during our implementation of the To-Do application:

- The **model** layer, defining the structure of the app's data
- The **view** layer, describing the user interface
- The **controller** layer, supporting the business logic of the application

Next, we will learn how to set up access control security and, finally, we will add some description and branding information to the module.

Note that the concept of the term controller mentioned here is different from the Odoo web development controllers. These are program endpoints that web pages can call to perform actions.

With this approach, you will be able to gradually learn about the basic building blocks that make up an application and experience the iterative process of building an Odoo module from scratch.

Essential concepts

You're probably just getting started with Odoo, so now is obviously a good time to explain Odoo modules and how they are used in an Odoo development.

Understanding applications and modules

It's common to hear about Odoo modules and applications. But what exactly is the difference between them?

Module addons are the building blocks for Odoo applications. A module can add new features to Odoo, or modify existing ones. It is a directory containing a manifest, or descriptor file, named `__manifest__.py`, plus the remaining files that implement its features.

Applications are the way major features are added to Odoo. They provide the core elements for a functional area, such as Accounting or HR, based on which additional addon modules modify or extend features. Because of this, they are highlighted in the Odoo **Apps** menu.

If your module is complex, and adds new or major functionality to Odoo, you might consider creating it as an application. If your module just makes changes to existing functionality in Odoo, it is likely not an application.

Whether a module is an application or not is defined in the manifest. Technically it does not have any particular effect on how the addon module behaves. It is only used for a highlight in the **Apps** list.

Modifying and extending modules

In the example that we are going to follow, we will create a new module with as few dependencies as possible.

This will not be the typical case, however. Mostly, we will either modify or extend an already existing module.

As a general rule, it's considered a bad practice to modify existing modules by changing their source code directly. This is especially true for the official modules provided by Odoo. Doing so does not allow you to have a clear separation between the original module code and the modifications, and this makes it difficult to apply upgrades since they would overwrite the modifications.

Instead, we should create the extension modules to be installed next to the modules we want to modify, implementing the changes we need. In fact, one of Odoo's main strengths is the **inheritance** mechanism, which allows custom modules to extend existing modules, either officially or from the community. The inheritance is possible at all levels: data models, business logic, and user interface layers.

In this chapter, we will create a completely new module, without extending any existing module, to focus on the different parts and steps involved in module creation. We will have just a brief look at each part since each one of them will be studied in more detail in the later chapters.

Once we are comfortable with creating a new module, we can dive into the inheritance mechanism, which will be introduced in `Chapter 3`, *Inheritance – Extending Existing Applications*.

To get productive developing for Odoo we should be comfortable with the development workflow: managing the development environment, applying code changes, and checking the results. This section will guide you through these basics.

Creating the module basic skeleton

Following the instructions in `Chapter 1`, *Getting Started with Odoo Development*, we should have the Odoo server at `~/odoo-dev/odoo/`. To keep things tidy, we will create a new directory alongside it to host our custom modules, at `~/odoo-dev/custom-addons`.

Odoo includes a `scaffold` command to automatically create a new module directory, with a basic structure already in place. You can learn more about it with the following command:

```
$ ~/odoo-dev/odoo/odoo-bin scaffold --help
```

You might want to keep this in mind when you start working on your next module, but we won't be using it right now since we will prefer to manually create all the structure for our module.

An Odoo addon module is a directory containing a `__manifest__.py` descriptor file.

In previous versions, this descriptor file was named `__openerp__.py`. This name is still supported but is deprecated.

It also needs to be Python importable, so it must also have a `__init__.py` file.

The module's directory name is its technical name. We will use `todo_app` for it. The technical name must be a valid Python identifier: it should begin with a letter and can only contain letters, numbers, and the underscore character.

The following commands will create the module directory and create an empty `__init__.py` file in it, `~/odoo-dev/custom-addons/todo_app/__init__.py`.

In case you would like to do that directly from the command line, this is what you would use:

```
$ mkdir ~/odoo-dev/custom-addons/todo_app
$ touch ~/odoo-dev/custom-addons/todo_app/__init__.py
```

Next, we need to create the manifest file. It should contain only a Python dictionary with about a dozen possible attributes; of this, only the `name` attribute is required. The `description` attribute, for a longer description, and the `author` attribute provide better visibility and are advised.

We should now add a `__manifest__.py` file alongside the `__init__.py` file with the following content:

```
{
    'name': 'To-Do Application',
    'description': 'Manage your personal To-Do
    tasks.',
    'author': 'Daniel Reis',
    'depends': ['base'],
    'application': True,
}
```

The `depends` attribute can have a list of other modules that are required. Odoo will have them automatically installed when this module is installed. It's not a mandatory attribute, but it's advised to always have it. If no particular dependencies are needed, we should depend on the core `base` module.

You should be careful to ensure all dependencies are explicitly set here; otherwise, the module may fail to install in a clean database (due to missing dependencies) or have loading errors if by chance the other required modules are loaded afterward.

For our application, we don't need any specific dependencies, so we depend on the `base` module only.

To be concise, we chose to use very few descriptor keys, but, in a real word scenario, we recommend that you also use the additional keys, since they are relevant for the Odoo apps store:

- `summary` is displayed as a subtitle for the module.
- `version`, by default, is `1.0`. It should follow semantic versioning rules (see `http://semver.org/` for details).
- `license` identifier, by default is `LGPL-3`.
- `website` is a URL to find more information about the module. This can help people find more documentation or the issue tracker to file bugs and suggestions.
- `category` is the functional category of the module, which defaults to `Uncategorized`. The list of existing categories can be found in the security groups form (**Settings** | **User** | **Groups**), in the **Application** field drop-down list.

These other descriptor keys are also available:

- `installable` is by default `True` but can be set to `False` to disable a module.
- `auto_install` if set to `True`, this module will be automatically installed, provided all its dependencies are already installed. It is used for the glue modules.

Since Odoo 8.0, instead of the `description` key, we can use an `README.rst` or `README.md` file in the module's top directory.

A word about licenses

Choosing a license for your work is very important, and you should consider carefully what is the best choice for you, and its implications. The most used licenses for Odoo modules are the **GNU Lesser General Public License** (**LGLP**) and the **Affero General Public License** (**AGPL**). The LGPL is more permissive and allows commercial derivate work, without the need to share the corresponding source code. The AGPL is a stronger open source license, and requires derivate work and service hosting to share their source code. Learn more about the GNU licenses at `https://www.gnu.org/licenses/`.

Adding to the addons path

Now that we have a minimalistic new module, we want to make it available to the Odoo instance.

For this, we need to make sure the directory containing the module is in the addons path, then update the Odoo module list.

Both actions have been explained in detail in the previous chapter, but here, we will continue with a brief overview of what is needed.

We will position in our work directory and start the server with the appropriate addons path configuration:

```
$ cd ~/odoo-dev
$ ./odoo/odoo-bin -d todo --addons-path="custom-addons,odoo/addons" --save
```

The `--save` option saves the options you used in a configuration file. This spares us from repeating them every time we restart the server: just run `./odoo-bin` and the last saved option will be used.

Look closely at the server log. It should have an `INFO ? odoo: addons paths:[...]` line. It should include our `custom-addons` directory.

Remember to also include any other addon directories you might be using. For instance, if you also have a `~/odoo-dev/extra` directory containing additional modules to be used, you might want to include them also using the `--addons-path` option:

```
--addons-path="custom-addons,extra,odoo/addons"
```

Now we need the Odoo instance to acknowledge the new module we just added.

Installing the new module

In the **Apps** top menu, select the **Update Apps List** option. This will update the module list, adding any modules that may have been added since the last update to the list. Remember that we need the developer mode enabled for this option to be visible. That is done in the **Settings** dashboard, in the link at the bottom-right, below the Odoo version number information.

Make sure your web client session is working with the right database. You can check that at the top-right: the database name is shown in parenthesis, right after the username. A way to enforce using the correct database is to start the server instance with the additional option `--db-filter=^MYDB$`.

The **Apps** option shows us the list of available modules. By default, it shows only the application modules. Since we have created an application module, we don't need to remove that filter to see it. Type `todo` in the search and you should see our new module, ready to be installed:

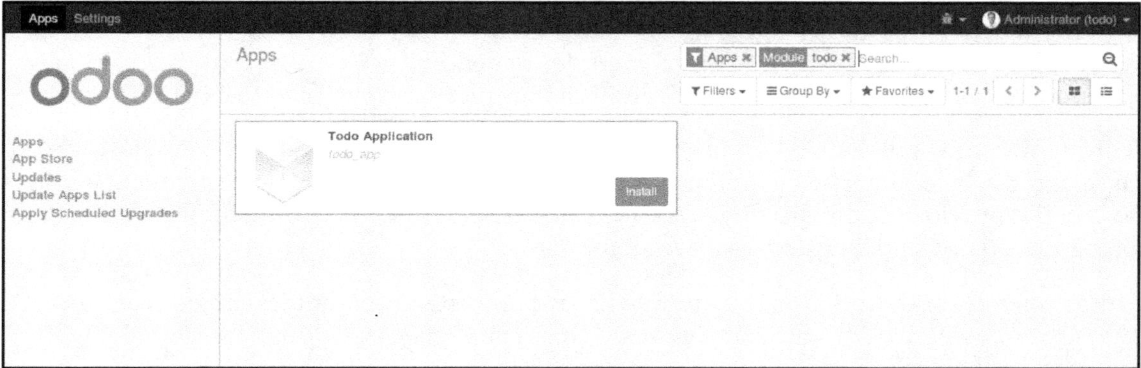

Now click on the module's **Install** button and we're ready!

Upgrading a module

Developing a module is an iterative process, and you will want changes made on source files to be applied to and made visible in Odoo.

In many cases, this is done by upgrading the module: look up the module in the **Apps** list and once it is already installed, you will have an **Upgrade** button available.

However, when the changes are only in Python code, the upgrade may not have an effect. Instead of a module upgrade, an application server restart is needed. Since Odoo loads Python code only once, any later changes to code require a server restart to be applied.

In some cases, if the module changes were in both data files and Python code, you might need both the operations. This is a common source of confusion for new Odoo developers.

But fortunately, there is a better way. The safest and fastest way to make all our changes to a module effective is to stop and restart the server instance, requesting our modules to be upgraded to our work database.

In the terminal where the server instance is running, use *Ctrl* + *C* to stop it. Then, start the server and upgrade the `todo_app` module using the following command:

```
$ ./odoo-bin -d todo -u todo_app
```

The `-u` option (or `--update` in the long form) requires the `-d` option and accepts a comma-separated list of modules to update. For example, we could use `-u todo_app,mail`. When a module is updated, all other installed modules depending on it are also updated. This is essential to maintain the integrity of the inheritance mechanisms, used to extend features.

Throughout the book, when you need to apply the work done in modules, the safest way is to restart the Odoo instance with the preceding command. Pressing the up arrow key brings to you the previous command that was used. So, most of the time, you will find yourself using the *Ctrl* + *C*, up, and *Enter* key combination.

Unfortunately, both updating the module list and uninstalling modules are both actions that are not available through the command line. These need to be done through the web interface in the **Apps** menu.

The server development mode

In Odoo 10 a new option was introduced providing developer-friendly features. To use it start the server instance with the additional option `--dev=all`.

This enables a few handy features to speed up our development cycle. The most important are:

- Reload Python code automatically, once a Python file is saved, avoiding a manual server restart
- Read view definitions directly from the XML files, avoiding manual module upgrades

The `--dev` option accepts a comma-separated list of options, although the `all` option will be suitable most of the time. We can also specify the debugger we prefer to use. By default the Python debugger, `pdb` , is used. Some people might prefer to install and use alternative debuggers. Here also supported are `ipdb` and `pudb`.

The model layer

Now that Odoo knows about our new module, let's start by adding a simple model to it.

Models describe business objects, such as an opportunity, sales order, or partner (customer, supplier, and so on). A model has a list of attributes and can also define its specific business.

Models are implemented using a Python class derived from an Odoo template class. They translate directly to database objects, and Odoo automatically takes care of this when installing or upgrading the module. The mechanism responsible for this is the **Object Relational Model** (**ORM**).

Our module will be a very simple application to keep to-do tasks. These tasks will have a single text field for the description and a checkbox to mark them as complete. We should later add a button to clean the to-do list of the old, completed tasks.

Creating the data model

The Odoo development guidelines state that the Python files for models should be placed inside a `models` subdirectory. For simplicity, we won't be following this here, so let's create a `todo_model.py` file in the main directory of the `todo_app` module.

Add the following content to it:

```
# -*- coding: utf-8 -*-
from odoo import models, fields
class TodoTask(models.Model):
    _name = 'todo.task'
    _description = 'To-do Task'
    name = fields.Char('Description', required=True)
    is_done = fields.Boolean('Done?')
    active = fields.Boolean('Active?', default=True)
```

The first line is a special marker telling the Python interpreter that this file has UTF-8 so that it can expect and handle non-ASCII characters. We won't be using any, but it's a good practice to have it anyway.

The second line is a Python code import statement, making available the `models` and `fields` objects from the Odoo core.

The third line declares our new model. It's a class derived from `models.Model`.

The next line sets the `_name` attribute defining the identifier that will be used throughout Odoo to refer to this model. Note that the actual Python class name, `TodoTask` in this case, is meaningless to other Odoo modules. The `_name` value is what will be used as an identifier.

Notice that this and the following lines are indented. If you're not familiar with Python, you should know that this is important: indentation defines a nested code block, so these four lines should all be equally indented.

Then we have the `_description` model attribute. It is not mandatory, but it provides a user-friendly name for the model records, that can be used for better user messages.

The last three lines define the model's fields. It's worth noting that `name` and `active` are special field names. By default, Odoo will use the `name` field as the record's title when referencing it from other models. The `active` field is used to inactivate records, and by default, only active records will be shown. We will use it to clear away completed tasks without actually deleting them from the database.

Right now, this file is not yet used by the module. We must tell Python to load it with the module in the `__init__.py` file. Let's edit it to add the following line:

```
from . import todo_model
```

That's it! For our Python code changes to take effect, the server instance needs to be restarted (unless it was using the `--dev` mode).

We won't see any menu option to access this new model since we didn't add them yet. Still, we can inspect the newly created model using the **Technical** menu. In the **Settings** top menu, go to **Technical** | **Database Structure** | **Models**, search for the `todo.task` model on the list, and click on it to see its definition:

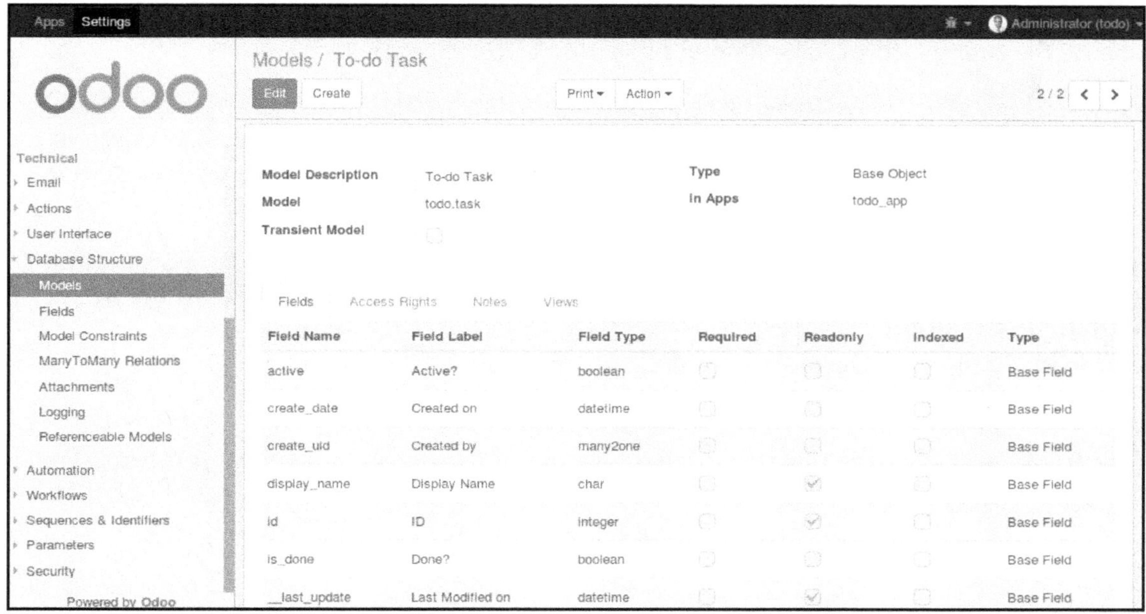

If everything goes right, it is confirmed that the model and fields were created. If you can't see them here, try a server restart with a module upgrade, as described before.

We can also see some additional fields we didn't declare. These are reserved fields Odoo automatically adds to every new model. They are as follows:

- `id` is a unique numeric identifier for each record in the model.
- `create_date` and `create_uid` specify when the record was created and who created it respectively.
- `write_date` and `write_uid` confirm when the record was last modified and who modified it respectively.
- `__last_update` is a helper that is not actually stored in the database. It is used for concurrency checks.

Adding automated tests

Programming best practices include having automated tests for your code. This is even more important for dynamic languages such as Python. Since there is no compilation step, you can't be sure there are no syntactic errors until the code is actually run by the interpreter. A good editor can help us spot these problems ahead of time, but can't help us ensure the code performs as intended like automated tests can.

Odoo supports two ways to describe tests: either using YAML data files or using Python code, based on the `Unittest2` library. YAML tests are a legacy from older versions, and are not recommended. We will prefer using Python tests and will add a basic test case to our module.

The test code files should have a name starting with `test_` and should be imported from `tests/__init__.py`. But the `tests` directory (or Python submodule) should not be imported from the module's top `__init__.py`, since it will be automatically discovered and loaded only when tests are executed.

Tests must be placed in a `tests/` subdirectory. Add a `tests/__init__.py` file with the following:

```
from . import test_todo
```

Now add the actual test code, available in the `tests/test_todo.py` file:

```
# -*- coding: utf-8 -*-
from odoo.tests.common import TransactionCase

class TestTodo(TransactionCase):

    def test_create(self):
        "Create a simple Todo"
        Todo = self.env['todo.task']
        task = Todo.create({'name': 'Test Task'})
        self.assertEqual(task.is_done, False)
```

This adds a simple test case to create a new to-do task and verifies that the **Is Done?** field has the correct default value.

Now we want to run our tests. This is done by adding the `--test-enable` option while installing the module:

```
$ ./odoo-bin -d todo -i todo_app --test-enable
```

The Odoo server will look for a `tests/` subdirectory in the upgraded modules and will run them. If any of the tests fail, the server log will show that.

The view layer

The view layer describes the user interface. Views are defined using XML, which is used by the web client framework to generate data-aware HTML views.

We have menu items that can activate actions that can render views. For example, the **Users** menu item processes an action also called **Users**, that in turn renders a series of views. There are several view types available, such as the list and form views, and the filter options made available are also defined by a particular type of view, the search view.

The Odoo development guidelines states that the XML files defining the user interface should be placed inside a `views/` subdirectory.

Let's start creating the user interface for our To-Do application.

Adding menu items

Now that we have a model to store our data, we should make it available on the user interface.

For that, we should add a menu option to open the `To-do Task` model so that it can be used.

Create the `views/todo_menu.xml` file to define a menu item and the action performed by it:

```
<?xml version="1.0"?>
<odoo>
  <!-- Action to open To-do Task list -->
  <act_window id="action_todo_task"
    name="To-do Task"
    res_model="todo.task"
    view_mode="tree,form" />
  <!-- Menu item to open To-do Task list -->
  <menuitem id="menu_todo_task"
    name="Todos"
    action="action_todo_task" />
</odoo>
```

The user interface, including menu options and actions, is stored in database tables. The XML file is a data file used to load those definitions into the database when the module is installed or upgraded. The preceding code is an Odoo data file, describing two records to add to Odoo:

- The `<act_window>` element defines a client-side window action that will open the `todo.task` model with the `tree` and `form` views enabled, in that order.
- The `<menuitem>` defines a top menu item calling the `action_todo_task` action, which was defined before.

Both elements include an `id` attribute. This `id` attribute also called an **XML ID**, is very important: it is used to uniquely identify each data element inside the module, and can be used by other elements to reference it. In this case, the `<menuitem>` element needs to reference the action to process, and needs to make use of the `<act_window>` ID for that. XML IDs are discussed in greater detail in `Chapter 4`, *Module Data*.

Our module does not yet know about the new XML data file. This is done by adding it to the `data` attribute in the `__manifest__.py` file. It holds the list of files to be loaded by the module. Add this attribute to the manifest's dictionary:

```
'data': ['views/todo_menu.xml'],
```

Now we need to upgrade the module again for these changes to take effect. Go to the **Todos** top menu and you should see our new menu option available:

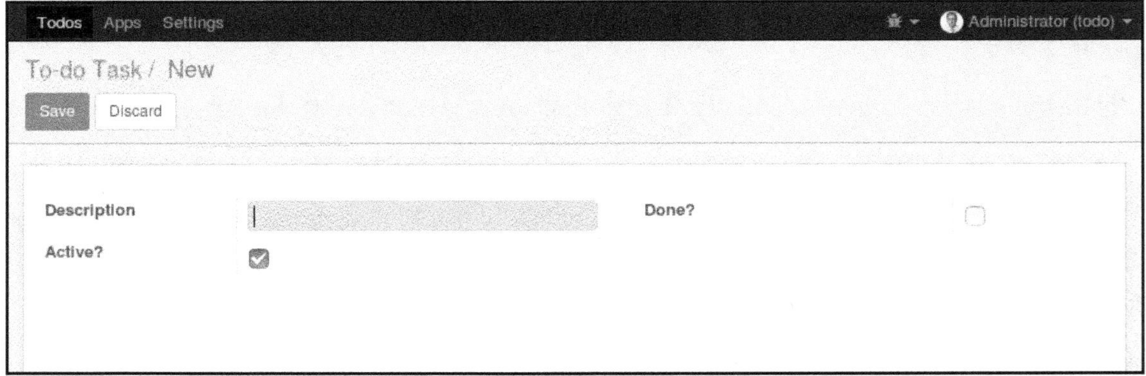

Even though we haven't defined our user interface view, clicking on the **Todos** menu will open an automatically generated form for our model, allowing us to add and edit records.

Odoo is nice enough to automatically generate them so that we can start working with our model right away.

So far, so good! Let's improve our user interface now. Try making gradual improvements as shown in the next sections, doing frequent module upgrades, and don't be afraid to experiment. You might also want to try the `--dev=all` server option. Using it the view definitions are read directly from the XML files so that your changes can be immediately available to Odoo without the need of a module upgrade.

If an upgrade fails because of an XML error, don't panic! Comment out the last edited XML portions or remove the XML file from `__manifest__.py` and repeat the upgrade. The server should start correctly. Now read the error message in the server log carefully: it should point you to where the problem is.

Odoo supports several types of views, but the three most important ones are: `tree` (usually called list views), `form`, and `search` views. We'll add an example of each to our module.

Creating the form view

All views are stored in the database, in the `ir.ui.view` model. To add a view to a module, we declare a `<record>` element describing the view in an XML file, which is to be loaded into the database when the module is installed.

Add this new `views/todo_view.xml` file to define our form view:

```
<?xml version="1.0"?>
<odoo>
  <record id="view_form_todo_task" model="ir.ui.view">
    <field name="name">To-do Task Form</field>
    <field name="model">todo.task</field>
    <field name="arch" type="xml">
      <form string="To-do Task">
        <group>
          <field name="name"/>
          <field name="is_done"/>
          <field name="active" readonly="1"/>
        </group>
      </form>
    </field>
  </record>
</odoo>
```

Remember to add this new file to the `data` key in the manifest file, otherwise, our module won't know about it and it won't be loaded.

This will add a record to the `ir.ui.view` model with the identifier `view_form_todo_task`. The view is for the `todo.task` model and is named `To-do Task Form`. The name is just for information; it does not have to be unique, but it should allow one to easily identify which record it refers to. In fact, the name can be entirely omitted, in that case, it will be automatically generated from the model name and the view type.

The most important attribute is `arch`, and it contains the view definition, highlighted in the XML code above. The `<form>` tag defines the view type, and in this case, contains three fields. We also added an attribute to the `active` field to make it read only.

Business document form views

The preceding section provided a basic form view, but we can make some improvements on it. For document models, Odoo has a presentation style that mimics a paper page. This form contains two elements: `<header>` to contain action buttons and `<sheet>` to contain the data fields.

We can now replace the basic `<form>` defined in the previous section with this one:

```
<form>
  <header>
  <!-- Buttons go here-->
  </header>
  <sheet>
    <!-- Content goes here: -->
    <group>
      <field name="name"/>
      <field name="is_done"/>
      <field name="active" readonly="1"/>
    </group>
  </sheet>
</form>
```

Adding action buttons

Forms can have buttons to perform actions. These buttons are able to run window actions such as opening another form or run Python functions defined in the model.

They can be placed anywhere inside a form, but for document-style forms, the recommended place for them is the `<header>` section.

For our application, we will add two buttons to run the methods of the `todo.task` model:

```
<header>
  <button name="do_toggle_done" type="object"
    string="Toggle Done" class="oe_highlight" />
  <button name="do_clear_done" type="object"
    string="Clear All Done" />
</header>
```

The basic attributes of a button comprise the following:

- `string` with the text to display on the button
- `type` of action it performs
- `name` is the identifier for that action
- `class` is an optional attribute to apply CSS styles, like in regular HTML

Using groups to organize forms

The `<group>` tag allows you to organize the form content. Placing `<group>` elements inside a `<group>` element creates a two column layout inside the outer group. Group elements are advised to have a `name` attribute so that its easier for other modules to extend them.

We will use this to better organize our content. Let's change the `<sheet>` content of our form to match this:

```
<sheet>
  <group name="group_top">
    <group name="group_left">
      <field name="name"/>
    </group>
    <group name="group_right">
      <field name="is_done"/>
      <field name="active" readonly="1"/>
    </group>
  </group>
</sheet>
```

The complete form view

At this point, our `todo.task` form view should look like this:

```
<form>
  <header>
    <button name="do_toggle_done" type="object"
      string="Toggle Done" class="oe_highlight" />
    <button name="do_clear_done" type="object"
      string="Clear All Done" />
  </header>
  <sheet>
    <group name="group_top">
      <group name="group_left">
        <field name="name"/>
      </group>
      <group name="group_right">
        <field name="is_done"/>
        <field name="active" readonly="1" />
      </group>
    </group>
  </sheet>
</form>
```

Remember that, for the changes to be loaded to our Odoo database, a module upgrade is needed. To see the changes in the web client, the form needs to be reloaded: either click again on the menu option that opens it or reload the browser page (*F5* in most browsers).

The action buttons won't work yet since we still need to add their business logic.

Adding list and search views

When viewing a model in list mode, a `<tree>` view is used. Tree views are capable of displaying lines organized in hierarchies, but most of the time, they are used to display plain lists.

We can add the following `tree` view definition to `todo_view.xml`:

```
<record id="view_tree_todo_task" model="ir.ui.view">
  <field name="name">To-do Task Tree</field>
  <field name="model">todo.task</field>
  <field name="arch" type="xml">
    <tree colors="decoration-muted:is_done==True">
      <field name="name"/>
```

```
        <field name="is_done"/>
      </tree>
    </field>
  </record>
```

This defines a list with only two columns: `name` and `is_done`. We also added a nice touch: the lines for done tasks (`is_done==True`) are shown grayed out. This is done applying the Bootstrap class `muted`. Check `http://getbootstrap.com/css/#helper-classes-colors` for more information on Bootstrap and its contextual colors.

At the top-right corner of the list, Odoo displays a search box. The fields it searches in and the available filters are defined by a `<search>` view.

As before, we will add this to `todo_view.xml`:

```
  <record id="view_filter_todo_task" model="ir.ui.view">
    <field name="name">To-do Task Filter</field>
    <field name="model">todo.task</field>
    <field name="arch" type="xml">
      <search>
        <field name="name"/>
        <filter string="Not Done"
          domain="[('is_done','=',False)]"/>
        <filter string="Done"
          domain="[('is_done','!=',False)]"/>
      </search>
    </field>
  </record>
```

The `<field>` elements define fields that are also searched when typing in the search box. The `<filter>` elements add predefined filter conditions, that can be toggled with a user click, defined using a specific syntax.

The business logic layer

Now we will add some logic to our buttons. This is done with Python code, using the methods in the model's Python class.

Adding business logic

We should edit the `todo_model.py` Python file to add to the class the methods called by the buttons. First, we need to import the new API, so add it to the import statement at the top of the Python file:

```
from odoo import models, fields, api
```

The action of the **Toggle Done** button will be very simple: just toggle the **Is Done?** flag. For logic on records, use the `@api.multi` decorator. Here, `self` will represent a recordset, and we should then loop through each record.

Inside the `TodoTask` class, add this:

```
@api.multi
def do_toggle_done(self):
    for task in self:
        task.is_done = not task.is_done
    return True
```

The code loops through all the to-do task records and, for each one, modifies the `is_done` field, inverting its value. The method does not need to return anything, but we should have it to at least return a `True` value. The reason is that clients can use XML-RPC to call these methods, and this protocol does not support server functions returning just a `None` value.

For the **Clear All Done** button, we want to go a little further. It should look for all active records that are done, and make them inactive. Usually form buttons are expected to act only on the selected record, but in this case, we will want it also act on records other than the current one:

```
@api.model
def do_clear_done(self):
    dones = self.search([('is_done', '=', True)])
    dones.write({'active': False})
    return True
```

On methods decorated with `@api.model`, the `self` variable represents the model with no record in particular. We will build a `dones` recordset containing all the tasks that are marked as done. Then, we set the `active` flag to `False` on them.

The `search` method is an API method that returns the records that meet some conditions. These conditions are written in a domain, which is a list of triplets. We'll explore domains in more detail in `Chapter 6`, *Views – Designing the User Interface*.

The write method sets the values at once on all the elements of the recordset. The values to write are described using a dictionary. Using write here is more efficient than iterating through the recordset to assign the value to each of them one by one.

Adding tests

Now we should add tests for the business logic. Ideally, we want every line of code to be covered by at least one test case. In tests/test_todo.py, add a few more lines of code to the test_create() method:

```
# def test_create(self):
        # ...
        # Test Toggle Done
        task.do_toggle_done()
        self.assertTrue(task.is_done)
        # Test Clear Done
        Todo.do_clear_done()
        self.assertFalse(task.active)
```

If we now run the tests and the model methods are correctly written, we should see no error messages in the server log:

```
$ ./odoo-bin -d todo -i todo_app --test-enable
```

Setting up access security

You might have noticed that, upon loading, our module is getting a warning message in the server log:

```
The model todo.task has no access rules, consider adding one.
```

The message is pretty clear: our new model has no access rules, so it can't be used by anyone other than the admin superuser. As a superuser, the admin ignores data access rules, and that's why we were able to use the form without errors. But we must fix this before other users can use our model.

Another issue we have yet to address is that we want the to-do tasks to be private to each user. Odoo supports row-level access rules, which we will use to implement that.

Testing access security

In fact, our tests should be failing right now due to the missing access rules. They aren't because they are done with the admin user. So, we should change them so that they use the Demo user instead.

For this, we should edit the `tests/test_todo.py` file to add a `setUp` method:

```
# class TestTodo(TransactionCase):

    def setUp(self, *args, **kwargs):
        result = super(TestTodo, self).setUp(*args, \
        **kwargs)
        user_demo = self.env.ref('base.user_demo')
        self.env= self.env(user=user_demo)
        return result
```

This first instruction calls the `setUp` code of the parent class. The next ones change the environment used to run the tests, `self.env`, to a new one using the Demo user. No further changes are needed to the tests we already wrote.

We should also add a test case to make sure that users can see only their own tasks. For this, first, add an additional import at the top:

```
from odoo.exceptions import AccessError
```

Next, add an additional method to the test class:

```
    def test_record_rule(self):
        "Test per user record rules"
        Todo = self.env['todo.task']
        task = Todo.sudo().create({'name': 'Admin Task'})
        with self.assertRaises(AccessError):
            Todo.browse([task.id]).name
```

Since our `env` method is now using the Demo user, we used the `sudo()` method to change the context to the admin user. We then use it to create a task that should not be accessible to the Demo user.

When trying to access this task data, we expect an `AccessError` exception to be raised.

If we run the tests now, they should fail, so let's take care of that.

Adding access control security

To get a picture of what information is needed to add access rules to a model, use the web client and go to **Settings** | **Technical** | **Security** | **Access Controls List**:

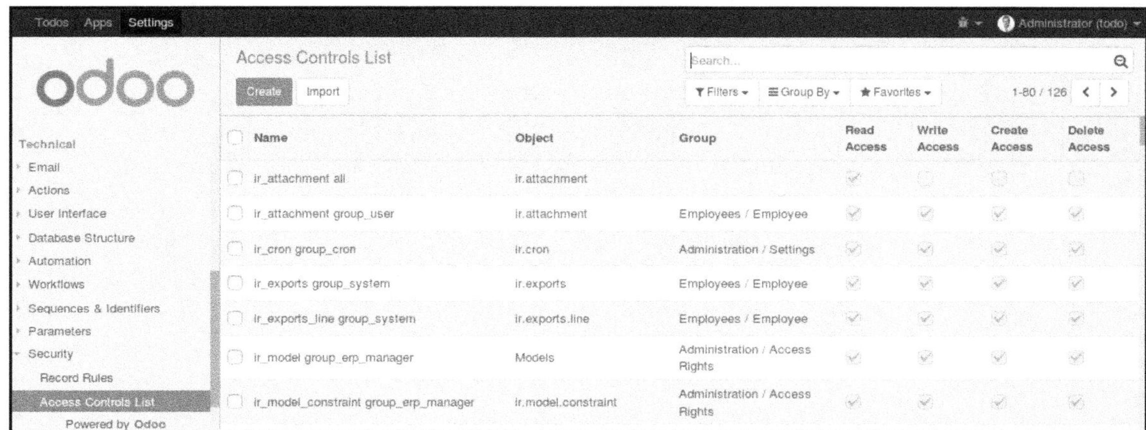

Here we can see the ACL for some models. It indicates, per security group, what actions are allowed on records.

This information has to be provided by the module using a data file to load the lines into the `ir.model.access` model. We will add full access to the employee group on the model. Employee is the basic access group nearly everyone belongs to.

This is done using a CSV file named `security/ir.model.access.csv`. Let's add it with the following content:

```
id,name,model_id:id,group_id:id,perm_read,perm_write,perm_create,perm_unlin
k
acess_todo_task_group_user,todo.task.user,model_todo_task,base.group_user,1
,1,1,1
```

The filename corresponds to the model to load the data into, and the first line of the file has the column names. These are the columns provided in our CSV file:

- `id` is the record external identifier (also known as XML ID). It should be unique in our module.
- `name` is a description title. It is only informative and it's best if it's kept unique. Official modules usually use a dot-separated string with the model name and the group. Following this convention, we used `todo.task.user`.
- `model_id` is the external identifier for the model we are giving access to. Models have XML IDs automatically generated by the ORM: for `todo.task`, the identifier is `model_todo_task`.
- `group_id` identifies the security group to give permissions to. The most important ones are provided by the `base` module. The Employee group is such a case and has the identifier `base.group_user`.
- `perm` fields flag the access to grant `read`, `write`, `create`, or `unlink` (delete) access.

We must not forget to add the reference to this new file in the `__manifest__.py` descriptor's `data` attribute. It should look like this:

```
'data': [
    'security/ir.model.access.csv',
    'views/todo_view.xml',
    'views/todo_menu.xml',
],
```

As before, upgrade the module for these additions to take effect. The warning message should be gone, and we can confirm that the permissions are OK by logging in with the user `demo` (password is also `demo`). If we run our tests now they should only fail the `test_record_rule` test case.

Row-level access rules

We can find the **Record Rules** option in the **Technical** menu, alongside **Access Control List**.

Record rules are defined in the `ir.rule` model. As usual, we need to provide a distinctive name. We also need the model they operate on and the domain filter to use for the access restriction. The domain filter uses the usual list of tuples syntax used across Odoo.

Usually, rules apply to some particular security groups. In our case, we will make it apply to the Employees group. If it applies to no security group, in particular, it is considered global (the `global` field is automatically set to `True`). Global rules are different because they impose restrictions that non-global rules can't override.

To add the record rule, we should create a `security/todo_access_rules.xml` file with the following content:

```
<?xml version="1.0" encoding="utf-8"?>
<odoo>
  <data noupdate="1">
    <record id="todo_task_user_rule" model="ir.rule">
      <field name="name">ToDo Tasks only for owner</field>
      <field name="model_id" ref="model_todo_task"/>
      <field name="domain_force">
          [('create_uid','=',user.id)]
      </field>
      <field name="groups" eval="
      [(4,ref('base.group_user'))]"/>
    </record>
  </data>
</odoo>
```

Notice the `noupdate="1"` attribute. It means this data will not be updated in module upgrades. This will allow it to be customized later since module upgrades won't destroy user-made changes. But be aware that this will also be the case while developing, so you might want to set `noupdate="0"` during development until you're happy with the data file.

In the `groups` field, you will also find a special expression. It's a one-to-many relational field, and they have a special syntax to operate with. In this case, the `(4, x)` tuple indicates to append `x` to the records, and here `x` is a reference to the Employees group, identified by `base.group_user`. This one-to-many writing special syntax is discussed in more detail in `Chapter 4`, *Module Data*.

As before, we must add the file to `__manifest__.py` before it can be loaded into the module:

```
'data': [
  'security/ir.model.access.csv',
  'security/todo_access_rules.xml',
  'todo_view.xml',
  'todo_menu.xml',
],
```

If we did everything right, we can run the module tests and now they should pass.

Better describing the module

Our module is looking good. Why not add an icon to it to make it look even better? For this, we just need to add to the module a `static/description/icon.png` file with the icon to use.

We will be reusing the icon of the existing **Notes** application, so we should copy the `odoo/addons/static/description/icon.png` file into the `custom-addons/todo_app/static/description` directory.

The following commands should do that trick for us:

```
$ mkdir -p ~/odoo-dev/custom-addons/todo_app/static/description
$ cp ~/odoo-dev/odoo/addons/note/static/description/icon.png ~/odoo-dev/custom-addons/todo_app/static/description
```

Now, if we update the module list, our module should be displayed with the new icon.

We can also add a better description to it to explain what it does and how great it is. This can be done in the `description` key of the `__manifest__.py` file. However, the preferred way is to add a `README.rst` file to the module root directory.

Summary

We created a new module from the start, covering the most frequently used elements in a module: models, the three basic types of views (form, list, and search), business logic in model methods, and access security.

In the process, we got familiar with the module development process, which involves module upgrades and application server restarts to make the gradual changes effective in Odoo.

Always remember, when adding model fields, an upgrade is needed. When changing Python code, including the manifest file, a restart is needed. When changing XML or CSV files, an upgrade is needed; also, when in doubt, do both: restart the server and upgrade the modules.

In the next chapter, you will learn how to build modules that will stack on existing ones in order to add features.

3
Inheritance – Extending Existing Applications

One of Odoo's most powerful feature is the ability to add features without directly modifying the underlying objects.

This is achieved through inheritance mechanisms, functioning as modification layers on top of existing objects. These modifications can happen at all levels: models, views, and business logic. Instead of directly modifying an existing module, we create a new module to add the intended modifications.

In this chapter, you will learn how to write your own extension modules, empowering you to leverage the existing core or community applications. As a relevant example, you will learn how to add Odoo's social and messaging features to your own modules.

Adding sharing capabilities to the To-Do app

Our To-Do application now allows users to privately manage their own to-do tasks. Won't it be great to take the app to another level by adding collaboration and social networking features to it? We will be able to share tasks and discuss them with other people.

We will do this with a new module to extend the previously created To-Do app and add these new features using the inheritance mechanisms. Here is what we expect to achieve by the end of this chapter:

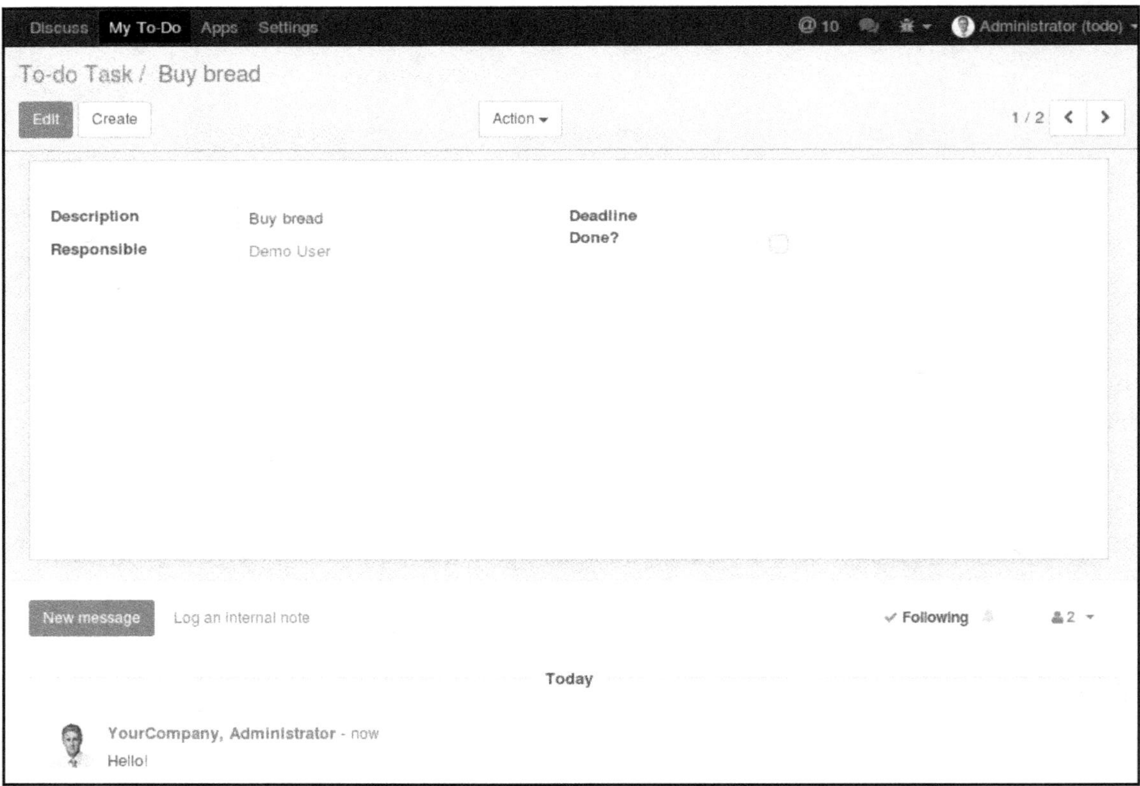

This will be our work plan for the feature extensions to be implemented:

- Extend the Task model, such as the user who is responsible for the task
- Modify the business logic to operate only on the current user's tasks, instead of all the tasks the user is able to see
- Extend the views to add the necessary fields to the views
- Add social networking features: a message wall and the followers

We will start creating the basic skeleton for a new `todo_user` module alongside the `todo_app` module. Following the installation example in `Chapter 1`, *Getting Started with Odoo Development*, we are hosting our modules at `~/odoo-dev/custom-addons/`. We should add there a new `todo_user` directory for the module, containing an empty `__init__.py` file.

Now create `todo_user/__manifest__.py`, containing this code:

```
{  'name': 'Multiuser To-Do',
   'description': 'Extend the To-Do app to multiuser.',
   'author': 'Daniel Reis',
   'depends': ['todo_app'], }
```

We haven't done this here, but including the `summary` and `category` keys can be important when publishing modules to the Odoo online app store.

Notice that we added the explicit dependency on `todo_app` module. This is necessary and important for the inheritance mechanism to work properly. And from now on, when the `todo_app` module is updated, all modules depending on it, such as `todo_user` module, will also be updated.

Next, install it. It should be enough to update the module list using the **Update Apps List** menu option under **Apps**; find the new module in the **Apps** list and click on its **Install** button. Note that this time you will need to remove the default **Apps** filter in order to see the new module in the list, since it is not flagged as being an application. For more detailed instructions on discovering and installing a module, refer to `Chapter 1`, *Getting Started with Odoo Development*.

Now, let's start adding new features to it.

Extending models

New models are defined through Python classes. Extending them is also done through Python classes, but with the help of an Odoo-specific inheritance mechanism.

To extend an existing model, we use a Python class with a `_inherit` attribute. This identifies the model to be extended. The new class inherits all the features of the parent Odoo model, and we only need to declare the modifications we want to introduce.

In fact, Odoo models exist outside our particular Python module, in a central registry. This registry, can be accessed from model methods using `self.env[<model name>]`. For example, to get a reference to the object representing the `res.partner` model, we would write `self.env['res.partner']`.

To modify an Odoo model, we get a reference to its registry class and then perform in-place changes on it. This means that these modifications will also be available everywhere else where this new model is used.

During the Odoo server startup, the module loading the sequence is relevant: modifications made by one add-on module will only be visible to the add-on modules loaded afterward. So it's important for the module dependencies to be correctly set, ensuring that the modules providing the models we use are included in our dependency tree.

Adding fields to a model

We will extend the `todo.task` model to add a couple of fields to it: the user responsible for the task and a deadline date.

The coding style guidelines recommended having a `models/` subdirectory with one file per Odoo model. So we should start by creating the model subdirectory, making it Python-importable.

Edit the `todo_user/__init__.py` file to have this content:

```
from .import models
```

Create `todo_user/models/__init__.py` with the following code:

```
from . import todo_task
```

The preceding line directs Python to look for a file called `odoo_task.py` in the same directory and imports it. You would usually have a `from` line for each Python file in the directory:

Now create the `todo_user/models/todo_task.py` file to extend the original model:

```
# -*- coding: utf-8 -*-
from odoo import models, fields, api
class TodoTask(models.Model):
    _inherit = 'todo.task'
    user_id = fields.Many2one('res.users', 'Responsible')
    date_deadline = fields.Date('Deadline')
```

The class name `TodoTask` is local to this Python file and, in general, is irrelevant for other modules. The `_inherit` class attribute is the key here: it tells Odoo that this class is inheriting and thus modifying the `todo.task` model.

Notice the `_name` attribute is absent. It is not needed because it is already inherited from the parent model.

The next two lines are regular field declarations. The `user_id` field represents a user from the users model `res.users`. It's a `Many2one` field, which is equivalent to a foreign key in database jargon. The `date_deadline` is a simple date field. In `Chapter 5`, *Models – Structuring the Application Data*, we will explain the types of fields available in Odoo in more detail.

To have the new fields added to the model's supporting database table, we need to perform a module upgrade. If everything goes as expected, you should see the new fields when inspecting the `todo.task` model in the **Technical** | **Database Structure** | **Models** menu option.

Modifying existing fields

As you can see, adding new fields to an existing model is quite straightforward. Since Odoo 8, modifying the attributes on existing inherited fields is also possible. It's done by adding a field with the same name and setting values only for the attributes to be changed.

For example, to add a help tooltip to the `name` field, we would add this line to `todo_task.py`, described previously:

```
name = fields.Char(help="What needs to be done?")
```

This modifies the field with the specified attributes, leaving unmodified all the other attributes not explicitly used here. If we upgrade the module, go to a to-do task form and pause the mouse pointer over the **Description** field; the tooltip text will be displayed.

Modifying model methods

Inheritance also works at the business logic level. Adding new methods is simple: just declare their functions inside the inheriting class.

To extend or change the existing logic, the corresponding method can be overridden by declaring a method with the exact same name. The new method will replace the previous one, and it can also just extend the code of the inherited class, using Python's `super()` method to call the parent method. It can then add new logic around the original logic both before and after `super()` method is called.

It's best to avoid changing the method's function signature (that is, keep the same arguments) to be sure that the existing calls on it will keep working properly. In case you need to add additional parameters, make them optional keyword arguments (with a default value).

The original **Clear All Done** action is not appropriate for our task-sharing module anymore since it clears all the tasks, regardless of their user. We need to modify it so that it clears only the current user tasks.

For this, we will override (or replace) the original method with a new version that first finds the list of completed tasks for the current user and then inactivates them:

```
@api.multi
def do_clear_done(self):
    domain = [('is_done', '=', True),
              '|', ('user_id', '=', self.env.uid),
                   ('user_id', '=', False)]
    dones = self.search(domain)
    dones.write({'active': False})
    return True
```

For clarity, we first build the filter expression to be used to find the records to be cleared.

This filter expression follows an Odoo-specific syntax referred to as `domain`: it is a list of conditions, where each condition is a tuple.

These conditions are implicitly joined with the AND (`&`) operator. For the OR operation, a pipe, `|`, is used in the place of a tuple, and it joins the next two conditions. We will go into more details about domains in `Chapter 6`, *Views – Designing the User Interface.*

The domain used here filters all the done tasks (`'is_done', '=', True`) that either have the current user as responsible (`'user_id', '=', self.env.uid`) or don't have a current user set (`'user_id', '=', False`).

We then use the `search` method to get a recordset with the done records to act upon and, finally, do a bulk write on them setting the `active` field to `False`. The Python `False` value here represents the database `NULL` value.

In this case, we completely overwrote the parent method, replacing it with a new implementation, but that is not what we usually want to do. Instead, we should extend the existing logic with some additional operations. Otherwise, we might break the already existing features.

To have the overriding method keep the already existing logic, we use Python's `super()` construct to call the parent's version of the method. Let's see an example of this.

We can improve the `do_toggle_done()` method so that it only performs its action on the tasks assigned to the current user. This is the code to achieve that:

```
from odoo.exceptions import ValidationError
# ...
# class TodoTask(models.Model):
# ...
@api.multi
def do_toggle_done(self):
    for task in self:
        if task.user_id != self.env.user:
            raise ValidationError(
                'Only the responsible can do this!')
    return super(TodoTask, self).do_toggle_done()
```

The method in the inheriting class starts with a `for` loop to check that none of the tasks to toggle belongs to another user. If these checks pass, it then goes on calling the parent class method, using `super()`. If not an error is raised, and we should use for this the Odoo built-in exceptions. The most relevant are `ValidationError`, used here, and `UserError`.

These are the basic techniques for overriding and extending business logic defined in model classes. Next, we will see how to extend the user interface views.

Extending views

Forms, lists, and search views are defined using the `arch` XML structures. To extend views, we need a way to modify this XML. This means locating XML elements and then introducing modifications at those points.

Inherited views allow just that. An inherited view declaration looks like this:

```
<record id="view_form_todo_task_inherited"
  model="ir.ui.view">
  <field name="name">Todo Task form - User
    extension</field>
  <field name="model">todo.task</field>
  <field name="inherit_id"
    ref="todo_app.view_form_todo_task"/>
  <field name="arch" type="xml">
    <!-- ...match and extend elements here! ... -->
  </field
</record>
```

The `inherit_id` field identifies the view to be extended by referring to its external identifier using the special `ref` attribute. External identifiers will be discussed in more detail in `Chapter 4`, *Module Data*.

Being XML, the best way to locate elements in XML is to use XPath expressions. For example, taking the form view defined in the previous chapter, one XPath expression to locate the `<field name="is_done">` element is `//field[@name]='is_done'`. This expression finds any `field` element with a `name` attribute that is equal to `is_done`. You can find more information on XPath at `https://docs.python.org/2/library/xml.etree.elementtree.html#xpath-support`.

If an XPath expression matches multiple elements, only the first one will be modified. So they should be made as specific as possible, using unique attributes. Using the `name` attribute is the easiest way to ensure we find the exact elements we want to use an extension point. Thus, it is important to set them on our view XML elements.

Once the extension point is located, you can either modify it or have XML elements added near it. As a practical example, to add the `date_deadline` field before the `is_done` field, we would write the following in `arch`:

```
<xpath expr="//field[@name]='is_done'" position="before">
  <field name="date_deadline" />
</xpath>
```

Fortunately, Odoo provides shortcut notation for this, so most of the time we can avoid the XPath syntax entirely. Instead of the preceding XPath element, we can just use information related to the type of element type to locate and its distinctive attributes, and instead of the preceding XPath, we write this:

```
<field name="is_done" position="before">
  <field name="date_deadline" />
</field>
```

Just be aware that if the field appears more than once in the same view, you should always use the XPath syntax. This is because Odoo will stop at the first occurrence of the field and it may apply your changes to the wrong field.

Often, we want to add new fields next to the existing ones, so the `<field>` tag will be used as the locator frequently. But any other tag can be used: `<sheet>`, `<group>`, `<div>`, and so on. The `name` attribute is usually the best choice for matching elements, but sometimes, we may need to use something else: the CSS `class` element, for example. Odoo will find the first element that has at least all the attributes specified.

Before version 9.0, the `string` attribute (for the displayed label text) could also be used as an extension locator. Since 9.0, this is not allowed anymore. This limitation is related to the language translation mechanism operating on those strings.

The `position` attribute used with the locator element is optional and can have the following values:

- `after` adds the content to the parent element, after the matched node.
- `before` adds the content, before the matched node.
- `inside` (default value) appended the content inside matched node.

- `replace` replaces the matched node. If used with empty content, it deletes an element. Since Odoo 10 it also allows to wrap an element with other markup, by using $0 in the content to represent the element being replaced.
- `attributes` modifies the XML attributes of the matched element. This is done using in the element content `<attribute name="attr-name">` elements with the new attribute values to set.

For Example, in the Task form, we have the `active` field, but having it visible is not that useful. We could hide it from the user. This can be done by setting its `invisible` attribute:

```
<field name="active" position="attributes">
  <attribute name="invisible">1</attribute>
</field>
```

Setting the `invisible` attribute to hide an element is a good alternative to using the `replace` locator to remove nodes. Removing nodes should be avoided since it can break depending modules that may be depending on the deleted node as a placeholder to add other elements.

Extending the form view

Putting together all the previous form elements, we can add the new fields and hide the `active` field. The complete inheritance view to extend the to-do tasks form is this:

```
<record id="view_form_todo_task_inherited"
  model="ir.ui.view">
  <field name="name">Todo Task form - User
    extension</field>
  <field name="model">todo.task</field>
  <field name="inherit_id"
    ref="todo_app.view_form_todo_task"/>
  <field name="arch" type="xml">
    <field name="name" position="after">
      <field name="user_id">
    </field>
    <field name="is_done" position="before">
      <field name="date_deadline" />
    </field>
    <field name="active" position="attributes">
      <attribute name="invisible">1</attribute>
    </field>
  </field>
</record>
```

This should be added to a `views/todo_task.xml` file in our module, inside the `<odoo>` element, as shown in the previous chapter.

Inherited views can also be inherited, but since this creates more intricate dependencies, it should be avoided. You should prefer to inherit from the original view whenever possible.

Also, we should not forget to add the `data` attribute to the `__manifest__.py` descriptor file:

```
'data': ['views/todo_task.xml'],
```

Extending the tree and search views

Tree and search view extensions are also defined using the `arch` XML structure, and they can be extended in the same way as form views. We will continue our example by extending the list and search views.

For the list view, we want to add the `user` field to it:

```
<record id="view_tree_todo_task_inherited"
  model="ir.ui.view">
  <field name="name">Todo Task tree - User
  extension</field>
  <field name="model">todo.task</field>
  <field name="inherit_id"
    ref="todo_app.view_tree_todo_task"/>
  <field name="arch" type="xml">
    <field name="name" position="after">
      <field name="user_id" />
    </field>
  </field
</record>
```

For the search view, we will add the search by the user and predefined filters for the user's own tasks and the tasks not assigned to anyone:

```
<record id="view_filter_todo_task_inherited"
  model="ir.ui.view">
  <field name="name">Todo Task tree - User
    extension</field>
  <field name="model">todo.task</field>
  <field name="inherit_id"
  ref="todo_app.view_filter_todo_task"/>
```

```
    <field name="arch" type="xml">
      <field name="name" position="after">
        <field name="user_id" />
        <filter name="filter_my_tasks" string="My Tasks"
          domain="[('user_id','in',[uid,False])]" />
        <filter name="filter_not_assigned" string="Not
          Assigned" domain="[('user_id','=',False)]" />
      </field>
    </field
  </record>
```

Don't worry too much about the specific syntax for these views. We'll cover them in more detail in `Chapter 6`, *Views – Designing the User Interface.*

More model inheritance mechanisms

We have seen the basic extension of models, called **class inheritance** in the official documentation. This is the most frequent use of inheritance, and it's easiest to think about it as **in-place extension**. You take a model and extend it. As you add new features, they are added to the existing model. A new model isn't created. We can also inherit from multiple parent models, setting a list of values to the `_inherit` attribute. With this, we can make use of **mixin classes.** Mixin classes are models that implement generic features we can add to other models. They are not expected to be used directly, and are like a container of features ready to be added to other models.

If we also use the `_name` attribute with a value different from the parent model, we get a new model reusing the features from the inherited one but with its own database table and data. The official documentation calls this **prototype inheritance**. Here you take a model and create a brand new one that is a copy of the old one. As you add new features, they are added to the new model. The existing model isn't changed.

There is also the **delegation inheritance** method, using the `_inherits` attribute. It allows a model to contain other models in a transparent way for the observer while, behind the scenes, each model handles its own data. You take a model and extend it. As you add new features, they are added to the new model. The existing module isn't changed. Records in the new model have a link to a record in the original model, and the fields of the original model are exposed and can be used directly in the new model.

Let's explore these possibilities in more detail.

Copying features with prototype inheritance

The method we used before to extend a model used just the _inherit attribute. We defined a class inheriting the todo.task model and added some features to it. The class attribute _name was not explicitly set; implicitly, it was todo.task.

However, using the _name attribute allows us to create a new model copying the features from the inherited ones. Here is an example:

```
from odoo import models
class TodoTask(models.Model):
    _name = 'todo.task'
    _inherit = 'mail.thread'
```

This extends the todo.task model by copying into it the features from the mail.thread model. The mail.thread model implements the Odoo messages and followers features and is reusable so that it's easy to add those features to any model.

Copying means that the inherited methods and fields will also be available in the inheriting model. For fields, this means that they will also be created and stored in the target model's database tables. The data records of the original (inherited) and the new (inheriting) models are kept unrelated. Only the definitions are shared.

In a moment, we will discuss in detail how to use this to add mail.thread and its social networking features to our module. In practice, when using mixins, we rarely inherit from regular models because this causes duplication of the same data structures.

Odoo also provides the delegation inheritance mechanism that avoids data structure duplication, so it is usually preferred when inheriting from regular models. Let's look at it in more detail.

Embedding models using delegation inheritance

Delegation inheritance is less frequently used, but it can provide very convenient solutions. It is used through the _inherits attribute (note the additional s) with dictionary mapping inherited models with fields linking to them.

A good example of this is the standard user's model, `res.users`; it has a Partner model embedded in it:

```
from odoo import models, fields
class User(models.Model):
    _name = 'res.users'
    _inherits = {'res.partner': 'partner_id'}
    partner_id = fields.Many2one('res.partner')
```

With delegation inheritance, the `res.users` model embeds the inherited model `res.partner` so that when a new `User` class is created, a partner is also created and a reference to it is kept in the `partner_id` field of the `User` class. It has some similarities with the polymorphism concept in object-oriented programming.

Through the delegation mechanism, all fields from the inherited model and Partner are available as if they were `User` fields. For example, the Partner `name` and `address` fields are exposed as `User` fields, but in fact, they are being stored in the linked Partner model, and no data duplication occurs.

The advantage of this, compared to prototype inheritance, is that there is no need to repeat data structures, such as addresses, across several tables. Any new model that needs to include an address can delegate that to an embedded Partner model. And if modifications are introduced in Partner address fields, these are immediately available to all the models embedding it!

Note that with delegation inheritance, fields are inherited, but methods are not.

Adding the social network features

The social network module (technical name `mail`) provides the message board found at the bottom of many forms and the **Followers** feature, as well as the logic regarding messages and notifications. This is something we will often want to add to our models, so let's learn how to do it.

The social network messaging features are provided by the `mail.thread` model of the `mail` module. To add it to a custom model, we need to do the following:

- Have the module depend on `mail`
- Have the class inherit from `mail.thread`
- Have the followers and thread widgets added to the form view
- Optionally, we need to set up record rules for followers.

Let's follow this checklist.

Regarding the first point, our extension module will need the additional `mail` dependency on the module `__manifest__.py` manifest file:

```
'depends': ['todo_app', 'mail'],
```

Regarding the second point, the inheritance on `mail.thread` is done using the `_inherit` attribute we used before. But our to-do task extension class is already using the `_inherit` attribute. Fortunately, it can accept a list of models to inherit from, so we can use this to make it also include the inheritance on `mail.thread`:

```
_name = 'todo.task'
_inherit = ['todo.task', 'mail.thread']
```

The `mail.thread` is an abstract model. **Abstract models** are just like regular models, except that they don't have a database representation; no actual tables are created for them. Abstract models are not meant to be used directly. Instead, they are expected to be used as mixin classes, as we just did. We can think of them as templates with ready-to-use features. To create an abstract class, we just need it to use `models.AbstractModel` instead of `models.Model` for the class defining them.

For the third point, we want to add the social network widgets at the bottom of the form. This is done by extending the form view definition. We can reuse the inherited view we already created, `view_form_todo_task_inherited`, and add this to its `arch` data:

```
<sheet position="after">
  <div class="oe_chatter">
    <field name="message_follower_ids"
      widget="mail_followers" />
    <field name="message_ids" widget="mail_thread" />
  </div>
</sheet>
```

The two fields added here haven't been explicitly declared by us, but they are provided by the `mail.thread` model.

The final step, that is step four, is to set up record rules for followers: row-level access control. This is only needed if our model is required to limit other users from accessing the records. In this case, we want each to-do task record to also be visible to any of its followers.

We already have a Record Rules defined on the to-do task model, so we need to modify it to add this new requirement. That's one of the things we will be doing in the next section.

Modifying data

Unlike views, regular data records don't have an XML `arch` structure and can't be extended using XPath expressions. But they can still be modified replacing the values in their fields.

The `<record id="x" model="y">` data loading elements actually perform an `insert` or `update` operation on the model `y`: if model `x` does not exist, it is created; otherwise, it is updated/written over.

Since records in other modules can be accessed using a `<model>.<identifier>` global identifier, it's possible for our module to overwrite something that was written before by another module.

Note that since the dot is reserved to separate the module name from the object identifier, it can't be used in identifier names. Instead, use the underscore option.

Modifying menu and action records

As an example, let's change the menu option created by the `todo_app` module to `My To-Do`. For this, we can add the following to the `todo_user/views/todo_task.xml` file:

```
<!-- Modify menu item -->
<record id="todo_app.menu_todo_task" model="ir.ui.menu">
  <field name="name">My To-Do</field>
</record>
```

We can also modify the action used in the menu item. Actions have an optional context attribute. It can provide default values for view fields and filters. We will use it to have enabled by default the **My Tasks** filter, defined earlier in this chapter:

```
<!-- Action to open To-Do Task list -->
<record model="ir.actions.act_window"
  id="todo_app.action_todo_task">
  <field name="context">
    {'search_default_filter_my_tasks': True}
  </field>
</record>
```

Modifying security record rules

The To-Do application included a record rule to ensure that each task would only be visible to the user that created it. But now, with the addition of social features, we need the task followers to also access them. The social network module does not handle this by itself.

Also, now tasks can have users assigned to them, so it makes more sense to have the access rules to work on the responsible user instead of the user who created the task.

The plan would be the same as we did for the menu item: overwrite `todo_app.todo_task_user_rule` to modify the `domain_force` field to a new value.

The convention is to keep security-related files in a `security` subdirectory, so we will create a `security/todo_access_rules.xml` file with the following content:

```
<?xml version="1.0" encoding="utf-8"?>
<odoo>
  <data noupdate="1">
    <record id="todo_app.todo_task_per_user_rule"
      model="ir.rule">
      <field name="name">ToDo Tasks for owner and
        followers</field>
      <field name="model_id" ref="model_todo_task"/>
      <field name="groups" eval="[(4,
        ref('base.group_user'))]"/>
      <field name="domain_force">
        ['|',('user_id','in', [user.id,False]),
        ('message_follower_ids','in',
        [user.partner_id.id])]
      </field>
    </record>
  </data>
</odoo>
```

This overwrites the `todo_task_per_user_rule` record rule from the `todo_app` module. The new domain filter now makes a task visible to the responsible user, `user_id`, or to everyone if the responsible user is not set (equals `False`); it is visible to all the task followers as well.

The record rule runs in a context where a `user` variable is available and represents the record for the current session user. Since Followers are partners, not `users`, instead of `user.id`, we need to use `user.partner_id`.

The groups field is a to-many relation. Editing data in these fields uses a special notation. The code `4` used here is to append to the list of related records. Also used often is code `6`, to instead completely replace the related records with a new list. We well discuss this notation in more detail in `Chapter 4`, *Module Data*.

The `noupdate="1"` attribute of the record element means that this record data will only be written on installation actions and will be ignored on module upgrades. This allows for it to be customization, without taking those risk of overwriting customizations and losing them when doing an module upgrade sometime in the future.

Working on data files with `<data noupdate="1">` at development time can be tricky because later edits on the XML definition will be ignored on module upgrades. To avoid this, you can instead reinstall the module. This is easier done through the command line using the `-i`

As usual, we must not forget to add the new file to data attribute in the the `__manifest__.py`:

```
'data': ['views/todo_task.xml', 'security/todo_access_rules.xml'],
```

Summary

You should now be able to create your own modules by extending the existing ones.

To demonstrate how to do this, we extended the To-Do module we created in the previous chapter, adding new features to the several layers that make up an application.

We extended an Odoo model to add new fields and extended its business logic methods. Next, we modified the views to make the new fields available to them. Finally, we learned how to inherit features from other models and use them to add the social network features to the To-Do app.

The first three chapters gave us an overview of the common activities involved in Odoo development, from Odoo installation and setup to module creation and extension.

The next chapters will each focus on a specific area of Odoo development, most of which we briefly visited in these first chapters. In the following chapter, we will address data serialization and the usage of XML and CSV data files in more detail.

4
Module Data

Most Odoo module definitions, such as user interfaces and security rules, are actually data records stored in specific database tables. The XML and CSV files found in modules are not used by Odoo applications at runtime. They are instead a means to load those definitions into the database tables.

Because of this, an important part of Odoo modules is about representing (serializing) that data using files so that can be later loaded into a database.

Modules can also have default and demonstration data. Data representation allows adding that to our modules. Additionally, understanding Odoo data representation formats is important in order to export and import business data in the context of a project implementation.

Before we go into practical cases, we will first explore the external identifier concept, which is the key to Odoo data representation.

Understanding external identifiers

An **external identifier** (also called XML ID) is a human-readable string identifier that uniquely identifies a particular record in Odoo. They are important when loading data into Odoo.

One reason for that is when upgrading a module, its data files will be loaded again into the database, and we need to detect the already existing records, in order to update them instead of creating new duplicate records.

Another reason supporting interrelated data: data records must be able to reference other data records. The actual database identifier is a sequential number automatically assigned by the database, during module installation. The external identifiers provides a way to reference a related record without the need to know beforehand what database ID it will be assigned, allowing us to define data relations in Odoo data files.

Odoo takes care of translating the external identifier names into actual database IDs assigned to them. The mechanism behind this is quite simple: Odoo keeps a table with the mapping between the named external identifiers and their corresponding numeric database IDs: the `ir.model.data` model.

To inspect the existing mappings, go to the **Technical** section of the **Settings** top menu and select the **External Identifiers** menu item under **Sequences & Identifiers**.

For example, if we visit the **External Identifiers** list and filter it by the `todo_app` module, we will see the external identifiers generated by the module created previously:

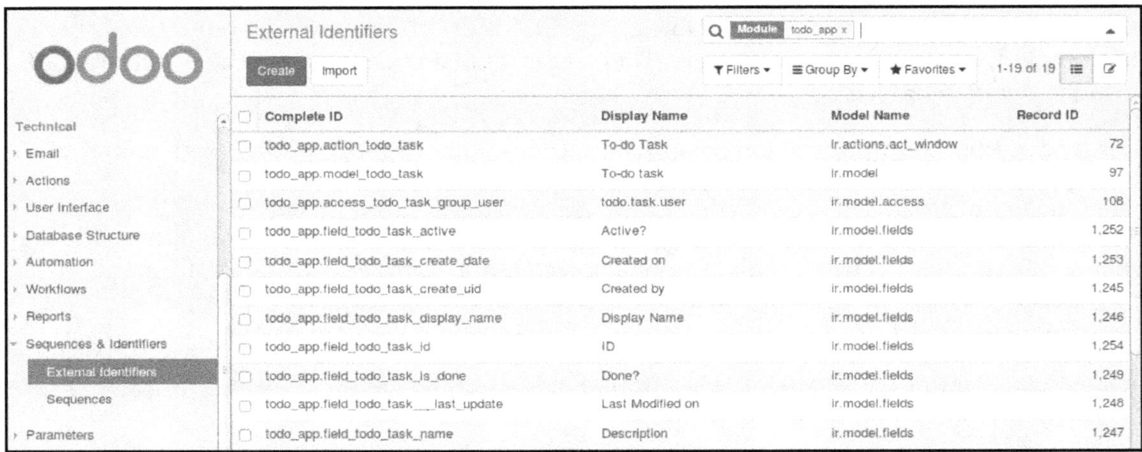

We can see that the external identifiers have a **Complete ID** label. Notice how it is composed of the module name and the identifier name joined by a dot, for example, `todo_app.action_todo_task`.

External identifiers need to be unique only inside an Odoo module, so that there is no risk of two modules conflicting because they accidentally chose the same identifier name. To build a global unique identifier Odoo joins together the modules name with the actual external identifier name. This is what you can see in the **Complete ID** field.

When using an external identifier in a data file, you can choose to use either the complete identifier or just the external identifier name. Usually it's simpler to just use the external identifier name, but the complete identifier enables us to reference data records from other modules. When doing so, make sure that those modules are included in the module dependencies, to ensure that those records are loaded before ours.

At the top of the list, we have the `todo_app.action_todo_task` complete identifier. This is the menu action we created for the module, which is also referenced in the corresponding menu item. By clicking on it, we go to the form view with its details; the `action_todo_task` external identifier in the `todo_app` module maps to a specific record ID in the `ir.actions.act_window` model, `72` in this case:

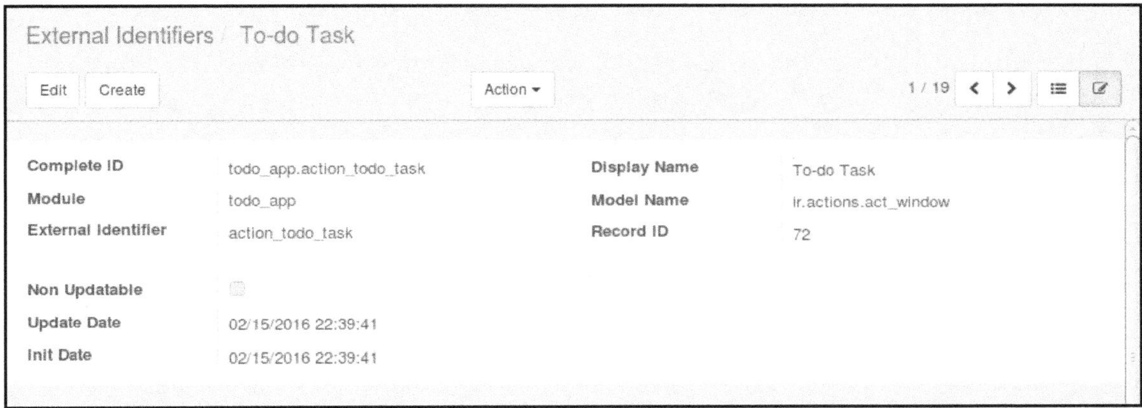

Besides providing a way for records to easily reference other records, external identifiers also allow you to avoid data duplication on repeated imports. If the external identifier is already present, the existing record will be updated; you'd not need to create a new record. This is why on subsequent module upgrades, previously loaded records are updated instead of being duplicated.

Finding external identifiers

When preparing definition and demonstration data files for the modules, we frequently need to look up existing external identifiers that are needed for references.

We can use the **External Identifiers** menu shown earlier, but the **Developer** menu can provide a more convenient method for this. As you may recall from `Chapter 1`, *Getting Started with Odoo Development*, the **Developer** menu is activated in the **Settings** dashboard, in an option at the bottom-right.

To find the external identifier for a data record, on the corresponding form view, select the **View Metadata** option from the **Developer** menu. This will display a dialog with the record's database ID and external identifier (also known as XML ID).

As an example, to look up the `Demo` user ID, we can navigate to form view, at **Settings** | **Users** and select the **View Metadata** option, and this will be shown:

To find the external identifier for view elements, such as form, tree, search, or action, the **Developer** menu is also a good source of help. For this, we can either use its **Manage Views** option or open the information for the desired view using the **Edit <view type>** option. Then, select their **View Metadata** option.

Exporting and importing data

We will start exploring how data exporting and importing work from Odoo's user interface, and from there, we will move on to the more technical details on how to use the data files in our addon modules.

Exporting data

Data exporting is a standard feature available in any list view. To use it, we must first pick the rows to export by selecting the corresponding checkboxes on the far left and then select the **Export** option from the **More** button.

Here is an example, using the recently created to-do tasks:

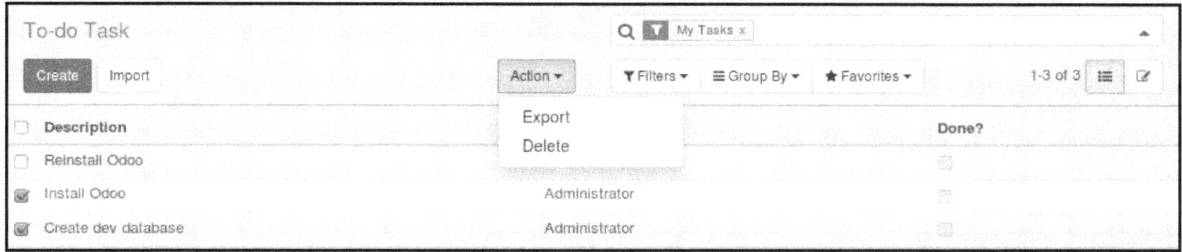

We can also tick the checkbox in the header of the column. It will check all the records at once, and will export all the records that match the current search criteria.

In previous Odoo versions, only the records seen on the screen (the current page) would actually be exported. Since Odoo 9, this was changed and ticked checkbox in the header will export all records that match the current filter, not just the ones currently displayed. This is very useful to export large sets of records that do not fit on the screen.

The **Export** option takes us to a dialog form, where we can choose what to export. The **Import-Compatible Export** option makes sure that the exported file can be imported back to Odoo. We will need to use this.

The export format can be either CSV or Excel. We will prefer a CSV file to get a better understanding of the export format. Next, we pick the columns we want to export and click on the **Export To File** button. This will start the download of a file with the exported data:

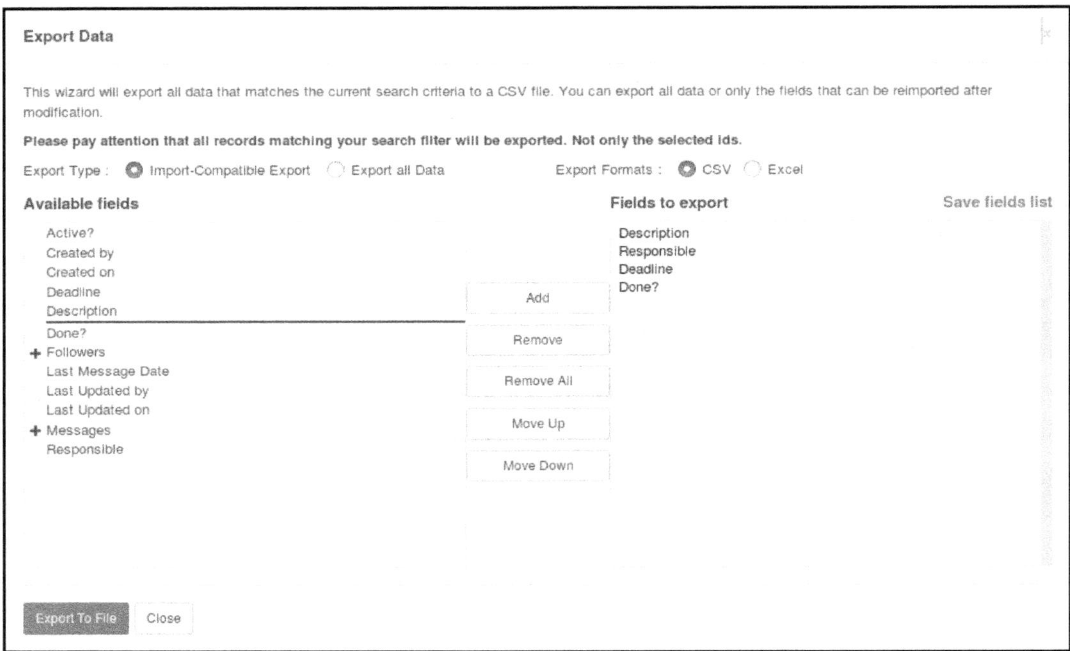

If we follow these instructions and select the fields shown in the preceding screenshot, we should end up with a CSV text file similar to this:

```
"id","name","user_id/id","date_deadline","is_done"
"todo_user.todo_task_a","Install
Odoo","base.user_root","2015-01-30","False"
"__export__.todo_task_9","Create my first
module","base.user_root","","False"
```

Notice that Odoo automatically exported an additional `id` column. This is an external identifier assigned to each record. If none is already assigned, a new one is automatically generated using `__export__` in place of an actual module name. New identifiers are only assigned to records that don't already have one, and from there on, they are kept bound to the same record. This means that subsequent exports will preserve the same external identifiers.

Importing data

First we have to make sure the import feature is enabled. Since Odoo 9 it is enabled by default. If not, the option is available from the **Settings** top menu, **General Settings** option. Under the **Import | Export** section there is **a Allow users to import data from CSV/XLS/XLSX/ODS files** checkbox that should be enabled.

This feature is provided by the **Initial Setup Tools** addon (`base_setup` is the technical name). The actual effect of the **Allow users to import...** checkbox is to install or uninstall `base_setup`.

With this option enabled list views show an **Import** option next to the **Create** button at the top of the list.

Let's perform a bulk edit on our to-do data first. Open the CSV file we just downloaded in a spreadsheet or a text editor and change a few values. Also, add some new rows, leaving the `id` column blank.

As mentioned before, the first column, `id`, provides a unique identifier for each row. This allows already existing records to be updated instead of duplicating them when we import the data back to Odoo. For new rows added to the CSV file, we can choose to either provide an external identifier of our choice, or to leave blank the `id` column, a new record will be created for them.

After saving the changes to the CSV file, click on the **Import** option (next to the **Create** button) and we will be presented with the import assistant.

There, we should select the CSV file location on the disk and click on **Validate** to check its format for correctness. Since the file to import is based on an Odoo export, chances are that it will be valid:

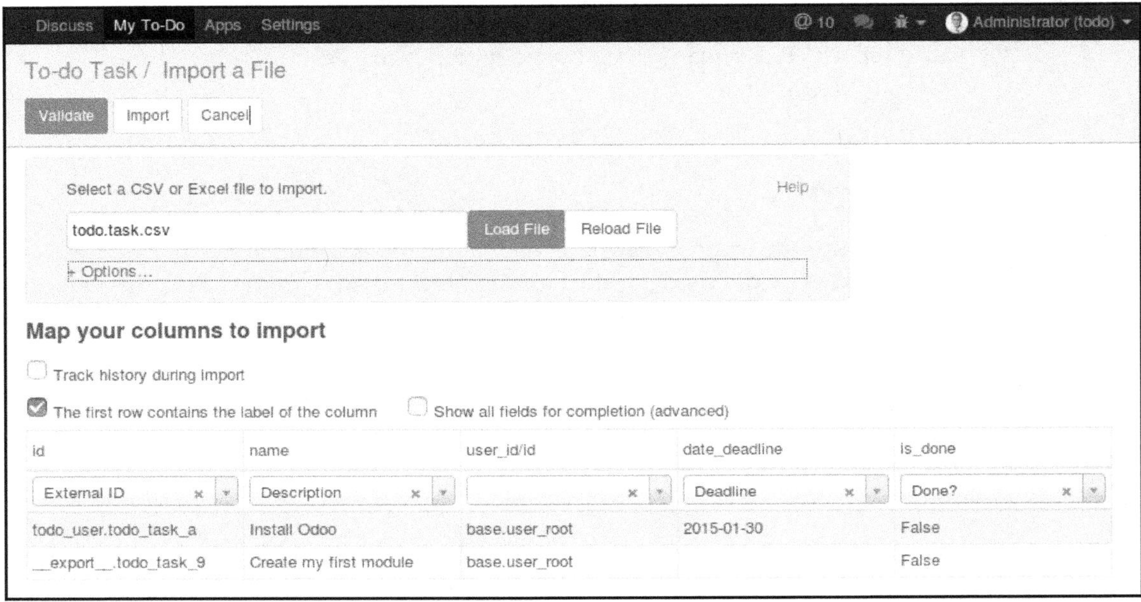

Now we can click on **Import**, and there you go; our modifications and new records should have been loaded into Odoo.

Related records in CSV data files

In the preceding example, the user responsible for each task is a related record in the users model, with a many-to-one (or a foreign key) relation. The column name used for it was `user_id/id` and the field values were external identifiers for the related records, such as `base.user_root` for the administrator user.

Using database IDs is only recommended if you are exporting and importing from/to the same database. Usually you will prefer to use external identifiers.

Relation columns should have `/id` appended to their name if using external identifiers or `/.id` if using database (numeric) IDs. Alternatively, a colon (`:`) can be used in place of a slash for the same effect.

Similarly, many-to-many relations are also supported. An example of a many-to-many relation is the one between users and groups: each user can be in many groups, and each group can have many users. The column name for this type of field should have `/id` appended. The field values accept a comma-separated list of external identifiers, surrounded by double quotes.

For example, the to-do task followers have a many-to-many relation between to-do tasks and partners. Its column name should be `follower_ids/id`, and a field value with two followers could look like this:

```
"__export__.res_partner_1,__export__.res_partner_2"
```

Finally, one-to-many relations can also be imported through a CSV. The typical example for this type of relation is a document *head* with several *lines*. Notice that a one-to-many relation is always the inverse of a many-to-one relations. Each document *head* can have many *lines*. And inversely every *line* has one *head*.

We can see an example of such a relation in the company model (the form view is available in the **Settings** menu): each company can have several bank accounts, each with its own details; inversely, each bank account record belongs to and has a many-to-one relation with only one company.

We can import companies along with their bank accounts in a single file. Here is an example where we load a company with three banks:

```
id,name,bank_ids/id,bank_ids/acc_number,bank_ids/state
base.main_company,YourCompany,__export__.res_partner_bank_4,123456789,bank
,,__export__.res_partner_bank_5,135792468,bank
,,__export__.res_partner_bank_6,1122334455,bank
```

We can see that the first two columns, `id` and `name`, have values in the first line and are empty in the next two lines. They have data for the `head` record, which is the company.

The other three columns are all prefixed with `bank_ids/` and have values on all three lines. They have data for the three related lines for the company's bank accounts. The first line has data of both the company and the first bank, and the next two lines have data only for the additional company and banks.

These are essentials while working with export and import from the GUI. It is useful to set up data in new Odoo instances or to prepare data files to be included in Odoo modules. Next, we will learn more about using data files in modules.

Module data

Modules use data files to load their configurations into the database, default data, and demonstration data. This can be done using both CSV and XML files. For completeness, the YAML file format can also be used, but it is very rare for it to be used to load data; therefore, we won't be discussing it.

CSV files used by modules are exactly the same as those we have seen and used for the import feature. When using them in modules, one additional restriction is that the filename must match the name of the model to which the data will be loaded so the system can infer the model into which the data should be imported.

A common usage of data CSV files is for accessing security definitions, loaded into the `ir.model.access` model. They usually use CSV files that are named `ir.model.access.csv`.

Demonstration data

Odoo addon modules may install demonstration data, and it is considered good practice to do so. This is useful to provide usage examples for a module and datasets to be used in tests. Demonstration data for a module is declared using the `demo` attribute of the `__manifest__.py` manifest file. Just like the `data` attribute, it is a list of filenames with the corresponding relative paths inside the module.

It's time to add some demonstration data to our `todo_user` module. We can start by exporting some data from the to-do tasks, as explained in the previous section. The convention is to place data files in a `data/` subdirectory. So we should save these data files in the `todo_user` addon module as `data/todo.task.csv`. Since this data will be owned by our module, we should edit the `id` values to remove the `__export__` prefix in the identifiers.

As an example, our `todo.task.csv` data file might look like this:

```
id,name,user_id/id,date_deadline
todo_task_a,"Install Odoo","base.user_root","2015-01-30"
todo_task_b","Create dev database","base.user_root",""
```

We must not forget to add this data file to the `__manifest__.py` manifest `demo` attribute:

```
'demo': ['data/todo.task.csv'],
```

Next time we update the module, as long as it is installed with demo data enabled, the content of the file will be imported. Note that this data will be reimported whenever a module upgrade is performed.

XML files are also used to load module data. Let's learn more about what XML data files can do that CSV files can't.

XML data files

While CSV files provide a simple and compact format to represent data, XML files are more powerful and give more control over the loading process. Their filenames are not required to match the model to be loaded. This is because the XML format is much richer and that information is provided by the XML elements inside the file.

We already used XML data files in the previous chapters. The user interface components, such as views and menu items, are in fact records stored in system models. The XML files in the modules are the means used to load these records into the server.

To showcase this, we will add a second data file to the `todo_user` module, `data/todo_data.xml`, with the following content:

```
<?xml version="1.0"?>
<odoo>
  <!-- Data to load -->
  <record model="todo.task" id="todo_task_c">
    <field name="name">Reinstall Odoo</field>
    <field name="user_id" ref="base.user_root" />
    <field name="date_deadline">2015-01-30</field>
    <field name="is_done" eval="False" />
  </record>
</odoo>
```

This XML is equivalent to the CSV data file we just saw in the previous section.

XML data files have a `<odoo>` top element, inside of which we can have several `<record>` elements that correspond to the CSV data rows.

The <odoo> top element in data files was introduced in version 9.0 and replaces the former <openerp> tag. The <data> section inside the top element is still supported, but it's now optional. In fact, now <odoo> and <data> are equivalent, so we could use either one as top elements for our XML data files.

A <record> element has two mandatory attributes, namely `model` and `id` (the external identifier for the record), and contains a <field> tag for each field to write on.

Note that the slash notation in field names is not available here; we can't use <field name="user_id/id">. Instead, the `ref` special attribute is used to reference external identifiers. We'll discuss the values of the relational to-many fields in a moment.

The data noupdate attribute

When data loading is repeated, records loaded from the previous run are rewritten. It is important to keep in mind that this means that upgrading a module will overwrite any manual changes that might have been made inside the database. Notably, if views were modified with customizations, then these changes will be lost with the next module upgrade. The correct procedure is to instead create inherited views for the changes we need, as discussed in `Chapter 3`, *Inheritance – Extending Existing Applications*.

This re-import behavior is default, but it can be changed, so that when an module is upgraded, some data file records are left untouched. This is done by the `noupdate="1"` attribute of the <odoo> or <data> element. These records will be created when the addon module is installed, but in subsequent module upgrades nothing will be done to them.

This allows you to ensure that manually made customizations are kept safe from module upgrades. It is often used with record access rules, allowing them to be adapted to implementation-specific needs.

It is possible to have more than one <data> section in the same XML file. We can take advantage of this to separate data to import only one, with `noupdate="1"`, and data to be re-imported on each upgrade, with `noupdate="0"`.

The `noupdate` flag is stored in the **External Identifier** information for each record. It's possible to manually edit it directly using the **External Identifier** form available in the **Technical** menu, using the **Non Updatable** checkbox.

The `noupdate` attribute can be tricky when developing modules, because changes made to the data later will be ignored. A solution is to, instead of upgrading the module with the `-u` option, reinstall it using the `-i` option. Reinstalling from the command line using the `-i` option ignores the `noupdate` flags on data records.

Defining records in XML

Each `<record>` element has two basic attributes, `id` and `model`, and contains `<field>` elements that assign values to each column. As mentioned before, the `id` attribute corresponds to the record's external identifier and the `model` attribute to the target model where the record will be written. The `<field>` elements have a few different ways to assign values. Let's look at them in detail.

Setting field values

The `<record>` element defines a data record and contains `<field>` elements to set values on each field.

The `name` attribute of the `field` element identifies the field to be written.

The value to write is the element content: the text between the field's opening and closing tag. For dates and datetimes, strings with `"YYYY-mm-dd"` and `"YYYY-mm-dd HH:MM:SS"` will be converted properly. But for Boolean fields any non-empty value will be converted as `True`, and the `"0"` and `"False"` values are converted to `False`.

The way Boolean `False` values are read from data files is improved in Odoo 10. In previous versions, any non-empty values, including `"0"` and `"False"` were converted to `True`. For Booleans using the `eval` attribute discussed next was recommended.

Setting values using expressions

A more elaborate alternative to define a field value is the `eval` attribute. It evaluates a Python expression and assigns the resulting value to the field.

The expression is evaluated in a context that, besides Python built-ins, also has some additional identifiers available. Let's have a look at them.

To handle dates, the following modules are available: `time`, `datetime`, `timedelta`, and `relativedelta`. They allow you to calculate date values, something that is frequently used in demonstration and test data, so that the dates used are close to the module installation date. For example, to set a value to yesterday, we will use this:

```
<field name="date_deadline"
  eval="(datetime.now() + timedelta(-1)).strftime('%Y-%m-%d')" />
```

Also available in the evaluation context is the `ref()` function, which is used to translate an external identifier into the corresponding database ID. This can be used to set values for relational fields. As an example, we have used it before to set the value for `user_id`:

```
<field name="user_id" eval="ref('base.group_user')" />
```

Setting values for relation fields

We have just seen how to set a value on a many-to-one relation field, such as `user_id`, using the `eval` attribute with a `ref()` function. But there is a simpler way.

The `<field>` element also has a `ref` attribute to set the value for a many-to-one field, using an external identifier. With this, we can set the value for `user_id` using just this:

```
<field name="user_id" ref="base.user_demo" />
```

For one-to-many and many-to-many fields, a list of related IDs is expected, so a different syntax is needed; Odoo provides a special syntax to write on this type of fields.

The following example, taken from the official Fleet app, replaces the list of related records of a `tag_ids` field:

```
<field name="tag_ids"
  eval="[(6,0,
    [ref('vehicle_tag_leasing'),
    ref('fleet.vehicle_tag_compact'),
    ref('fleet.vehicle_tag_senior')]
  )]" />
```

To write on a to-many field, we use a list of triples. Each triple is a write command that does different things according to the code used:

- `(0,_ ,{'field': value})` creates a new record and links it to this one
- `(1,id,{'field': value})` updates the values on an already linked record
- `(2,id,_)` unlinks and deletes a related record
- `(3,id,_)` unlinks but does not delete a related record
- `(4,id,_)` links an already existing record
- `(5,_,_)` unlinks but does not delete all the linked records
- `(6,_,[ids])` replaces the list of linked records with the provided list

The underscore symbol used in the preceding list represents irrelevant values, usually filled with `0` or `False`.

Shortcuts for frequently used models

If we go back to `Chapter 2`, *Building Your First Odoo Application*, we will find elements other than `<record>`, such as `<act_window>` and `<menuitem>`, in the XML files.

These are convenient shortcuts for frequently used models that can also be loaded using regular `<record>` elements. They load data into base models supporting the user interface and will be explored in more detail later, specifically in `Chapter 6`, *Views – Designing the User Interface*.

For reference, the following shortcut elements are available with the corresponding models they load data into:

- `<act_window>` is the window action model, `ir.actions.act_window`
- `<menuitem>` is the menu items model, `ir.ui.menu`
- `<report>` is the report action model, `ir.actions.report.xml`
- `<template>` is for QWeb templates stored in the model `ir.ui.view`
- `<url>` is the URL action model, `ir.actions.act_url`

Other actions in XML data files

Until now, we have seen how to add or update data using XML files. But XML files also allow you to perform other types of actions that are sometimes needed to set up data. In particular, they can delete data, execute arbitrary model methods, and trigger workflow events.

Deleting records

To delete a data record, we use the `<delete>` element, providing it with either an ID or a search domain to find the target record. For example, using a search domain to find the record to delete looks like this:

```
<delete
  model="ir.rule"
  search="
  [('id','=',ref('todo_app.todo_task_user_rule'))]"
/>
```

Since in this case we know the specific ID to delete, we could have used it directly for the same effect:

```
<delete model="ir.rule" id="todo_app.todo_task_user_rule" />
```

Triggering functions and workflows

An XML file can also execute methods during its load process through the `<function>` element. This can be used to set up demo and test data. For example, the CRM app uses it to set up demonstration data:

```
<function
  model="crm.lead"
  name="action_set_lost"
  eval="[ref('crm_case_7'), ref('crm_case_9')
        , ref('crm_case_11'), ref('crm_case_12')]
        , {'install_mode': True}" />
```

This calls the `action_set_lost` method of the `crm.lead` model, passing two arguments through the `eval` attribute. The first is the list of IDs to work on, and the next is the context to use.

Another way XML data files can perform actions is by triggering Odoo workflows through the `<workflow>` element. Workflows can, for example, change the state of a sales order or convert it into an invoice. The `sale` app no longer uses workflows, but this example can still be found in the demo data:

```
<workflow model="sale.order"
  ref="sale_order_4"
  action="order_confirm" />
```

The `model` attribute is self-explanatory by now, and `ref` identifies the workflow instance we are acting upon. The `action` is the workflow signal sent to this workflow instance.

Summary

You have learned all the essentials about data serialization and gained a better understanding of the XML aspects we saw in the previous chapters. We also spent some time understanding external identifiers, a central concept of data handling in general and module configurations in particular. XML data files were explained in detail. You learned about the several options available to set values on fields and also to perform actions, such as deleting records and calling model methods. CSV files and the data import/export features were also explained. These are valuable tools for Odoo's initial setup or for mass editing of data.

In the next chapter, we will explore how to build Odoo models in detail and learn more about building their user interfaces.

5
Models – Structuring the Application Data

In the previous chapters, we had an end-to-end overview of creating new modules for Odoo. In `Chapter 2`, *Building Your First Odoo Application*, we built a completely new application, and in `Chapter 3`, *Inheritance – Extending Existing Applications*, we explored inheritance and how to use it to create an extension module for our application. In `Chapter 4`, *Module Data*, we discussed how to add initial and demonstration data to our modules.

In these overviews, we touched upon all the layers involved in building a backend application for Odoo. Now, in the following chapters, it's time to explain these several layers that make up an application in more detail: models, views, and business logic.

In this chapter, you will learn how to design the data structures that support an application and how to represent the relationships between them.

Organizing application features into modules

As before, we will use an example to help explain the concepts.

Odoo's inheritance features provide an effective extensibility mechanism. It allows you to extend existing third-party apps without changing them directly. This composability also enables a module-oriented development pattern, where large apps can be split into smaller features, rich enough to stand on their own.

This can be helpful to limit complexity, both at the technical level and the user experience level. From a technical perspective, splitting a large problem into smaller parts makes it easier to solve and is friendlier for incremental feature development. From the user experience perspective, we can choose to activate only the features that are really needed for them, for a simpler user interface. So we will be improving our To-Do application through additional addon modules to finally form a fully featured application.

Introducing the todo_ui module

In the previous chapter, we first created an app for personal to-dos and then extended it so that the to-dos could be shared with other people.

Now we want to take our app to the next level by improving its user interface, including a kanban board. The kanban board is a simple workflow tool that organizes items in columns, where these items flow from the left-hand column to the right, until they are completed. We will organize our Tasks into columns, according to their Stages, such as **Waiting**, **Ready**, **Started**, or **Done**.

We will start by adding the data structures to enable this vision. We need to add stages, and it will be good to add support for tags as well, allowing the tasks to be categorized by subject. In this chapter, we will focus on the data models only. The user interface for these features will be discussed in `Chapter 6`, *Views – Designing the User Interface*, and kanban views in `Chapter 9`, *QWeb and Kanban Views*.

The first thing to figure out is how our data will be structured so that we can design the supporting models. We already have the central entity: the To-do Task. Each task will be in one Stage at a time, and tasks can also have one or more tags on them. We will need to add these two additional models, and they will have these relationships:

- Each task has a stage, and there can be many tasks in each stage
- Each task can have many tags, and each tag can be attached to many tasks

This means that Tasks have many-to-one relationship with Stages, and many-to-many relationships with Tags. On the other hand, the inverse relationships are: Stages have a one-to-many relationship with Tasks and Tags have a many-to-many relationship with Tasks.

We will start by creating the new `todo_ui` module and add the To-do Stages and To-do Tags models to it.

We've been using the `~/odoo-dev/custom-addons/` directory to host our modules. We should create a new `todo_ui` directory inside it for the new addons. From the shell, we could use the following commands:

```
$ cd ~/odoo-dev/custom-addons
$ mkdir todo_ui
$ cd todo_ui
```

We begin adding the `__manifest__.py` manifest file, with this content:

```
{
  'name': 'User interface improvements to the To-Do app',
  'description': 'User friendly features.',
  'author': 'Daniel Reis',
  'depends': ['todo_user'] }
```

We should also add a `__init__.py` file. It is perfectly fine for it to be empty for now.

Now we can install the module in our Odoo work database and get started with the models.

Creating models

For the to-do tasks to have a kanban board, we need Stages. Stages are board columns, and each task will fit into one of these columns:

1. Edit `todo_ui/__init__.py` to import the `models` submodule:

   ```
   from . import models
   ```

2. Create the `todo_ui/models` directory and add to it an `__init__.py` file with this:

   ```
   from . import todo_model
   ```

3. Now let's add the `todo_ui/models/todo_model.py` Python code file:

```
# -*- coding: utf-8 -*-
from odoo import models, fields, api

class Tag(models.Model):
    _name = 'todo.task.tag'
    _description = 'To-do Tag'
    name = fields.Char('Name', 40, translate=True)
class Stage(models.Model):
    _name = 'todo.task.stage'
    _description = 'To-do Stage'
    _order = 'sequence,name'

name = fields.Char('Name', 40, translate=True)
    sequence = fields.Integer('Sequence')
```

Here we created the two new models that will be referenced in the to-do tasks.

Focusing on the task stages, we have a Python class, `Stage`, based on the `models.Model` class, which defines a new Odoo model called `todo.task.stage`. We also have two fields: `name` and `sequence`. We can see some model attributes (prefixed with an underscore) that are new to us. Let's have a closer look at them.

Model attributes

Model classes can use additional attributes that control some of their behaviors. These are the most commonly used attributes:

- `_name` is the internal identifier for the Odoo model we are creating. Mandatory when creating a new model.
- `_description` is a user friendly title for the model's records, shown when the model is viewed in the user interface. Optional but recommended.
- `_order` sets the default order to use when the model's records are browsed, or shown in a list view. It is a text string to be used as the SQL `order by` clause, so it can be anything you could use there, although it has a smart behavior and supports translatable and many-to-one field names.

For completeness, there are a couple of more attributes that can be used in advanced cases:

- `_rec_name` indicates the field to use as the record description when referenced from related fields, such as a many-to-one relationship. By default, it uses the `name` field, which is a commonly found field in models. But this attribute allows us to use any other field for that purpose.
- `_table` is the name of the database table supporting the model. Usually, it is left to be calculated automatically, and is the model name with the dots replaced by underscores. But it's possible to set to indicate a specific table name.

We can also have the `_inherit` and `_inherits` attributes, as explained in `Chapter 3`, *Inheritance – Extending Existing Applications*.

Models and Python classes

Odoo models are represented by Python classes. In the preceding code, we have a Python class `Stage`, based on the `models.Model` class, that defines a new Odoo model called `todo.task.stage`.

Odoo models are kept in a central registry, also referred to as `pool` in the older Odoo versions. It is a dictionary that keeps references to all the model classes available in the instance, and it can be referenced by a model name. Specifically, the code in a model method can use `self.env['x']` to get a reference to a class representing the model `x`.

You can see that model names are important since they are the keys used to access the registry. The convention for model names is to use a list of lowercase words joined with dots, such as `todo.task.stage`. Other examples from the core modules are `project.project`, `project.task`, or `project.task.type`. We should use the singular form `todo.task` model instead of `todo.tasks`. For historical reasons, it is possible to find some core models that don't follow this, such as `res.users`, but it is not the rule.

Model names must be globally unique. Because of this, the first word should correspond to the main application the module relates to. In our example, it is `todo`. Other examples from the core modules are `project`, `crm`, or `sale`.

Python classes, on the other hand, are local to the Python file where they are declared. The identifier used for them is only significant for the code in that file. Because of this, class identifiers are not required to be prefixed by the main application they relate to. For example, there is no problem to name our class `Stage` for the `todo.task.stage` model. There is no risk of collision with possible classes with the same name on other modules.

Two different conventions for class identifiers can be used: `snake_case` or `CamelCase`. Historically, Odoo code used the snake case, and it is still possible to find classes that use this convention. But the trend is to use camel case, since it is the Python standard defined by the PEP8 coding conventions. You may have noticed that we are using the latter form.

Transient and Abstract models

In the preceding code and in the vast majority of Odoo models, classes are based on the `models.Model` class. These type of models have permanent database persistence: database tables are created for them and their records are stored until explicitly deleted.

But Odoo also provides two other model types to be used: Transient and Abstract models.

- **Transient models** are based on the `models.TransientModel` class and are used for wizard-style user interaction. Their data is still stored in the database, but it is expected to be temporary. A vacuum job periodically clears old data from these tables. For example, the **Load a Language** dialog window, found in the **Settings** | **Translations** menu, uses a Transient model to store user selections and implement wizard logic.
- **Abstract models** are based on the `models.AbstractModel` class and have no data storage attached to them. They act as reusable feature sets to be mixed in with other models, using the Odoo inheritance capabilities. For example, `mail.thread` is an Abstract model, provided by the `Discuss` addon, used to add message and follower features to other models.

Inspecting existing models

The models and fields created through the Python classes have their metadata available through the user interface. In the **Settings** top menu, navigate to the **Technical** | **Database Structure** | **Models** menu item. Here, you will find the list of all the models available in the database. Clicking on a model in the list will open a form with its details:

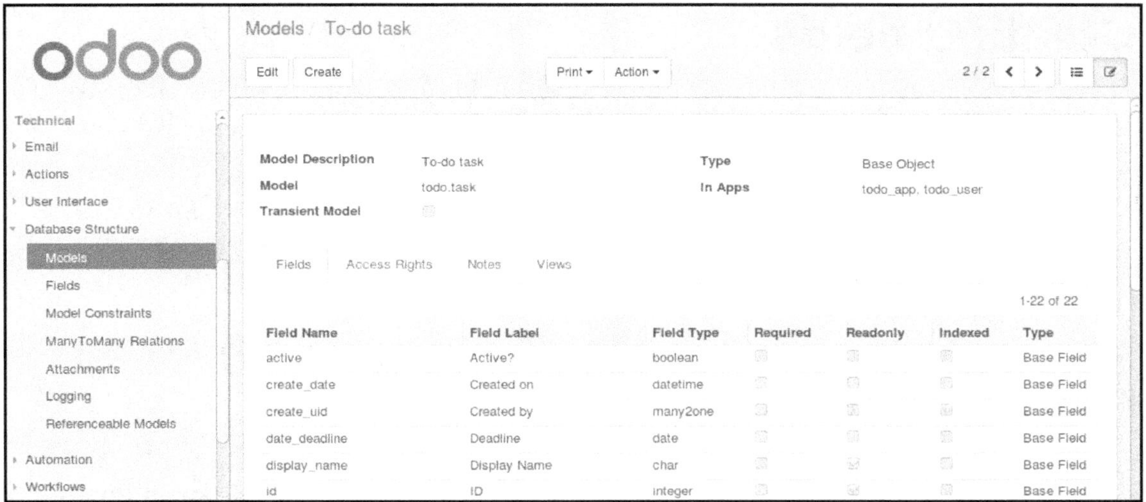

This is a good tool to inspect the structure of a model since in one place, you can see the results of all the customizations from different modules. In this case, as you can see at the top-right corner in the **In Apps** field, the `todo.task` definitions for this model come from both the `todo_app` and `todo_user` modules.

In the lower area, we have some information tabs available: a quick reference for the model's **Fields**, the **Access Rights** granted on security groups, and also list the **Views** available for this model.

We can find the model's **External Identifier** using, from the **Developer** menu, the **View Metadata** option. The model external identifiers, or XML IDs, are automatically generated by the ORM but fairly predictable: for the `todo.task` model, the external identifier is `model_todo_task`.

The **Models** form is editable! It's possible to create and modify models, fields, and views from here. You can use this to build prototypes before persisting them in modules.

Creating fields

After creating a new model, the next step is to add fields to it. Odoo supports all the basic data types expected, such as text strings, integers, floating point numbers, Booleans, dates, datetimes, and image/binary data.

Some field names are special, wither because they are reserved by the ORM for special purposes, or because some built-in features by default use some default field names.

Let's explore the several types of fields available in Odoo.

Basic field types

We now have a `Stage` model and we will expand it to add some additional fields. We should edit the `todo_ui/models/todo_model.py` file and add extra field definitions to make it look like this:

```
class Stage(models.Model):
    _name = 'todo.task.stage'
    _description = 'To-do Stage'
    _order = 'sequence,name'
    # String fields:
    name = fields.Char('Name', 40)
    desc = fields.Text('Description')
    state = fields.Selection(
        [('draft','New'), ('open','Started'),
        ('done','Closed')],'State')
    docs = fields.Html('Documentation')
    # Numeric fields:
    sequence = fields.Integer('Sequence')
    perc_complete = fields.Float('% Complete', (3, 2))
    # Date fields:
    date_effective = fields.Date('Effective Date')
    date_changed = fields.Datetime('Last Changed')
    # Other fields:
    fold = fields.Boolean('Folded?')
    image = fields.Binary('Image')
```

Here, we have a sample of the non-relational field types available in Odoo with the positional arguments expected by each one.

In most cases, the first argument is the field title, corresponding to the `string` field argument; this is used as the default text for the user interface labels. It's optional, and if not provided, a title will be automatically generated from the field name.

For date field names, there is a convention to use date as a prefix. For example, we should use `date_effective` field instead of `effective_date`. Similar conventions also apply to other fields, such as `amount_`, `price_`, or `qty_`.

These are the standard positional arguments expected by each of the field types:

- `Char` expects a second, optional, argument size, for the maximum text size. It's recommended to not use it unless there is business requirement that requires it, such as a social security number with a fixed length.
- `Text` differs from `Char`, in that, it can hold multiline text content, but expects the same arguments.
- `Selection` is a drop-down selection list. The first argument is the list of selectable options and the second is the string title. The selection item is a list of `('value', 'Title')` tuples, for the value stored in the database and the corresponding user interface description. When extending through inheritance, the `selection_add` argument is available to append new items to an existing selection list.
- `Html` is stored as a text field, but has specific handling on the user interface, for HTML content presentation. For security reasons, they are sanitized by default, but this behavior can be overridden.
- `Integer` just expects a string argument for the field title.
- `Float` has a second optional argument, an `(x,y)` tuple with the field's precision: `x` is the total number of digits; of those, `y` are decimal digits.
- `Date` and `Datetime` fields expect only the string text as a positional argument. For historical reasons, the ORM handles their values in a string format. Helper functions should be used to convert them to actual date objects. Also the datetime values are stored in the database in UTC time but presented in local time, using the user's time zone preferences. This is discussed in more detail in `Chapter 6`, *Views – Designing the User Interface*.

- `Boolean` holds `True` or `False` values, as you might expect, and only have one positional argument for the string text.
- `Binary` stores file-like binary data, and also expects only the string argument. They can be handled by Python code using `base64` encoded strings.

Other than these, we also have the relational fields, which will be introduced later in this chapter. But now, there is still more to learn about these field types and their attributes.

Common field attributes

Fields have attributes that can be set when defining them. Depending on the field type, a few attributes can be passed positionally, without an argument keyword, as shown in the previous section.

For example, `name=fields.Char('Name', 40)` could make use of positional arguments. Using the keyword arguments, the same could be written as `name=fields.Char(size=40, string='Name')`. More information on keyword arguments can be found in the Python official documentation at `https://docs.python.org/2/tutorial/controlflow.html#keyword-arguments`.

All the available attributes can be passed as a keyword argument. These are the generally available attributes and the corresponding argument keywords:

- `string` is the field default label, to be used in the user interface. Except for selection and relational fields, it is the first positional argument, so most of the time it is not used as a keyword argument.
- `default` sets a default value for the field. It can be a static value, such as a string, or a callable reference, either a named function or an anonymous function (a lambda expression).
- `size` applies only to `Char` fields, and can set a maximum size allowed. Current best practice is to not use it unless it's really needed.
- `translate` applies only to `Char`, `Text`, and `Html` fields, and makes the field contents translatable, holding different values for different languages.
- `help` provides the text for tooltips displayed to the users.
- `readonly=True` makes the field by default not editable on the user interface. This is not enforced at the API level; it is only a user interface setting.

- `required=True` makes the field by default mandatory in the user interface. This is enforced at the database level by adding a `NOT NULL` constraint on the column.
- `index=True` will create a database index on the field.
- `copy=False` has the field ignored when using the duplicate record feature, `copy()` ORM method. The non-relational fields are `copyable` by default.
- `groups` allows limiting the field's access and visibility to only some groups. It expects a comma separated list of XML IDs for security groups, such as `groups='base.group_user,base.group_system'`.
- `states` expects a dictionary mapping values for UI attributes depending on values of the `state` field. For example: `states={'done':[('readonly',True)]}`. Attributes that can be used are `readonly`, `required`, and `invisible`.

Note that the `states` field attribute is equivalent to the `attrs` attribute in views. Note that views support a `states` attribute, but it has a different usage: it accepts a comma-separated list of states to control when the element should be visible.

For completeness, two other attributes are sometimes used when upgrading between Odoo major versions:

- `deprecated=True` logs a warning whenever the field is being used.
- `oldname='field'` is used when a field is renamed in a newer version, enabling the data in the old field to be automatically copied into the new field.

Special field names

A few field names are reserved to be used by the ORM.

The `id` field is an automatic number uniquely identifying each record, and used as the database primary key. It's automatically added to every model.

The following fields are automatically created on new models, unless the `_log_access=False` model attribute is set:

- `create_uid` is for the user that created the record
- `create_date` is for the date and time when the record is created
- `write_uid` is for the last user to modify the record
- `write_date` is for the last date and time when the record was modified

This information is available from the web client, navigating to the **Developer Mode** menu and selecting the **View Metadata** option.

Some API built-in features by default expect specific field names. We should avoid using these field names for purposes other than the intended ones. Some of them are even reserved and can't be used for other purposes at all:

- `name` is used by default as the display name for the record. Usually it is a `Char`, but can also be a `Text` or a `Many2one` field type. We can still set another field to be used for display name, using the `_rec_name` model attribute.
- `Active`, of type `Boolean`, allows inactivating records. Records with `active==False` will automatically be excluded from queries. To access them an `('active','=',False)` condition must be added to the search domain, or `'active_test': False` should be added to the current context.
- `Sequence`, of type `Integer`, if present in a list view, allows to manually define the order of the records. To work properly you should not forget to use it with the model's `_order` attribute.
- `State`, of type `Selection`, represents basic states of the record's life cycle, and can be used by the state's field attribute to dynamically modify the view: some form fields can be made `readonly`, `required`, or `invisible` in specific record states.
- `parent_id`, `parent_left`, and `parent_right`, of type `Integer`, have special meaning for parent/child hierarchical relations. We will discuss them in detail in the next section.

So far, we've discussed non-relational fields. But a good part of an application data structure is about describing the relationships between entities. Let's look at that now.

Relationships between models

Looking again at our module design, we have these relationships:

- Each Task has a Stage. That's a many-to-one relationship, also known as a foreign key. The inverse is a one-to-many relationship, meaning that each Stage can have many Tasks.
- Each Task can have many Tags. That's a many-to-many relationship. The inverse relationship, of course, is also a many-to-many, since each Tag can be in many Tasks.

The following Entity Relationship Diagram can help visualizing the relationships we are about to create on the model. The lines ending with a triangle represent a many sides of the relationships:

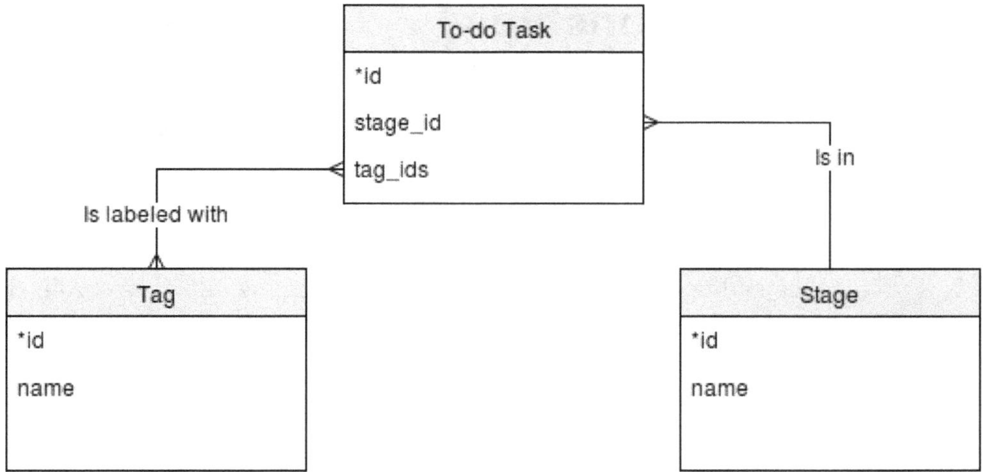

Let's add the corresponding relationship fields to the to-do tasks in our `todo_model.py` file:

```
class TodoTask(models.Model):
    _inherit = 'todo.task'
    stage_id = fields.Many2one('todo.task.stage', 'Stage')
    tag_ids = fields.Many2many('todo.task.tag', string='Tags')
```

The preceding code shows the basic syntax of these fields, setting the related model and the field's title `string`. The convention for relational field names is to append `_id` or `_ids` to the field names, for to-one and to-many relationships, respectively.

As an exercise, you may try to also add the corresponding inverse relationships to the related models:

- The inverse of the `Many2one` relationship is a `One2many` field on Stages, since each Stage can have many tasks. We should add this field to the Stage class.
- The inverse of the `Many2many` relationship is also a `Many2many` field on Tags, since each Tag can also be used on many Tasks.

Let's have a closer look at relational field definitions.

Many-to-one relationships

The `Many2one` relationship accepts two positional arguments: the related model (corresponding to the `comodel` keyword argument) and the title `string`. It creates a field in the database table with a foreign key to the related table.

Some additional named arguments are also available to use with this type of field:

- `ondelete` defines what happens when the related record is deleted. Its default is `set null`, meaning that an empty value is set when the related record is deleted. Other possible values are `restrict`, raising an error preventing the deletion, and `cascade` also deleting this record.
- `context` is a dictionary of data, meaningful for the web client views, to carry information when navigating through the relationship. For example, to set default vales. It will be better explained in the `Chapter 6`, *Views – Designing the User Interface*.
- `domain` is a domain expression, a list of tuples, used filter the records available for the relation field.
- `auto_join=True` allows the ORM to use SQL joins when doing searches using this relationship. If used, the access security rules will be bypassed, and the user could have access to related records the security rules wouldn't allow, but the SQL queries will be more efficient and run faster.

Many-to-many relationships

The Many2many minimal signature accepts one argument for the related model, and it is recommended to also provide the string argument with the field title.

At the database level, it does not add any columns to the existing tables. Instead, it automatically creates a new relationship table that has only two ID fields with the foreign keys for the related tables. The relationship table name and the field names are automatically generated. The relationship table name is the two table names joined with an underscore with _rel appended to it.

On some occasions we may need to override these automatic defaults.

One such case is when the related models have long names, and the name for the automatically generated relationship table is too long, exceeding the 63 characters PostgreSQL limit. In these cases we need to manually choose a name for the relationship table, to conform to the table name size limit.

Another case is when we need a second many-to-many relationship between the same models. In these cases we need to manually provide a name for the relationship table, so that it doesn't collide with the table name already being used for the first relationship.

There are two alternatives to manually override these values: either using positional arguments or keyword arguments.

Using positional arguments for the field definition we have:

```
# Task <-> Tag relation (positional args):
tag_ids = fields.Many2many(
    'todo.task.tag',      # related model
    'todo_task_tag_rel',  # relation table name
    'task_id',            # field for "this" record
    'tag_id',             # field for "other" record
    string='Tags')
```

Note that the additional arguments are optional. We could just set the name for the relationship table and let the field names use the automatic defaults.

We can instead use keyword arguments, which some people prefer for readability:

```
# Task <-> Tag relation (keyword args):
tag_ids = fields.Many2many(
    comodel_name='todo.task.tag',  # related model
    relation='todo_task_tag_rel',# relation table name
    column1='task_id',       # field for "this" record
    column2='tag_id',        # field for "other" record
    string='Tags')
```

Just like many-to-one fields, many-to-many fields also support the `domain` and `context` keyword attributes.

There is currently a limitation in the ORM design, regarding Abstract models, that when you force the names of the relationship table and columns, they cannot be cleanly inherited anymore. So this should not be done in Abstract models.

The inverse of the `Many2many` relationship is also a `Many2many` field. If we also add a `Many2many` field to the `Tags` model, Odoo infers that this many-to-many relationship is the inverse of the one in the `Task` model.

The inverse relationship between Tasks and Tags can be implemented like this:

```
class Tag(models.Model):
    _name = 'todo.task.tag'
    # Tag class relationship to Tasks:
    task_ids = fields.Many2many(
        'todo.task',    # related model
        string='Tasks')
```

One-to-many inverse relationships

An inverse of a `Many2one` can be added to the other end of the relationship. This has no impact on the actual database structure, but allows us easily browse from the **one** side of the **many** related records. A typical use case is the relationship between a document header and its lines.

In our example, a `One2many` inverse relationship on Stages allows us to easily list all the Tasks in that Stage. The code to add this inverse relationship to Stages is:

```
class Stage(models.Model):
    _name = 'todo.task.stage'
    # Stage class relationship with Tasks:
    tasks = fields.One2many(
        'todo.task',    # related model
        'stage_id', # field for "this" on related model
        'Tasks in this stage')
```

The `One2many` accepts three positional arguments: the related model, the field name in that model referring this record, and the title string. The first two positional arguments correspond to the `comodel_name` and `inverse_name` keyword arguments.

The additional keyword parameters available are the same as for `Many2one`: `context`, `domain`, `ondelete` (here acting on the **many** side of the relationship), and `auto_join`.

Hierarchic relationships

Parent-child tree relationships are represented using a `Many2one` relationship with the same model, so that each record references its parent. And the inverse `One2many` makes it easy for a parent to keep track of its children.

Odoo provides improved support for these hierarchic data structures, for faster browsing through tree siblings, and for easier search using the additional `child_of` operator in domain expressions.

To enable these features we need to set the `_parent_store` flag attribute and add to the model the helper fields: `parent_left` and `parent_right`. Mind that this additional operation comes at storage and execution time penalties, so it's best used when you expect to read more frequently than write, such as a the case of a category tree.

Revisiting the `Tags` model, defined in the `todo_model.py` file, we should now edit it to look like this:

```
class Tags(models.Model):
    _name = 'todo.task.tag'
    _description = 'To-do Tag'
    _parent_store = True
    # _parent_name = 'parent_id'
    name = fields.Char('Name')
    parent_id = fields.Many2one(
       'todo.task.tag', 'Parent Tag', ondelete='restrict')
    parent_left = fields.Integer('Parent Left', index=True)
    parent_right = fields.Integer('Parent Right', index=True)
```

Here, we have a basic model, with a `parent_id` field to reference the parent record, and the `additional _parent_store` attribute to add hierarchic search support. When doing this, the `parent_left` and `parent_right` fields must also be added.

The field referring to the parent is expected to be named `parent_id`, but any other field name can be used as long as we declare that in the `_parent_name` attribute.

Also, it is often convenient to add a field with the direct children of the record:

```
child_ids = fields.One2many(
    'todo.task.tag', 'parent_id', 'Child Tags')
```

Reference fields using dynamic relationships

Regular relational fields reference one fixed comodel. The Reference field type does not have this limitation and supports dynamic relationships, so that the same field is able to refer to more than one model.

For example, we can use it to add a `Refers to` field to To-do Tasks, that can either refer to a `User` or a `Partner`:

```
# class TodoTask(models.Model):
    refers_to = fields.Reference(
    [('res.user', 'User'), ('res.partner', 'Partner')],
    'Refers to')
```

As you can see, the field definition is similar to a Selection field, but here the selection list holds the models that can be used. On the user interface, the user will first pick a model from the av available list, and then pick a record from that model.

This can be taken to another level of flexibility: a **Referenceable Models** configuration table exists to configure the models that can be used in **Reference** fields. It is available in the **Settings** | **Technical** | **Database Structure** menu. When creating such a field we can set it to use any model registered there, with the help of the `referenceable_models()` function in the `odoo.addons.res.res_request` module.

Using the **Referenceable Models** configuration, an improved version of the `Refers to` field would look like this:

```
from odoo.addons.base.res.res_request import referenceable_models
# class TodoTask(models.Model):
    refers_to = fields.Reference(
        referenceable_models, 'Refers to')
```

Note that in Odoo 9.0 this function used a slightly different spelling, and was still using the old API. So in version 9.0, before using the code shown before, we have to add some code at the top of our Python file to wrap it so that it uses the new API:

```
from openerp.addons.base.res import res_request
    def referenceable_models(self):
        return res_request.referencable_models(
            self, self.env.cr, self.env.uid, context=self.env.context)
```

Computed fields

Fields can have values calculated by a function, instead of simply reading a database stored value. A computed field is declared just like a regular field, but has the additional `compute` argument defining the function used to calculate it.

In most cases computed fields involve writing some business logic, so we will develop this topic more in `Chapter 7`, *ORM Application Logic – Supporting Business Processes*. We will still explain them here, but will keep the business logic side as simple as possible.

Let's work on an example: Stages have a `fold` field. We will add to To-do Tasks a computed field with the **Folded?** flag for the corresponding Stage.

We should edit the `TodoTask` model in the `todo_model.py` file to add the following:

```
# class TodoTask(models.Model):
    stage_fold = fields.Boolean(
        'Stage Folded?',
        compute='_compute_stage_fold')

    @api.depends('stage_id.fold')
    def _compute_stage_fold(self):
        for task in self:
            task.stage_fold = task.stage_id.fold
```

The preceding code adds a new `stage_fold` field and the `_compute_stage_fold` method used to compute it. The function name was passed as a string, but it's also allowed to pass it as a callable reference (the function identifier with no quotes). In this case we should make sure the function is defined in the Python file before the field is.

The `@api.depends` decorator is needed when the computation depends on other fields, as it usually does. It lets the server know when to recompute stored or cached values. One or more field names are accepted as arguments and dot-notation can be used to follow field relationships.

The computation function is expected to assign a value to the field or fields to compute. If it doesn't, it will error. Since `self` is a record object, our computation here is simply to get the **Folded?** field using `stage_id.fold`. The result is achieved by assigning that value (writing it) to the computed field, `stage_fold`.

We won't be working yet on the views for this module, but you can make right now a quick edit on the task form to confirm if the computed field is working as expected: using the **Developer Mode** pick the **Edit View** option and add the field directly in the form XML. Don't worry: it will be replaced by the clean module view on the next upgrade.

Searching and writing on computed fields

The computed field we just created can be read, but it can't be searched or written. To enable these operations, we first need to implement specialized functions for them. Along with the `compute` function, we can also set a `search` function, implementing the search logic, and the `inverse` function, implementing the write logic.

Using these, our computed field declaration becomes like this:

```
# class TodoTask(models.Model):
    stage_fold = fields.Boolean(
        string='Stage Folded?',
        compute='_compute_stage_fold',
        # store=False,  # the default
        search='_search_stage_fold',
        inverse='_write_stage_fold')
```

And the supporting functions are:

```
def _search_stage_fold(self, operator, value):
    return [('stage_id.fold', operator, value)]

def _write_stage_fold(self):
    self.stage_id.fold = self.stage_fold
```

The `search` function is called whenever a `(field, operator, value)` condition on this field is found in a search domain expression. It receives the `operator` and `value` for the search and is expected to translate the original search element into an alternative domain search expression.

The `inverse` function performs the reverse logic of the calculation, to find the value to write on the computation's source fields. In our example, this means writing back on the `stage_id.fold` field.

Storing computed fields

Computed field's values can also be stored on the database, by setting `store = True` on their definition. They will be recomputed when any of their dependencies change. Since the values are now stored, they can be searched just like regular fields, and a search function is not needed.

Related fields

The computed field we implemented in the previous section just copies a value from a related record into a model's own field. However this is a common usage that can be automatically handled by Odoo.

The same effect can be achieved using related fields. They make available, directly on a model, fields that belong to a related model, accessible using a dot-notation chain. This makes them usable in situations where dot-notation can't be used, such as UI form views.

To create a related field, we declare a field of the needed type, just like with regular computed fields, but instead of compute we use the related attribute with the dot-notation field chain to reach the desired field.

To-do Tasks are organized in customizable Stages and these is turn map into basic States. We will make the State value available directly on the Task model, so that it can be used for some client-side logic in the next chapter.

Similarly to `stage_fold`, we will add a computed field on the task model, but this time using the simpler related field:

```
# class TodoTask(models.Model):
    stage_state = fields.Selection(
        related='stage_id.state',
        string='Stage State')
```

Behind the scenes, related fields are just computed fields that conveniently implement `search` and `inverse` methods. This means that we can search and write on them out of the box, without having to write any additional code.

Model Constraints

To enforce data integrity, models also support two types of constraints: SQL and Python

SQL constraints are added to the database table definition and are enforced directly by PostgreSQL. They are defined using the `_sql_constraints` class attribute. It is a list of tuples with: the constraint identifier name; the SQL for the constraint; and the error message to use.

A common use case is to add unique constraints to models. Suppose we don't want to allow two active tasks with the same title:

```
# class TodoTask(models.Model):
    _sql_constraints = [
        ('todo_task_name_uniq',
         'UNIQUE (name, active)',
         'Task title must be unique!')]
```

Python constraints can use a piece of arbitrary code to check the conditions. The checking function should be decorated with `@api.constraints`, indicating the list of fields involved in the check. The validation is triggered when any of them is modified and will raise an exception if the condition fails.

For example, to validate that a Task name is at least five characters long, we could add the following constraint:

```
from odoo.exceptions import ValidationError
# class TodoTask(models.Model):
    @api.constrains('name')
    def _check_name_size(self):
        for todo in self:
            if len(todo.name) < 5:
                raise ValidationError('Must have 5
                chars!')
```

Summary

We went through a detailed explanation of models and fields, using them to extend the To-Do app with Tags and Stages on tasks. You learned how to define relationships between models, including hierarchical parent/child relationships. Finally, we saw simple examples of computed fields and constraints using Python code.

In the next chapter, we will work on the user interface for these backend model features, making them available in the views used to interact with the application.

6

Views - Designing the User Interface

This chapter will help you learn how to build the graphical interface for users to interact with the To-Do application. You will discover the distinct types of views and widgets available, understand what context and domain are, and learn how to use them to provide a good user experience.

We will continue working with the `todo_ui` module. It already has the Model layer ready, and now it needs the View layer for the user interface.

Defining the user interface with XML files

Each component of the user interface is stored in a database record, just like business records are. Modules add UI elements to the database loading the corresponding data from XML files.

This means that a new XML data file for our UI needs to be added to the `todo_ui` module. We can start by editing the `__manifest__.py` file to declare these new data files:

```
{
  'name': 'User interface improvements to the To-Do app',
  'description': 'User friendly features.',
  'author': 'Daniel Reis',
  'depends': ['todo_user'],
  'data': [
    'security/ir.model.access.csv',
    'views/todo_view.xml',
    'views/todo_menu.xml',
  ]}
```

Remember that the data files are loaded in the order you specify. This is important because you can only reference XML IDs that were defined before they are being used.

We might also create the subdirectory and the `views/todo_view.xml` and `views/todo_menu.xml` files with a minimal structure:

```
<?xml version="1.0"?>
<odoo>
  <!-- Content will go here... -->
</odoo>
```

In `Chapter 3`, *Inheritance – Extending Existing Applications*, a basic menu was given to our application, but we now want to improve it. So we will be adding new menu items and the corresponding window actions, to be triggered when they are selected.

Menu items

Menu items are stored in the `ir.ui.menu` model and can be browsed via the **Settings** menu under **Technical** | **User Interface** | **Menu Items**.

The `todo_app` addon created a top-level menu to open the To-Do app tasks. Now we want to modify it to a second-level menu and have other menu options alongside it.

To do this, we will add a new top-level menu for the app and modify the existing To-Do task menu option. To `views/todo_menu.xml`, add:

```
<!-- Menu items -->
<!-- Modify top menu item -->
<menuitem id="todo_app.menu_todo_task" name="To-Do" />
<!-- App menu items -->
<menuitem id="menu_todo_task_view"
  name="Tasks"
  parent="todo_app.menu_todo_task"
  sequence="10"
  action="todo_app.action_todo_task" />
<menuitem id="menu_todo_config"
  name="Configuration"
  parent="todo_app.menu_todo_task"
  sequence="100"
  groups="base.group_system" />
<menuitem id="menu_todo_task_stage"
  name="Stages"
  parent="menu_todo_config"
```

```
    sequence="10"
    action="action_todo_stage" />
```

Instead of using `<record model="ir.ui.menu">` elements, we can use the more convenient `<menuitem>` shortcut element, that provides an abbreviated way to define the record to load.

Our first menu item is for the To-do app top menu entry, with only the `name` attribute, and will be used as the parent for the next two options.

Notice that it uses the existing XML ID `todo_app.menu_todo_task`, thus rewriting the menu item, defined in the `todo_app` module, without any action attached to it. This is because we will be adding child menu items, and the action to open the Task views will now be called from one of them.

Then next menu items are placed under the top level item, through the `parent="todo_app.menu_todo_task"` attribute.

The second menu is the one opening the Task views, through the `action="todo_app.action_todo_task"` attribute. As you can see from the XML ID used, it is reusing an action already created by the `todo_app` module.

The third menu item adds the **Configuration** section for our app. We want it to be available only for super users, so we also use the groups attribute to make it visible only to the **Administration** | **Settings** security group.

Finally, under the **Configuration** menu we add the option for the task Stages. We will use it to maintain the Stages to be used by the kanban feature we will be adding to the To-do Tasks.

At this point, if we try to upgrade the addon we should get errors because we haven't defined the XML IDs used in the `action` attributes. We will be adding them in the next section.

Window actions

A **window action** gives instructions to the GUI client, and is usually used by menu items or buttons in views. It tells the GUI what model to work on, and what views to make available. These actions can force for only a subset of the records to be visible, using a `domain` filter. They can also set default values and filters through the `context` attribute.

We will add window actions to the `views/todo_menu.xml` data file, which will be used by the menu items created in previous section. Edit the file, and make sure they are added before the menu items:

```
<!-- Actions for the menu items -->
<act_window id="action_todo_stage"
  name="To-Do Task Stages"
  res_model="todo.task.stage"
  view_mode="tree,form"
  target="current"
  context="{'default_state': 'open'}"
  domain="[]"
  limit="80"
/>
<act_window id="todo_app.action_todo_task"
  name="To-Do Tasks"
  res_model="todo.task"
  view_mode="tree,form,calendar,graph,pivot"
  target="current"
  context="{'search_default_filter_my_tasks': True}"
/>
<!-- Add option to the "More" button -->
<act_window id="action_todo_task_stage"
  name="To-Do Task Stages"
  res_model="todo.task.stage"
  src_model="todo.task"
  multi="False"
/>
```

Window actions are stored in the `ir.actions.act_window` model and can be defined in XML files using the `<act_window>` shortcut used in the preceding code.

The first action will open the Task Stages model and include the most relevant attributes for window actions:

- `name` is the title that will be displayed on the views opened through this action.
- `res_model` is the identifier of the target model.

- `view_mode` is the view type available and their order. The first is the one opened by default.
- `target`, if set to `new`, will open the view in a pop-up dialog window. By default it is `current`, opening the view inline, in the main content area.
- `context` sets context information on the target views, which can set default values or activate filters, among other things. We will see it in more details in a moment.
- `domain` is a domain expression forcing a filter for the records that will be browseable in the opened views.
- `limit` is the number of records for each page, in the list view.

The second action defined in the XML is replacing the original To-do Tasks action of the `todo_app` addon so that it displays the other view types we will explore later in this chapter: calendar and graph. After these changes are installed, you'll see additional buttons in the top-right corner, after the list and form buttons; however, these won't work until we create the corresponding views.

We also added a third action, not used in any of the menu items. It shows us how to add an option to the **More** menu, available at the top-right part of the list and form views. To do so, it uses two specific attributes:

- `src_model` indicates on what model this action should be made available.
- `multi`, when set to `True`, makes it available in the list view so that it can applied to a multiple selection of records. The default value is `False`, as in our example, it will make the option available only in the form view, and so can only be applied to one record at a time.

Context and domain

We have stumbled upon context and domain several times. We have seen that window actions are able to set them and relational fields in models can also have them as attributes.

Context data

The **context** is a dictionary carrying session data that can be used on both the client-side user interface and the server-side ORM and business logic.

On the client side it can carry information from one view to next, such as the ID of the record active on the previous view, after following a link or a button, or to provide default values to be used in the next view.

On the server side, some recordset field values can depend on the locale settings provided by the context. In particular the `lang` key affects the value of translatable fields. Context can also provide signals for server-side code. For example, the `active_test` key when set to `False` changes the behavior of ORM's `search()` method so that it does not filter out inactive records.

An initial context from the web client looks like this:

```
{'lang': 'en_US', 'tz': 'Europe/Brussels', 'uid': 1}
```

You can see the `lang` key with the user language, `tz` with the time zone information, and `uid` with the current user ID.

When opening a form from a link or a button in a previous view, an `active_id` key is added to the context, with the ID of record we were positioned at, in the origin form. In the particular case of list views, we have an `active_ids` context key containing a list of the record IDs selected in the previous list.

On the client side, the context can be used to set default values or activate default filters on the target view, using keys with the `default_` or `default_search_` prefixes. Here are some examples:

To set the current user as a default value of the `user_id` field, we will use the following:

```
{'default_user_id': uid}
```

To have a `filter_my_tasks` filter activated by default on the target view, we will use this:

```
{'default_search_filter_my_tasks': 1}
```

Domain expressions

The **domain** is used to filter data records. They use a specific syntax that the Odoo ORM parses to produce the SQL WHERE expressions that will query the database.

A domain expression is a list of conditions. Each condition is a `('field_name', 'operator', value')` tuple. For example, this is a valid domain expression, with only one condition: `[('is_done','=',False)]`.

Following is an explanation of each of these elements:

The **field name** is the field being filtered, and can use dot-notation for fields in related models.

The **value** is evaluated as a Python expression. It can use literal values, such as numbers, Booleans, strings, or lists, and can use fields and identifiers available in the evaluation context. There are actually two possible evaluation contexts for domains:

- When used in the client-side, such as in window actions or field attributes, the raw field values used to render the current view are available, but we can't use dot-notation on them.
- When used on the server-side, such as in security record rules and in server Python code, dot-notation can be used on fields, since the current record is an object.

The **operator** can be:

- The usual comparison operators are <, >, <= , >=, =, !=.
- `'=like'` matches against a pattern, where the underscore symbol, _, matches any single character, and the percentage symbol, `%`, matches any sequence of characters.
- `'like'` matches against a `'%value%'` pattern. The `'ilike'` is similar but case insensitive. The `'not like'` and `'not ilike'` operators are also available.
- `'child of'` finds the children values in a hierarchical relation, for the models configured to support them.
- `'in'` and `'not in'` are used to check for inclusion in a given list, so the value should be a list of values. When used on a "to-many" relation field the `in` operator behaves like a `contains` operator.

A domain expression is a list of items, and can contain several condition tuples. By default these condition will implicitly be combined using the AND logical operator. This means that it will only return records meeting all these conditions.

Explicit logic operators can also be used: the ampersand symbol, `'&'`, for AND operations (the default), and the pipe symbol,`'|'`, for OR operations. These will operate on the next two items, working in a recursive way. We'll look at this in more detail in a moment.

The exclamation point, `'!'`, represents the NOT operator, is also available and operates on the next item. So, it should be placed before the item to be negated. For example, the `['!', ('is_done','=',True)]` expression would filter all not done records.

The "next item" can also be an operator item acting on its next items, defining nested conditions. An example may help us to better understand this.

In server-side record rules, we can find domain expressions similar to this one:

```
['|', ('message_follower_ids', 'in',
      [user.partner_id.id]),
      '|', ('user_id', '=', user.id),
      ('user_id', '=', False)
]
```

This domain filters all the records where the current user is in the follower list, is the responsible user, or does not have a responsible user set.

The first `'|'` (OR) operator acts on the follower's condition plus the result of the next condition. The next condition is again the union of two other conditions: records where either the user ID is the current session user or it is not set.

The following diagram illustrates this nested operators resolution:

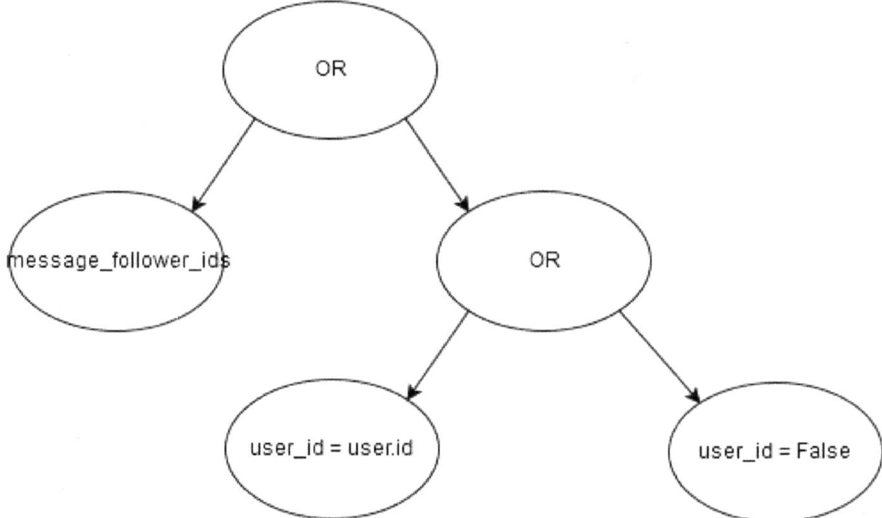

The form views

As we have seen in previous chapters, form views can follow a simple layout or a business document layout, similar to a paper document.

We will now see how to design these business document views and how to use the elements and widgets available. We would normally do this by inheriting and extending the `todo_app` views. But for the sake of clarity, we will instead create completely new views to override the original ones.

Dealing with several views of the same type

The same model can have more than one view of the same type. This can be useful since an window action can tell the specific view that should be used, through its XML ID. So we have the flexibility to have two different menu items to open the same model using different views. This is done adding a `view_id` attribute to the window action, with the XML ID of the view to use. For example, we could have used this in the `todo_app.action_todo_task` action, with something similar to: `view_id="view_form_todo_task_ui"`.

But what happens if no specific view is define? In that case the one used will be the first one returned when querying for views. This will be the one with the lower priority . If we add a new view and set it with a lower priority than the existing ones, it will be the one used. The final effect is that it looks like this new view is overriding the original one.

Since the default value for the view priority is 16, any lower value would do, so a 15 priority will work.

It's not the most commonly used route, to help keeping our examples as readable as possible, we will use the priority approach in our next examples.

Business document views

Business applications are often systems of record – for products in a warehouse, invoices in an accounting department, and many more. Most of the recorded data can be represented as a paper document. For a better user experience, form views can mimic these paper documents. For example, in our app, we could think of a To-Do Task as something that has a simple paper form to fill out. We will provide a form view that follows this design.

To add a view XML with the basic skeleton of a business document view, we should edit the `views/todo_views.xml` file and add it to the top:

```
<record id="view_form_todo_task_ui"
  model="ir.ui.view">
  <field name="model">todo.task</field>
  <field name="priority">15</field>
  <field name="arch" type="xml">
    <form>
      <header>
        <!-- To add buttons and status widget -->
      </header>
      <sheet>
        <!-- To add form content -->
      </sheet>
      <!-- Discuss widgets for history and
      communication: -->
      <div class="oe_chatter">
        <field name="message_follower_ids"
          widget="mail_followers" />
        <field name="message_ids" widget="mail_thread" />
      </div>
    </form>
  </field>
</record>
```

The view name is optional and automatically generated if missing. For simplicity, we took advantage of that and omitted the `<field name="name">` element from the view record.

We can see that business document views usually use three main areas: the **header** status bar, the **sheet** for the main content, and a bottom **history and communication** section, also known as **chatter**.

The history and communication section, at the bottom, uses the social network widgets provided by the mail addon module. To be able to use them, our model should inherit the `mail.thread` mixin model, as we saw in `Chapter 3`, *Inheritance – Extending Existing Applications*.

The header

The header at the top usually features the life cycle or steps that the document will move through and the action buttons.

These action buttons are regular form buttons, and the most important next steps can be highlighted, using `class="oe_highlight"`.

The document life cycle uses the `statusbar` widget on a field that represents the point in the life cycle where the document is currently at. This is usually a **State** selection field or a **Stage** many-to-one field. These two fields can be found across several Odoo core modules.

The stage is a many-to-one field which uses a supporting model to set up the steps of the process. Because of this it can be dynamically configured by end users to fit their specific business process, and is perfect to support kanban boards.

The state is a selection list featuring a few, rather stable, steps in a process, such as `New`, `In Progress`, and `Done`. It is not configurable by end users but, since it is static, it is much easier to be used in business logic. The view fields even have special support for it: the state attribute allows a field to be available to the user or not, depending on the document state.

Historically, stages were introduced later than states. Both have coexisted, but the trend in the Odoo core is for stages to replace states. But as seen in the preceding explanation, states still provide some features that stages don't.

It is still possible to benefit from the best of both worlds, by mapping the stages into states. This was what we did in the previous chapter, by adding a state field in the task Stages model, and making it also available in the To-do Task documents through a computed field, enabling the use of the state field attribute.

In the `views/todo_view.xml` file we can now expand the basic header to add a status bar:

```
<header>
  <field name="state" invisible="True" />
  <button name="do_toggle_done" type="object"
    attrs="{'invisible':[('state','in',['draft'])]}"
    string="Toggle Done"
    class="oe_highlight" />
  <field name="stage_id"
    widget="statusbar"
    clickable="True"
    options="{'fold_field': 'fold'}" />
</header>
```

Here we add `state` as a hidden field. We need this to force the client to also include that field in the data requests sent to the server. Otherwise it won't be available to be used in expressions.

It is important to remember that any field you wish to use, in a domain or `attrs` expression, must be loaded into the view, so you will make fields invisible any time you need them but don't need users to see them.

Next a button is added to the status bar, to let the user toggle the Task's **Done** flag.

The buttons displayed in the status bar should change based on the where in the life cycle the current document is.

We used the `attrs` attribute to hide the button when the document is in the `draft` state. The condition to do this uses the `state` field, not shown on the form, which is why we had to add it as a hidden field.

If we have a `state` selection field, we can instead use the `states` attribute. In this case we do, and the same effect could be achieved using `states="open,done"`. While it's not as flexible as `attrs` attribute, it is more concise.

These visibility features can be also used on other view elements, such as fields. We will explore them in more detail later in this chapter.

The `clickable` attribute allows the user to change the document stage by clicking on the status bar. We usually want to enable this, but there are also cases where we don't, such as when we need more control over the workflow, and require the users to progress through the stages using only the available action buttons, so that these can perform validations before moving between stages.

When using a status bar widget with stages, we can have the seldom used stages hidden in a More stage group. For this, the stages model must have a flag to configure the ones to hide, usually named `fold`. And the `statusbar` widget should use an `options` attribute, as shown in the preceding code, to provide that field name to the `fold_field` option.

When using the status bar widget with a state field, a similar effect can be achieved with the `statusbar_visible` attribute, used to list states that should be always visible and hide exception states necessary for less common cases. For example:

```
<field name="stage_id" widget="statusbar"
  clickable="True"
  statusbar_visible="draft,open" />
```

The sheet

The sheet canvas is the main area of the form where the actual data elements are placed. It is designed to look like an actual paper document, and it is common to see that the records in Odoo are referred to as **documents**.

Usually, a document sheet structure will have these areas:

- A document title and subtitle at the top.
- A button box at the top-right corner.
- Other document header fields.
- A notebook for additional fields organized in tabs or pages. Document lines would also go here, usually in the first notebook page.

Let's go through each of these areas.

Title and subtitle

Fields outside a `<group>` element don't automatically have labels rendered for them. This will be the case for the title elements, so the `<label for"..."/>` element should be used to render it. At the expense of some extra work, this has the advantage of giving more control over the label display.

Regular HTML, including CSS-style elements, can also be used to make the title shine. For best results, the title should be inside a `<div>` with the `oe_title` class.

Here is the `<sheet>` element expanded to include the title plus some additional fields as subtitles:

```
<sheet>
  <div class="oe_title">
    <label for="name" class="oe_edit_only"/>
    <h1><field name="name"/></h1>
    <h3>
      <span class="oe_read_only>By</span>
      <label for="user_id" class="oe_edit_only"/>
      <field name="user_id" class="oe_inline" />
    </h3>
  </div>
  <!-- More elements will be added from here... -->
</sheet>
```

Here we can see that we use regular HTML elements, such as `div`, `span`, `h1`, and `h2`. The `<label>` element allows us to control when and where it will be shown. The `for` attribute identifies the field we should get the label text from. Another possibility is to use the `string` attribute to provide a specific text to use for the label. Our example also uses the `class="oe_edit_only"` attribute so that it is visible only in edit mode.

In some cases, such as Partners or Products, a representative image is shown at the top-left corner. Supposing we had a `my_image` binary field, we could add before the `<div class="oe_title">` line, using:

```
<field name="my_image" widget="image" class="oe_avatar"/>
```

Smart buttons area

The top-right area can have an invisible box where buttons can be placed. The version 8.0 introduced smart buttons, shown as rectangles with a statistic indicator that can be followed through when clicked.

We can add the button box right after the end of the `oe_title` DIV, with the following:

```
<div name="buttons" class="oe_right oe_button_box">
  <!-- Smart buttons here ... -->
</div>
```

The container for the buttons is a `div` with the `oe_button_box` class and also `oe_right`, to align it to the right-hand side of the form. We will be discussing buttons in more detail in a later section, so we will wait until then to add actual buttons in this box.

Grouping content in a form

The main content of the form should be organized using `<group>` tags. The `group` tag inserts two columns in the canvas, and inside it, by default, fields will be displayed with labels.

A field value and field label takes two columns, so adding fields inside a group will have them stacked vertically. If we nest two `<group>` elements inside a top group, we will be able to get two columns of fields with labels, side by side.

Continuing with our form view, we can now add the main content after the smart buttons box:

```
<group name="group_top">
  <group name="group_left">
    <field name="date_deadline" />
    <separator string="Reference" />
    <field name="refers_to" />
  </group>
  <group name="group_right">
    <field name="tag_ids" widget="many2many_tags"/>
  </group>
</group>
```

It is a good practice to assign a `name` to group tags so that it's easier to reference them later to extend the view (either by you or another developer). The `string` attribute is also allowed, and if set, is used to display section title.

Inside a group, a `<newline>` element will force a new line and the next element will be rendered in the group's first column. Additional section titles can be added inside a group using the `<separator>` element.

Try the **Toggle Form Layout Outline** option from **Developer** menu: it draws lines around each group section, allowing for a better understanding of the current form layout.

We can have greater control over the layout of a group element using the `col` and `colspan` attributes.

The `col` attribute can be used on `<group>` elements to customize the number of columns it will contain. The default is `2`, but it can be changed to any other number. Even numbers work better since by default each field added takes up two columns, for the label plus the field value.

The elements placed inside the group, including `<field>` elements, can use a `colspan` attribute to set a specific number of columns they should take. By default one column is taken up.

Tabbed notebooks

Another way to organize content is using the `notebook` element, containing multiple tabbed sections, called pages. These can be used to keep less used data out of sight until needed, or to organize a large number of fields by topic.

We won't need to add this to our To-do Task form, but here is an example that could be added to a Task Stages form:

```
<notebook>
  <page string="Whiteboard" name="whiteboard">
    <field name="docs" />
  </page>
  <page>
    <!-- Second page content -->
  </page>
</notebook>
```

View semantic components

We have seen how to organize the content in a form, using structural components such as header, group, and notebook. Now we can take a closer look at the semantic components, fields and buttons, and what we can do with them.

Fields

View fields have a few attributes available for them. Most of them have values taken from their definition in the model, but these can be overridden in the view.

Attributes that are generic, and do not depend on the field type, are:

- `name` identifies the field database name.
- `string` is the label text, to be used if we want to override the label text provided by the model definition.
- `help` is a tooltip text shown when you hover the pointer over the field, and allows to override the help text provided by the model definition.
- `placeholder` is a suggestion text to display inside the field.
- `widget` allows us to override the default widget used for the field. We will explore the available widgets in a moment.

- `options` is a JSON data structure with additional options for the widget and depends on what each widget supports.
- `class` are the CSS classes to use for the field HTML rendering.
- `nolabel="True"` prevents the automatic field label from being presented. It only makes sense for the fields inside a `<group>` element and is often used along with a `<label for="...">` element.
- `invisible="True"` makes the field not visible, but it's data is fetched from the server and is available on the form.
- `readonly="True"` makes the field non-editable on the form.
- `required="True"` makes the field mandatory on the form.

Attributes specific to some field types are:

- `password="True"` is used for text fields. It is displayed as a password field, masking the characters typed in.
- `filename` is used for binary fields, and it is the name of the model field to be used to store the name of the uploaded file.
- `mode` is used for one-to-many fields. It specifies the view type to use to display the records. By default, it is `tree`, but can also be `form`, `kanban`, or `graph`.

Labels for fields

The `<label>` element can be used to better control the presentation of a field label. One case where this is used is to present the label only when the form is in edit mode:

```
<label for="name" class="oe_edit_only" />
```

When doing this, if the field is inside a `<group>` element, we usually want to also set `nolabel="True"` on it.

Relational fields

On relational fields, we can have some additional control on what the user can do. By default, the user can create new records from these fields (also known as "quick create") and open the related record form. This can be disabled using the `options` field attribute:

```
options={'no_open': True, 'no_create': True}
```

The context and domain are also particularly useful on relational fields. The context can define the default values for the related records, and the domain can limit the selectable records. A common example is top have the list of records selectable in a field to depend on the current value for another field of the current record. The domain can be defined in the model, but it can also be overridden in the View.

Field widgets

Each field type is displayed in the form with the appropriate default widget. But additional alternative widgets are available to be used.

For text fields, we have the following widgets:

- `email` is used to make the e-mail text an actionable "mail to" address.
- `url` is used to format the text as a clickable URL.
- `html` is used to render the text as HTML content; in edit mode, it features a WYSIWYG editor to allow the formatting of the content without the need for using the HTML syntax.

For numeric fields, we have the following widgets:

- `handle` is specifically designed for sequence fields in list views and displays a handle that allows you to drag lines to a custom order.
- `float_time` formats a float field with time quantities as hours and minutes.
- `monetary` displays a float field as the currency amount. It expects a `currency_id` companion field, but another field name can be provided with `options="{'currency_field': 'currency_id'}"`.
- `progressbar` presents a float as a progress percentage and can be useful for fields representing a completion rate.

For relational and selection fields, we have these additional widgets:

- `many2many_tags` displays values as a list of button-like labels.
- `selection` uses the `selection` field widget for a many-to-one field.
- `radio` displays the `selection` field options using radio buttons.

- `kanban_state_selection` shows a semaphore light for the kanban state selection list. The normal state is represented in gray, done is represented in green, and any other state is represented in red.

- `priority` represents the `selection` field as a list of clickable stars. The selection options are usually a numeric digit.

Buttons

Buttons support these attributes:

- `icon` is for icon image to use in the button to display; unlike smart buttons, the icons available for regular buttons are limited to the ones available in `addons/web/static/src/img/icons`.
- `string` is the button text label, or the HTML `alt` text when an icon is used.
- `type` is the typo of the action to perform. Possible values are:
    - `workflow` is used to trigger a workflow engine signal;
    - `object` is used for calling a Python method;
    - `action` is used to run a window action.
- `name` identifies the specific action to perform, according to the chosen type: either a workflow signal name, a model method name, or the database ID of window action to run. The `%(xmlid)d` formula can be used to translate the XML ID into the required Database ID.
- `args` is used when the `type` is `object`, to pass additional parameters to the method.
- `context` adds values to the context, that can have effects after the windows action is run, or in the Python code methods called.
- `confirm` displays a confirmation message box, with the text assigned to this attribute.
- `special="cancel"` is used on wizards, to cancel and close the wizard form.

Smart buttons

When designing the form structure, we included a top-right area to contain smart buttons. Let's now add a button inside it.

For our app, we will have a button displaying the total number of to-dos for the owner of the current to-do, and clicking on it would navigate to the list of those items.

First we need to add the corresponding computed field to `models/todo_model.py`. Add to the `TodoTask` class with the following:

```
def compute_user_todo_count(self):
    for task in self:
        task.user_todo_count = task.search_count(
            [('user_id', '=', task.user_id.id)])

user_todo_count = fields.Integer(
    'User To-Do Count',
    compute='compute_user_todo_count')
```

Next we add the button box and the button inside it. Right after the end of the `oe_title` DIV, replace the buttons box placeholder we added before, with the following:

```
<div name="buttons" class="oe_right oe_button_box">
  <button class="oe_stat_button"
    type="action" icon="fa-tasks"
    name="%(action_todo_task_button)d"
    context="{'default_user_id': user_id}"
    help="All to-dos for this user" >
    <field string="To-Dos" name="user_todo_count"
      widget="statinfo"/>
  </button>
</div>
```

This button displays the total number of To-do Tasks for the person responsible for this to-do task, computed by the `user_todo_count` field.

These are the attributes that we can use when adding smart buttons:

- `class="oe_stat_button"` renders a rectangle instead of a regular button.
- `icon` sets the icon to use, chosen from the Font Awesome set. Available icons can be browsed at `http://fontawesome.io`.
- `type` and `name` are the button type and the name of the action to trigger. For smart buttons the type will usually be `action`, for a window action, and `name` will be the ID of the action to execute. It expects an actual database ID, so we have to use a formula to convert an XML ID into a database ID: `"%(action-external-id)d"`. This action should open a view with the related records.
- `string` adds label text to the button. We have not used it here because the contained field already provides a text for it.
- `context` should be used to set default values on the target view, to be used on new records created on the view after clicking through the button.

- `help` adds a help tooltip displayed when the mouse pointer is over the button.

The `button` element itself is a container, with fields displaying statistics. Those are regular fields using the widget `statinfo`. The field should be a computed field defined in the underlying model. Other than fields, inside a button we can also use static text, such as:

```
<div>User's To-dos</div>
```

When clicking on the button, we want to see a list with only the Tasks for the current responsible user. That will be done by the `action_todo_task_button` action, not yet implemented. But it needs to know the current responsible user, to be able to perform the filter. For that we use the button's `context` attribute to store that value.

The Action used must to be defined before the Form, so we should add it at the top of the XML file:

```
<act_window id="action_todo_task_button"
  name="To-Do Tasks"
  res_model="todo.task"
  view_mode="tree,form,calendar,graph,pivot"
  domain="[('user_id','=',default_user_id)]" />
```

Notice how we use the `default_user_id` context key for the domain filter. This particular key will also set the default value on the `user_id` field when creating new Tasks after following the button link.

Dynamic views

View elements also support a few dynamic attributes that allow views to dynamically change their appearance or behavior depending on field values . We may have on change events, able change values on other fields while editing data on a form, or have fields to be mandatory or visible only when certain conditions are met.

On change events

The **on change** mechanism allows us to change values in other form fields when a particular field is changed. For example, the on change on a Product field can set the Price field with a default value whenever the product is changed.

In older versions the on change events were defined at the view level, but since version 8.0 they are defined directly on the Model layer, without the need for any specific markup on the views. This is done by creating methods to perform the calculations, and using `@api.onchange('field1', 'field2')` to bind it to fields. These onchange methods are discussed in more detail in `Chapter 7`, *ORM Application Logic – Supporting Business Processes*.

Dynamic attributes

The on change mechanism also takes care of the automatic recomputation of computed fields, to immediately react to the user input. Using the same example as before, if the Price field is changed when we changed the Product, a computed Total Amount field would also be automatically updated using the new price information. Dynamic attributes A couple of attributes provide an easy way to control the visibility of a particular user interface element:

- `groups` can make an element visible depending on the security Groups the current user belongs to. Only the members of the specified groups will see it. It expects a comma separated list of Group XML IDs.
- `states` can make an element visible depending on the record's State field. It expects a comma separated list of State values.

Other than these, we also have a flexible method available to set an element visibility depending on a client-side dynamically evaluated expression. This is the `attrs` special attribute, expecting for a value dictionary that maps the value of the `invisible` attribute to the result of an expression.

For example, to have the `refers_to` field visible in all states except draft, use the following code:

```
<field name="refers_to" attrs="{'invisible':
  state=='draft'}" />
```

The `invisible` attribute is available in any element, not only fields. For example, we can use it on notebook pages and in group elements.

The `attrs` can also set values for two other attributes: `readonly` and `required`. These only make sense for data fields, to make them not editable or mandatory. This allows us to implement some basic client-side logic, such as making a field mandatory depending on other record values, such as the State.

List views

At this point, list views should need little introduction, but we are still going to discuss the attributes that can be used with them. Here is an example of a list view for our To-Do Tasks:

```
<record id="todo_app.view_tree_todo_task"
  model="ir.ui.view">
  <field name="model">todo.task</field>
  <field name="arch" type="xml">
    <tree decoration-muted="is_done"
      decoration-bf="state=='open'"
      delete="false">
      <field name="name"/>
      <field name="user_id"/>
      <field name="is_done"/>
      <field name="state" invisible="1"/>
    </tree>
  </field>
</record>
```

The row text color and font can change dynamically depending on the results of a Python expression evaluation. This is done through `decoration-NAME` attributes, with the expression to evaluate based on field attributes. The `NAME` part can be `bf` or `it`, for bold and italic fonts, or any Bootstrap text contextual colors: `danger`, `info`, `muted`, `primary`, `success`, or `warning`. The Bootstrap documentation has examples on how these are presented: `http://getbootstrap.com/css/#helper-classes-colors`.

The `colors` and `fonts` attributes, available in version 8.0, were deprecated in version 9.0. The new decoration attributes should be used instead.

Remember that fields used in expressions must be declared in a `<field>` element, so that web client knows that that column needs to be retrieved from the server. If we don't want to have it displayed to the user, we should use the `invisible="1"` attribute on it.

Other relevant attributes of the tree element are:

- `default_order` allows to override the model's default sort order, and its value follows the same format as in order attribute used in model definitions.
- `create`, `delete`, and `edit`, if set to `false` (in lowercase) disables the corresponding action on the list view.
- `editable` makes records editable directly on the list view. Possible values are `top` and `bottom`, the location where the new records will be added.

A list view can contain fields and buttons, and most of their attributes for forms are also valid here.

In list views, numeric fields can display summary values for their column. For this add to the field one of the available aggregation attributes, `sum`, `avg`, `min`, or `max`, and assign to it the label text for the summary value. For example:

```
<field name="amount" sum="Total Amount" />
```

Search views

The search options available are defined through the `<search>` view type. We can choose the fields can be automatically searched when typing in the search box. We can also provide predefined filters, activated with a click, and predefined grouping options to be used in list views.

Here is a possible search view for the To-Do Tasks:

```
<record id="todo_app.view_filter_todo_task"
  model="ir.ui.view">
  <field name="model">todo.task</field>
  <field name="arch" type="xml">
    <search>
      <field name="name"/>
      <field name="user_id"/>
      <filter name="filter_not_done" string="Not Done"
        domain="[('is_done','=',False)]"/>
      <filter name="filter_done" string="Done"
        domain="[('is_done','!=',False)]"/>
      <separator/>
      <filter name="group_user" string="By User"
        context="{'group_by': 'user_id'}"/>
    </search>
  </field>
</record>
```

We can see two fields to be searched for – `name` and `user_id`. When the user starts typing on the search box, a drop-down will suggest searching on any of these fields. If the user types `ENTER` the search will be performed on the first of the filter fields.

Then we have two predefined filters, filtering not done and done tasks. These filters can be activated independently, and will be joined with an OR operator. Blocks of filters separated with a `<separator/>` element will be joined with an AND operator.

The third filter only sets a group by context. This tells the view to group the records by that field, `user_id` in this case.

The field elements can use the following attributes:

- `name` identifies the field to use.
- `string` is a label text which is used instead of the default.
- `operator` is used to change the operator from the default one (= for numeric fields and `ilike` for the other field types).
- `filter_domain` sets a specific domain expression to use for the search, providing one flexible alternative to the operator attribute. The searched text string is referred in the expression as self. A trivial example is: `filter_domain="[('name', 'ilike', self)]"`.
- `groups` makes the search on the field available only for users belonging to some security Groups. Expects a comma separated list of XML IDs.

For the filter elements, these are the attributes available:

- `name` is an identifier to use by inheritance or to enable it through window actions. Not mandatory, but it is a good practice to always provide it.
- `string` is the label text to display for the filter. Required.
- `domain` is the domain expression to be added to the current domain.
- `context` is a context dictionary to add to the current context. Usually sets a `group_id` key with the name of the field to group records.
- `groups` makes the search on the field available only for a list of security Groups (XML IDs).

Calendar views

As the name suggests, this view type presents the records in a calendar that can be viewed for month, week, or days periods of time. A calendar view for the To-Do Tasks could look like this:

```
<record id="view_calendar_todo_task" model="ir.ui.view">
  <field name="model">todo.task</field>
  <field name="arch" type="xml">
    <calendar date_start="date_deadline" color="user_id"
      display="[name], Stage [stage_id]" >
      <!-- Fields used for the display text -->
      <field name="name" />
      <field name="stage_id" />
    </calendar>
  </field>
</record>
```

The calendar attributes are:

- `date_start` is the field for the start date. Mandatory.
- `date_end` is the field for the end date. Optional.
- `date_delay` is the field with the duration in days, that can be used instead of `date_end`.
- `all_day` provides the name of a Boolean field that is to be used to signal full day events. In these events, the duration is ignored.
- `color` is the field used to group color the calendar entries. Each distinct value in this field will be assigned a color, and all its entries will have the same color.
- `display` is the display text for each calendar entry. It can user record values using the field names between square brackets, such as `[name]`. These fields must be declared as child of the calendar element, an in the preceding example.
- `mode` is the default display mode for the calendar, either `day`, `week`, or `month`.

Graph and pivot views

Graph views provide a graphical view of the data, in the form of a chart. The current fields available in the To-do Tasks are not good candidates for a chart, so we will add one to use on such a view.

In the `TodoTask` class, at the `todo_ui/models/todo_model.py` file, add:

```
effort_estimate = fields.Integer('Effort Estimate')
```

It also needs to be added to the To-do Task form, so that we can add values for it on the existing records, and are able to check this new view.

Now let's add the To-Do Tasks graph view:

```
<record id="view_graph_todo_task" model="ir.ui.view">
  <field name="model">todo.task</field>
    <field name="arch" type="xml">
      <graph type="bar">
        <field name="stage_id" />
        <field name="effort_estimate" type="measure" />
      </graph>
    </field>
</record>
```

The `graph` view element can have a `type` attribute that can be set to `bar` (the default), `pie`, or `line`. In the case of `bar`, the additional `stacked="True"` can be used to make it a stacked bar chart.

The data can also be seen in a pivot table, a dynamic analysis matrix. For this, we have the pivot view, introduced in version 9.0. Pivot tables were already available in version 8.0, but in 9.0, they moved into their own view type. Along with this, it improved the UI features of Pivot tables, and optimized the retrieval of pivot table data greatly.

To also add a pivot table to the To-Do Tasks, use this code:

```
<record id="view_pivot_todo_task" model="ir.ui.view">
  <field name="arch" type="xml">
    <pivot>
      <field name="stage_id" type="col" />
      <field name="user_id" />
      <field name="date_deadline" interval="week" />
      <field name="effort_estimate" type="measure" />
    </pivot>
  </field>
</record>
```

The graph and pivot views should contain field elements describing the axis and measures to use. Most of the available attributes are common to both the view types:

- `name` identifies the field to use in the graph, just like in other views
- `type` is how the field will be used, as a `row` group (default), a `measure`, or as `col` (only for pivot tables, use for column groups)
- `interval` is meaningful for date fields, and is the time interval used to group time data by `day`, `week`, `month`, `quarter`, or `year`

By default, the aggregation used is the sum of the values. This can be changed by setting the `group_operator` attribute on the Python field definition. The values that can be used include `avg`, `max`, and `min`.

Other view types

It's worth noting that we didn't cover three other view types that are also available: kanban, gantt, and diagram.

Kanban views will be covered in detail in `Chapter 9`, *QWeb and Kanban Views*.

The gantt view was available until version 8.0, but it was removed in version 9.0 Community edition because of license incompatibilities.

Finally, the diagram views are used for quite specific cases, and an addon module will need them rarely. Just in case, you might like to know that the reference material for the two view types can be found in the official documentation, `https://www.odoo.com/documentation/10.0/reference/views.html`.

Summary

Summary In this chapter, we learned more about Odoo views in order to build the user interface, covering the most important view types. In the next chapter, we will learn more about adding business logic to our applications.

7

ORM Application Logic – Supporting Business Processes

With the Odoo programming API, we can write complex logic and wizards to provide a rich user interaction for our apps. In this chapter, we will see how to write code to support business logic in our models, and we will also learn how to activate it on events and user actions.

We can perform computations and validations on events, such as creating or writing on a record, or perform some logic when a button is clicked. For example, we implemented button actions for the To-do Tasks, to toggle the **Is Done** flag and to clear all done tasks by inactivating.

Additionally, we can also use wizards to implement more complex interactions with the user, allowing to ask for inputs and provide feedback during the interaction.

We will start by building such a wizard for our To-Do app.

Creating a wizard

Suppose our To-Do app users regularly need to set the deadlines and person responsible for a large number of tasks. They could use an assistant to help with this. It should allow them to pick the tasks to be updated and then choose the deadline date and/or the responsible user to set on them.

Wizards are forms used to get input information from users, then use it for further processing. They can be used for simple tasks, such as asking for a few parameters and running a report, or for complex data manipulations, such as the use case described earlier.

This is how our wizard will look:

We can start by creating a new addon module for the `todo_wizard` feature.

Our module will have a Python file and an XML file, so the `todo_wizard/__manifest__.py` description will be as shown in the following code:

```
{   'name': 'To-do Tasks Management Assistant',
    'description': 'Mass edit your To-Do backlog.',
    'author': 'Daniel Reis',
    'depends': ['todo_user'],
    'data': ['views/todo_wizard_view.xml'], }
```

As in previous addons, the `todo_wizard/__init__.py` file is just one line:

```
from . import models
```

Next, we need to describe the data model supporting our wizard.

The wizard model

A wizard displays a form view to the user, usually as a dialog window, with some fields to be filled in. These will then be used by the wizard logic.

This is implemented using the same model/view architecture as for regular views, but the supporting model is based on `models.TransientModel` instead of `models.Model`.

This type of model has also a database representation and stores state there, but this data is expected to be useful only until the wizard completes its work. A scheduled job regularly cleans up the old data from wizard database tables.

The `models/todo_wizard_model.py` file will define the fields we need to interact with the user: the list of tasks to be updated, the user responsible, and the deadline date to set on them.

First add the `models/__init__.py` file with following line of code:

```
from . import todo_wizard_model
```

Then create the actual `models/todo_wizard_model.py` file:

```
# -*- coding: utf-8 -*-
from odoo import models, fields, api

class TodoWizard(models.TransientModel):
    _name = 'todo.wizard'
    _description = 'To-do Mass Assignment'
    task_ids = fields.Many2many('todo.task',
      string='Tasks')
    new_deadline = fields.Date('Deadline to Set')
    new_user_id = fields.Many2one(
      'res.users',string='Responsible to Set')
```

It's worth noting that one-to-many relations to regular models should not be used in transient models. The reason for this is that it would require the regular model to have the inverse many-to-one relation with the transient model, but this is not allowed, since there could be the need to garbage-collect the regular model records along with the transient records.

The wizard form

The wizard form views are the same as for regular models, except for two specific elements:

- A `<footer>` section can be used to place the action buttons
- A special `type= "cancel"` button available to interrupt the wizard without performing any action

This is the content of our `views/todo_wizard_view.xml` file:

```
<odoo>
  <record id="To-do Task Wizard" model="ir.ui.view">
    <field name="name">To-do Task Wizard</field>
    <field name="model">todo.wizard</field>
    <field name="arch" type="xml">

      <form>
        <div class="oe_right">
          <button type="object" name="do_count_tasks"
            string="Count" />
          <button type="object" name="do_populate_tasks"
            string="Get All" />
        </div>

        <field name="task_ids">
          <tree>
            <field name="name" />
            <field name="user_id" />
            <field name="date_deadline" />
          </tree>
        </field>

        <group>
          <group> <field name="new_user_id" /> </group>
          <group> <field name="new_deadline" /> </group>
        </group>

        <footer>
          <button type="object" name="do_mass_update"
            string="Mass Update" class="oe_highlight"
            attrs="{'invisible':
            [('new_deadline','=',False),
            ('new_user_id', '=',False)]
            }" />
          <button special="cancel" string="Cancel"/>
        </footer>
      </form>
```

```
    </field>
  </record>

  <!-- More button Action -->
  <act_window id="todo_app.action_todo_wizard"
    name="To-Do Tasks Wizard"
    src_model="todo.task" res_model="todo.wizard"
    view_mode="form" target="new" multi="True" />
</odoo>
```

The `<act_window>` window action we see in the XML adds an option to the **More** button of the To-do Task form by using the `src_model` attribute. The `target="new"` attribute makes it open as a dialog window.

You might also have noticed that `attrs` is used in the **Mass Update** button, to add the nice touch of making it invisible until either a new deadline or responsible user is selected.

The wizard business logic

Next, we need to implement the actions to perform on the form buttons. Excluding the **Cancel** button, we have three action buttons to implement, but now we will focus on the **Mass Update** button.

The method called by the button is `do_mass_update` and it should be defined in the `models/todo_wizard_model.py` file, as shown in the following code:

```
from odoo import exceptions
import logging
_logger = logging.getLogger(__name__)

# ...
# class TodoWizard(models.TransientModel):
# ...

    @api.multi
    def do_mass_update(self):
      self.ensure_one()
      if not (self.new_deadline or self.new_user_id):
        raise exceptions.ValidationError('No data to update!')
      _logger.debug('Mass update on Todo Tasks %s',
                    self.task_ids.ids)
      vals = {}
      if self.new_deadline:
        vals['date_deadline'] = self.new_deadline
      if self.new_user_id:
```

```
    vals['user_id'] = self.new_user_id
  # Mass write values on all selected tasks
  if vals:
    self.task_ids.write(vals)
  return True
```

Our code should handle one wizard instance at a time, so we used `self.ensure_one()` to make that clear. Here `self` represents the browse record for the data on the wizard form.

The method begins by validating if a new deadline date or responsible user was given, and raises an error if not. Next, we have an example of how to write a debug message to the server log.

Then the `vals` dictionary is built with the values to set with the mass update: the new date, new responsible, or both. And then the `write` method is used on a recordset to perform the mass update. This is more efficient than a loop performing individual writes on each record.

It is a good practice for methods to always return something. This is why it returns the `True` value at the end. The sole reason for this is that the XML-RPC protocol does not support `None` values, so those methods won't be usable using that protocol. In practice, you may not be aware of the issue because the web client uses JSON-RPC, not XML-RPC, but it is still a good practice to follow.

Next, we will have a closer look at logging, and then will work on the logic behind the two buttons at the top: **Count** and **Get All**.

Logging

These mass updates could be misused, so it might be a good idea to log some information when it is used. The preceding code initializes the `_logger` in the two lines before the `TodoWizard` class, using the Python `logging` standard library. The Python `__name__` internal variable is to identify the messages as coming from this module.

To write log messages in method code we can use:

```
_logger.debug('A DEBUG message')
_logger.info('An INFO message')
_logger.warning('A WARNING message')
_logger.error('An ERROR message')
```

When passing values to use in the log message, instead of using string interpolation, we should provide them as additional parameters. For example, instead of `_logger.info('Hello %s' % 'World')` we should use `_logger.info('Hello %s', 'World')`. You may notice that we did so in the `do_mass_update()` method.

An interesting thing to note about logging, is that log entries always print the timestamp in UTC. This may come as a surprise to new administrators, but is due to the fact that the server internally handles all dates in UTC.

Raising exceptions

When something is not right, we will want to interrupt the program with an error message. This is done by raising an exception. Odoo provides a few additional exception classes to the ones available in Python. These are examples for the most useful ones:

```
from odoo import exceptions
raise exceptions.Warning('Warning message')
raise exceptions.ValidationError('Not valid message')
```

The `Warning` message also interrupts execution but can sound less severe than a `ValidationError`. While it's not the best user interface, we take advantage of that on the **Count** button to display a message to the user:

```
@api.multi
def do_count_tasks(self):
    Task = self.env['todo.task']
    count = Task.search_count([('is done', '=', False)])
    raise exceptions.Warning(
          'There are %d active tasks.' %count)
```

As a side note, it looks like we could have used the `@api.model` decorator, since this method does not operate on the `self` recordset. But in this case we can't because the method needs to be called from a button.

Helper actions in wizards

Now suppose we want a button to automatically pick all the to-do tasks to spare the user from picking them one by one. That's the point of having the **Get All** button in the form. The code behind this button will get a recordset with all active tasks and assign it to the tasks in the many-to-many field.

But there is a catch here. In dialog windows, when a button is pressed, the wizard window is automatically closed. We didn't face this problem with the **Count** button because it uses an exception to display its message; so the action is not successful and the window is not closed.

Fortunately, we can work around this behavior by asking the client to reopen the same wizard. Model methods can return a window action to be performed by the web client, in the form of a dictionary object. This dictionary uses the same attributes used to define window actions in XML files.

We will define a helper function for the window action dictionary to reopen the wizard window, so that it can be easily reused in several buttons:

```
@api.multi
def _reopen_form(self):
    self.ensure_one()
    return {
        'type': 'ir.actions.act_window',
        'res_model': self._name,  # this model
        'res_id': self.id,  # the current wizard record
        'view_type': 'form',
        'view_mode': 'form',
        'target': 'new'}
```

It is worth noting that the window action could be something else, like jumping to a different wizard form to ask for additional user input, and that can be used to implement multi-page wizards.

Now the **Get All** button can do its job and still keep the user working on the same wizard:

```
@api.multi
def do_populate_tasks(self):
    self.ensure_one()
    Task = self.env['todo.task']
    open_tasks = Task.search([('is_done', '=', False)])
    # Fill the wizard Task list with all tasks
    self.task_ids = all_tasks
    # reopen wizard form on same wizard record
    return self._reopen_form()
```

Here we can see how to work with any other available model: we first use `self.env[]` to get a reference to the model, `todo.task` in this case, and can then perform actions on it, such as `search()` to retrieve records meeting some search criteria.

The transient model stores the values in the wizard form fields, and can be read or written just like any other model. The `all_tasks` variable is assigned to the model `task_ids` one-to-many field. As you can see, this is done just like we would for any other field type.

Working with the ORM API

From the previous section, we already got a taste of what it is like to use the ORM API. Next we will look at what more we can do with it.

Method decorators

During our journey, the several methods we encountered used API decorators like `@api.multi`. These are important for the server to know how to handle the method. Let's recap the ones available and when they should be used.

The `@api.multi` decorator is used to handle recordsets with the new API and is the most frequently used. Here `self` is a recordset, and the method will usually include a `for` loop to iterate it.

In some cases, the method is written to expect a singleton: a recordset containing no more than one record. The `@api.one` decorator was deprecated as of 9.0 and should be avoided. Instead we should still use `@api.multi` and add to the method code a line with `self.ensure_one()`, to ensure it is a singleton.

As mentioned, the `@api.one` decorator is deprecated but is still supported. For completeness, it might be worth knowing that it wraps the decorated method, feeding it one record at a time, doing the recordset iteration for. In our method `self` is guaranteed to be a singleton. The return values of each individual method call are aggregated as a list and returned.

The `@api.model` decorates a class-level static method, and it does not use any recordset data. For consistency, `self` is still a recordset, but its content is irrelevant. Note that this type of method cannot be used from buttons in the user interface.

A few other decorators have more specific purposes and are to be used together with the decorators described earlier:

- `@api.depends(fld1,...)` is used for computed field functions to identify on what changes the (re)calculation should be triggered
- `@api.constrains(fld1,...)` is used for validation functions to identify on what changes the validation check should be triggered
- `@api.onchange(fld1,...)` is used for on change functions to identify the fields on the form that will trigger the action

In particular, the `onchange` methods can send a warning message to the user interface. For example, this could warn the user that the product quantity just entered is not available in stock, without preventing the user from continuing. This is done by having the method return a dictionary describing the warning message:

```
return {
          'warning': {
          'title': 'Warning!',
          'message': 'You have been warned'}
         }
```

Overriding the ORM default methods

We have learned about the standard methods provided by the API but there uses don't end there! We can also extend them to add custom behavior to our models.

The most common case is to extend the `create()` and `write()` methods. This can be used to add logic to be triggered whenever these actions are executed. By placing our logic in the appropriate section of the custom method, we can have the code run before or after the main operations are executed.

Using the `TodoTask` model as an example, we can make a custom `create()`, which would look like this:

```
@api.model
def create(self, vals):
    # Code before create: can use the `vals` dict
    new_record = super(TodoTask, self).create(vals)
    # Code after create: can use the `new_record` created
    return new_record
```

A custom `write()` would follow this structure:

```
@api.multi
def write(self, vals):
    # Code before write: can use `self`, with the old values
    super(TodoTask, self).write(vals)
    # Code after write: can use `self`, with the updated values
    return True
```

These are common extension examples, but of course any standard method available for a model can be inherited in a similar way to add our custom logic to it.

These techniques open up a lot of possibilities, but remember that other tools are also available that can be better suited for common specific tasks:

- To have a field value calculated based on another, we should use computed fields. An example of this is to calculate a header total when the values of the lines are changed.
- To have field default values calculated dynamically, we can use a field default bound to a function instead of a fixed value.
- To have values set on other fields when a field is changed, we can use on change functions. An example of this is when picking a customer, setting its currency as the document's currency, that can later be manually changed by the user. Keep in mind that on change only works on form view interaction and not on direct `write` calls.
- For validations, we should use constraint functions decorated with `@api.constraints(fld1,fld2,...)`. These are like computed fields but, instead of computing values, they are expected to raise errors.

Methods for RPC and web client calls

We have seen the most important model methods used to generate recordsets and how to write on them. But there are a few more model methods available for more specific actions, as shown here:

- `read([fields])` is similar to the `browse` method, but instead of a recordset, it returns a list of rows of data with the fields given as its argument. Each row is a dictionary. It provides a serialized representation of the data that can be sent through RPC protocols and is intended to be used by client programs and not in server logic.
- `search_read([domain], [fields], offset=0, limit=None, order=None)` performs a search operation followed by a read on the resulting record list. It is intended to be used by RPC clients and saves them the extra round trip needed when doing a `search` followed by a `read` on the results.
- `load([fields], [data])` is used to import data acquired from a CSV file. The first argument is the list of fields to import, and it maps directly to a CSV top row. The second argument is a list of records, where each record is a list of string values to parse and import, and it maps directly to the CSV data rows and columns. It implements the features of CSV data import described in `Chapter 4`, *Module Data*, like the external identifiers support. It is used by the web client **Import** feature. It replaces the deprecated `import_data` method.
- `export_data([fields], raw_data=False)` is used by the web client **Export** function. It returns a dictionary with a data key containing the data; a list of rows. The field names can use the `.id` and `/id` suffixes used in CSV files, and the data is in a format compatible with an importable CSV file. The optional `raw_data` argument allows for data values to be exported with their Python types, instead of the string representation used in CSV.

The following methods are mostly used by the web client to render the user interface and perform basic interaction:

- `name_get()`: This returns a list of `(ID, name)` tuples with the text representing each record. It is used by default for computing the `display_name` value, providing the text representation of relation fields. It can be extended to implement custom display representations, such as displaying the record code and name instead of only the name.

- `name_search(name='', args=None, operator='ilike', limit=100)` returns a list of `(ID, name)` tuples, where the display name matches the text in the `name` argument. It is used in the UI while typing in a relation field to produce the list with the suggested records matching the typed text. For example, it is used to implement product lookup both by name and by reference, while typing in a field to pick a product.
- `name_create(name)` creates a new record with only the title name to use for it. It is used in the UI for the "quick-create" feature, where you can quickly create a related record by just providing its name. It can be extended to provide specific defaults for the new records created through this feature.
- `default_get([fields])` returns a dictionary with the default values for a new record to be created. The default values may depend on variables such as the current user or the session context.
- `fields_get()` is used to describe the model's field definitions, as seen in the **View Fields** option of the developer menu.
- `fields_view_get()` is used by the web client to retrieve the structure of the UI view to render. It can be given the ID of the view as an argument or the type of view we want using `view_type='form'`. For example, you might try this: `rset.fields_view_get(view_type='tree')`.

The shell command

Python has a command-line interface that is a great way to explore its syntax. Similarly, Odoo also has an equivalent feature, where we can interactively try out commands to see how they work. That is the `shell` command.

To use it, run Odoo with the `shell` command and the database to use, as shown here:

```
$ ./odoo-bin shell -d todo
```

You should see the usual server start up sequence in the terminal until it stops on a `>>>` Python prompt waiting for your input. Here, `self` will represent the record for the `Administrator` user, as you can confirm typing the following:

```
>>> self
res.users(1,)
>>> self._name
'res.users'
>>> self.name
u'Administrator'
```

In the preceding session, we do some inspection on our environment. The `self` represents a `res.users` recordset containing only the record with ID `1`. We can also confirm the recordset's model name inspecting `self._name`, and get the value for the record's `name` field, confirming that it is the `Administrator` user.

As with Python, you can exit the prompt using *Ctrl* + *D*. This will also close the server process and return to the system shell prompt.

The shell feature was added in version 9.0. For version 8.0 there is a community back-ported module to add it. Once downloaded and included in the addons path, no further installation is necessary. It can be downloaded from `https://www.odoo.com/apps/modules/8.0/shell/`.

The server environment

The server shell provides a `self` reference identical to what you would find inside a method of the Users model, `res.users`.

As we have seen, `self` is a recordset. **Recordsets** carry with them an environment information, including the user browsing the data and additional context information, such as the language and the time zone. This information is important and guage or time zone.

We can start inspecting our current environment with:

```
>>> self.env
<openerp.api.Environment object at 0xb3f4f52c>
```

The execution environment in `self.env` has the following attributes available:

- `env.cr` is the database cursor being used
- `env.uid` is the ID for the session user
- `env.user` is the record for the current user
- `env.context` is an immutable dictionary with a session context

The environment also provides access to the registry where all installed models are available. For example, `self.env['res.partner']` returns a reference to the Partners model. We can then use `search()` or `browse()` on it to retrieve recordsets:

```
>>> self.env['res.partner'].search([('name', 'like', 'Ag')])
res.partner(7, 51)
```

In this example, a recordset for the `res.partner` model contains two records, with IDs `7` and `51`.

Modifying the execution environment

The environment is immutable, and so it can't be modified. But we can create a modified environment and then run actions using it.

These methods can be used for that:

- `env.sudo(user)` is provided with a user record, and returns an environment with that user. If no user is provided, the `Administrator` superuser will be used, which allows running specific queries bypassing security rules.
- `env.with_context(dictionary)` replaces the context with a new one.
- `env.with_context(key=value,...)` modified the current context setting values for some of its keys.

Additionally, we have the `env.ref()` function, taking a string with an external identifier and returns a record for it, as shown here:

```
>>> self.env.ref('base.user_root')
res.users(1,)
```

Transactions and low-level SQL

Database writing operations are executed in the context of a database transaction. Usually, we don't have to worry about this as the server takes care of that while running model methods.

But in some cases, we may need a finer control over the transaction. This can be done through the database cursor `self.env.cr`, as shown here:

- `self.env.cr.commit()` commits the transaction's buffered write operations
- `self.env.savepoint()` sets a transaction savepoint to rollback to
- `self.env.rollback()` cancels the transaction's write operations since the last savepoint, or all if no savepoint was created

In a shell session, your data manipulation won't be made effective in the database until you use `self.env.cr.commit()`.

With the cursor `execute()` method, we can run SQL directly in the database. It takes a string with the SQL statement to run and a second optional argument with a tuple or list of values to use as parameters for the SQL. These values will be used where `%s` placeholders are found.

Caution!

With `cr.execute()` we should resist to directly add the parameter values to the query string. This is well known security risk that can be exploited through SQL injection attacks. Always use `%s` placeholders and the second parameter to pass values.

If you're using a `SELECT` query, records should then be fetched. The `fetchall()` function retrieves all the rows as a list of `tuples`, and `dictfetchall()` retrieves them as a list of dictionaries, as shown in the following example:

```
>>> self.env.cr.execute("SELECT id, login FROM res_users WHERE login=%s OR
id=%s", ('demo', 1))
>>> self.env.cr.fetchall() [(4, u'demo'), (1, u'admin')]
```

It's also possible to run **Data Manipulation Language** (**DML**) instructions such as `UPDATE` and `INSERT`. Since the server keeps data caches, they may become inconsistent with the actual data in the database. Because of that, while using raw DML, the caches should be cleared afterward by using `self.env.invalidate_all()`.

Caution!
Executing SQL directly in the database can lead to inconsistent data. You should use it only if you are sure of what you are doing.

Working with recordsets

We will now explore how the ORM works and learn about the most common operations performed with it. We will use the prompt provided by the `shell` command to interactively explore how recordsets work.

Querying models

With `self`, we can only access the method's recordset. But the `self.env` environment reference allows us to access any other model. For example, `self.env['res.partner']` returns a reference to the Partners model (which is actually an empty recordset). We can then use `search()` or `browse()` on it to generate recordsets.

The `search()` method takes a domain expression and returns a recordset with the records matching those conditions. An empty domain `[]` will return all records. For more details on domain expressions please refer back to `Chapter 6`, *Views – Designing the User Interface*. If the model has the `active` special field, by default only the records with `active=True` will be considered.

A few optional keyword arguments are available, as shown here:

- `order` is a string to be used as the `ORDER BY` clause in the database query. This is usually a comma-separated list of field names.
- `limit` sets a maximum number of records to retrieve.
- `offset` ignores the first `n` results; it can be used with `limit` to query blocks of records at a time.

Sometimes we just need to know the number of records meeting certain conditions. For that we can use `search_count()`, which returns the record count instead of a recordset. It saves the cost of retrieving a list of records just to count them, so it is much more efficient when we don't have a recordset yet and just want to count the number of records.

The `browse()` method takes a list of IDs or a single ID and returns a recordset with those records. This can be convenient for the cases where we already know the IDs of the records we want.

Some usage examples of this are shown here:

```
>>> self.env['res.partner'].search([('name', 'like', 'Ag')])
res.partner(7, 51)
>>> self.env['res.partner'].browse([7, 51])
res.partner(7, 51)
```

Singletons

The special case of a recordset with only one record is called a **singleton** recordset. Singletons are still a recordset, and can be used wherever a recordset is expected.

But unlike multi-element recordsets, singletons can access their fields using the dot notation, as shown here:

```
>>> print self.name
Administrator
```

In the next example, we can see the same `self` singleton recordset also behaves as a recordset, and we can iterate it. It has only one record, so only one name is printed out:

```
>>> for rec in self:
        print rec.name
Administrator
```

Trying to access field values on recordsets with more than one record will error, so this can be an issue in the cases we are not sure if we are working with a singleton recordset. On methods designed to work only with singleton, we can check this using `self.ensure_one()` at the beginning. It will raise an error if `self` is not singleton.

Note that an empty record is also a singleton.

Writing on records

Recordsets implement the active record pattern. This means that we can assign values on them, and these changes will be made persistent in the database. This is an intuitive and convenient way to manipulate data, as shown here:

```
>>> admin = self.env['res.users'].browse(1)
>>> print admin.name
Administrator
>>> admin.name = 'Superuser'
>>> print admin.name
Superuser
```

Recordsets also have three methods to act on their data: `create()`, `write()`, and `unlink()`.

The `create()` method takes a dictionary to map fields to values and returns the created record. Default values are automatically applied as expected, which is shown here:

```
>>> Partner = self.env['res.partner']
>>> new = Partner.create({'name': 'ACME', 'is_company': True})
>>> print new
res.partner(72,)
```

The `unlink()` method deletes the records in the recordset, as shown here:

```
>>> rec = Partner.search([('name', '=', 'ACME')])
>>> rec.unlink()
True
```

The `write()` method takes a dictionary to map fields to values. These are updated on all elements of the recordset and nothing is returned, as shown here:

```
>>> Partner.write({'comment': 'Hello!'})
```

Using the active record pattern has some limitations; it updates only one field at a time. On the other hand, the `write()` method can update several fields of several records at the same time by using a single database instruction. These differences should be kept in mind for cases where performance can be an issue.

It is also worth mentioning `copy()` to duplicate an existing record; it takes that as an optional argument and a dictionary with the values to write on the new record. For example, to create a new user copying from the Demo User:

```
>>> demo = self.env.ref('base.user_demo')
>>> new = demo.copy({'name': 'Daniel', 'login': 'dr', 'email':''})
```

Remember that fields with the `copy=False` attribute won't be copied.

Working with time and dates

For historical reasons, ORM recordsets handle `date` and `datetime` values using their strings representations, instead of actual Python `Date` and `Datetime` objects. In the database they are stored in date fields, but datetimes are stored in UTC time.

- `odoo.tools.DEFAULT_SERVER_DATE_FORMAT`
- `odoo.tools.DEFAULT_SERVER_DATETIME_FORMAT`

They map to `%Y-%m-%d` and `%Y-%m-%d %H:%M:%S` respectively.

To help handle dates, `fields.Date` and `fields.Datetime` provide few functions. For example:

```
>>> from odoo import fields
>>> fields.Datetime.now()
'2014-12-08 23:36:09'
>>> fields.Datetime.from_string('2014-12-08 23:36:09')
    datetime.datetime(2014, 12, 8, 23, 36, 9)
```

Dates and times are handled and stored by the server in a naive UTC format, which is not time zone aware and may be different from the time zone that the user is working on. Because of this we can make use of a few other functions to help us dealing with this:

- `fields.Date.today()` returns a string with the current date in the format expected by the server and using UTC as a reference. This is adequate to compute default values.
- `fields.Datetime.now()` returns a string with the current datetime in the format expected by the server using UTC as a reference. This is adequate to compute default values.

- `fields.Date.context_today(record, timestamp=None)` returns a string with the current date in the session's context. The time zone value is taken from the record's context, and the optional parameter to use is datetime instead of the current time.
- `fields.Datetime.context_timestamp(record, timestamp)` converts a naive datetime (without time zone) into a time zone aware datetime. The time zone is extracted from the record's context, hence the name of the function.

To facilitate conversion between formats, both `fields.Date` and `fields.Datetime` objects provide these functions:

- `from_string(value)` converts a string into a date or datetime object
- `to_string(value)` converts a date or datetime object into a string in the format expected by the server

Operations on recordsets

Recordsets support additional operations on them. We can check whether a record is included or not in a recordset. If `x` is a singleton recordset and `my_recordset` is a recordset containing many records, we can use:

- `x in my_recordset`
- `x not in my_recordset`

The following operations are also available:

- `recordset.ids` returns the list with the IDs of the recordset elements
- `recordset.ensure_one()` checks if it is a single record (singleton); if it's not, a `ValueError` exception is raised
- `recordset.filtered(func)` returns a filtered recordset
- `recordset.mapped(func)` returns a list of mapped values
- `recordset.sorted(func)` returns an ordered recordset

Here are some usage examples for these functions:

```
>>> rs0 = self.env['res.partner'].search([])
>>> len(rs0)  # how many records?
40
>>> starts_A = lambda r: r.name.startswith('A')
>>> rs1 = rs0.filtered(starts_A)
```

```
>>> print rs1
res.partner(8, 7, 19, 30, 3)
>>> rs2 = rs1.filtered('is_company')
>>> print rs2
res.partner(8, 7)
>>> rs2.mapped('name')
[u'Agrolait', u'ASUSTeK']
>>> rs2.mapped(lambda r: (r.id, r.name))
[(8, u'Agrolait'), (7, u'ASUSTeK')]
>> rs2.sorted(key=lambda r: r.id, reverse=True)
res.partner(8, 7)
```

Manipulating recordsets

We will surely want to add, remove, or replace the elements in these related fields, and so this leads to the question: how can recordsets be manipulated?

Recordsets are immutable, meaning that their values can't be directly modified. Instead, modifying a recordset means composing a new recordset based on existing ones.

One way to do this is using the supported set operations:

- `rs1 | rs2` is the **union** set operation, and results in a recordset with all elements from both recordsets.
- `rs1 + rs2` is the **addition** set operation, to concatenate both recordsets into one. It may result in a set with duplicate records.
- `rs1 & rs2` is the **intersection** set operation, and results in a recordset with only the elements present in both recordsets.
- `rs1 - rs2` is the **difference** set operation, and results in a recordset with the `rs1` elements not present in `rs2`

The slice notation can also be used, as shown in these examples:

- `rs[0]` and `rs[-1]` retrieve the first element and the last element, respectively.
- `rs[1:]` results in a copy of the recordset without the first element. This yields the same records as `rs - rs[0]` but preserves their order.

In Odoo 10, recordset manipulation preserves order. This is unlike previous Odoo versions, where recordset manipulation was not guaranteed to preserve the order, although addition and slicing are known to keep record order.

We can use these operations to change a recordset by removing or adding elements. Here are some examples:

- `self.task_ids |= task1` adds the `task1` record, if not in the recordset
- `self.task_ids -= task1` removes the specific record `task1`, if present in the recordset
- `self.task_ids = self.task_ids[:-1]` removes the last record

The relational fields contain recordset values. Many-to-one fields can contain a singleton recordset, and to-many fields contain recordsets with any number of records. We set values on them using a regular assignment statement, or using the `create()` and `write()` methods with a dictionary of values. In this last case, a special syntax is used to modify to-many fields. It is the same used in XML records to provide values for relational fields, and is described in `Chapter 4`, *Module Data*, in the section *Setting values for relation fields*.

As an example, the `write()` syntax equivalent to the three preceding assignment examples is:

- `self.write([(4, task1.id, None)])` adds the `task1` record
- `self.write([(3, task1.id, None)])` removes `task1` from the recordset
- `self.write([(3, self.task_ids[-1].id, False)])` removes the last record

Using relational fields

As we saw earlier, models can have relational fields: **many-to-one**, **one-to-many**, and **many-to-many**. These field types have recordsets as values.

In the case of many-to-one, the value can be a singleton or an empty recordset. In both cases, we can directly access their field values. As an example, the following instructions are correct and safe:

```
>>> self.company_id
res.company(1,)
>>> self.company_id.name
u'YourCompany'
>>> self.company_id.currency_id
res.currency(1,)
>>> self.company_id.currency_id.name
u'EUR'
```

Conveniently, an empty recordset also behaves like singleton, and accessing its fields does not return an error but just returns `False`. Because of this, we can traverse records using dot notation without worrying about errors from empty values, as shown here:

```
>>> self.company_id.country_id
res.country()
>>> self.company_id.country_id.name
False
```

Working with relational fields

While using the active record pattern, relational fields can be assigned recordsets.

For many-to-one fields, the value assigned must be a single record (a singleton recordset).

For to-many fields, their value can also be assigned with a recordset, replacing the list of linked records, if any, with a new one. Here a recordset with any size is allowed.

While using the `create()` or `write()` methods, where values are assigned using dictionaries, relational fields can't be assigned to recordset values. The corresponding ID or list of IDs should be used.

For example, instead of `self.write({'user_id': self.env.`**`user`**`})`, we should rather use `self.write({'user_id': self.env.`**`user.id`**`})`.

Summary

In the previous chapters, we saw how to build models and design views. Here we went a little further, learning how to implement business logic and use recordsets to manipulate model data.

We also saw how the business logic can interact with the user interface and learned to create wizards that communicate with the user and serve as a platform to launch advanced processes.

In the next chapter, we will learn about adding automated tests for our addon module, and some debugging techniques.

8
Writing Tests and Debugging Your Code

A good part of a developer's work is to test and debug code. Automated tests are an inestimable tool to build and maintain robust software. In this chapter, we will learn how to add automated tests to our addon modules, to make them more robust. Server side debugging techniques are also presented, allowing the developer to inspect and understand what is happening in his code.

Unit tests

Automated tests are generally accepted as a best practice in software. It does not only help us ensure our code is correctly implemented. More importantly, it provides a safety net for future code enhancements or rewrites.

In the case of dynamic programming languages, such as Python, since there is no compilation step, syntax errors can go unnoticed. This makes it even more important to have unit tests going through as many lines of code as possible.

The two goals described can provide a guiding light when writing tests. The first goal for your tests should be to provide a good test coverage, designing test cases that go through all lines of code. This alone will usually make good progress on the second goal – to show the functional correctness of the code.

This alone will usually make good progress on the second goal – to show the functional correctness of the code, since after this we will surely have a great starting point to build additional test cases for non obvious use cases.

Adding unit tests

Python tests are added to addon modules by using a `tests/` subdirectory. The test runner will automatically discover tests in the subdirectories with that particular name.

The tests on our `todo_wizard` addon will be in a `tests/test_wizard.py` file. We will need to add the `tests/__init__.py` file:

```
from . import test_wizard
```

And this would be the basic skeleton for the `tests/test_wizard.py`:

```
# -*- coding: utf-8 -*-
from odoo.tests.common import TransactionCase

class TestWizard(TransactionCase):

    def setUp(self, *args, **kwargs):
        super(TestWizard, self).setUp(*args, **kwargs)
        # Add test setup code here...

    def test_populate_tasks(self):
        "Populate tasks buttons should add two tasks"
        # Add test code
```

Odoo provides a few classes to use for tests. The `TransactionCase` tests uses a different transaction for each test, that is automatically rolled back at the end. We can also use the `SingleTransactionCase`, that runs all tests in a single transaction, that is rolled back only at the end of the last test. This can be useful when you want the final state of each test to be the initial state for the following test.

The `setUp()` method is where we prepare data and variables to be used. We will usually store them as class attributes, so that they are available to be used in the test methods.

Tests should then be implemented as class methods, like `test_populate_tasks()`. The test cases method names must begin with a `test_` prefix. They are automatically discovered, and this prefix is what identifies the methods implementing test cases.

Methods will be run in order of the test function names. When using the `TransactionCase` class, a rollback will be done at the end of each. The method's docstring is shown when the tests are run, and should provides a short description for it.

These test classes are wrappers around `unittest` testcases. This is part of the Python standard library, and you may refer to its documentation for more details at `https://docs.python.org/2/library/unittest.html`.

To be more precise, Odoo uses a `unittest` extension library, `unittest2`.

Writing test cases

Now let's expand the `test_populate_tasks()` method seen in our initial skeleton. The simplest tests we can write, run some code from the tested object, query for a result to verify, and then use an assert to compare with an expected result.

The `test_populate_tasks()` method will test the `do_populate_tasks()` Todo method. Since our setup made sure we have two open Todos, after running it we expect the wizard `task_ids` to be referencing these two records.

```
# class TestWizard(TransactionCase):
    def test_populate_tasks(self):
        "Populate tasks buttons should add two tasks"
        self.wizard.do_populate_tasks()
        count = len(self.wizard.task_ids)
        self.assertEqual(count, 2, 'Wrong number of populated
        tasks')
```

The docstring, at the first line of the method definition, is useful to describe the test and is printed out when running it.

The check verifying if the test succeeded or failed is the `self.assertEqual` statement. The last parameter is optional, but is recommended since it provides a more informative message when the test fails.

The `assertEquals` is one of the most used, but it is just one of the assert methods available. We should use the assert function appropriate for each case, since they will be more helpful to understand the cause of failing tests. For example, instead of comparing the length of `task_ids`, one could have prepared a recordset with the two expected tasks, and then use:

```
self.assertItemsEquals(
     self.wizard.task_ids, expected_tasks,
     'Incorrect set of populated tasks')
```

This would give the best output in case of failure, with a full comparison of the expected tasks versus the actual.

The `unittest` documentation provides a good reference on all the methods available at `https://docs.python.org/2/library/unittest.html#test-cases`.

To add a new test case, add to the class another method with it's implementation. Next we will test the `do_mass_update()` wizard method. This is the one doing the work when we click on the wizard's **OK** button:

```
def test_mass_change(self):
    "Mass change deadline date"
    self.wizard.do_populate_tasks()
    self.wizard.new_deadline = self.todo1.date_deadline
    self.wizard.do_mass_update()
    self.assertEqual(
        self.todo1.date_deadline,
        self.todo2.date_deadline)
```

We start by running `do_populate_tasks()` again. Remember that with `TransactionCase` tests, a rollback is done at the end of each test. So the operations done in the previous test were reverted, and we need to again populate the wizard's Todo Task list. Next we simulate the user filling in the new deadline field and performing the mass update. At the end our check is to see if both Todo Tasks ended up with the same date.

Setting up tests

We should begin by preparing the data to be used in the tests.

It is convenient to perform the test actions under a specific user, in order to also test that access control is properly configured. This is achieved using the `sudo()` model method. Recordsets carry that information with them, so after being created while using `sudo()`, later operations in the same recordset will be performed using that same context.

This is the code for the `setUp` method, and a few additional import statements that are also needed:

```
from datetime import date
from odoo.tests.common import TransactionCase
from odoo import fields

class TestWizard(TransactionCase):

    def setUp(self, *args, **kwargs):
        super(TestWizard, self).setUp(*args, **kwargs)
```

```
        # Close any open Todo tasks
        self.env['todo.task']\
            .search([('is_done', '=', False)])\
            .write({'is_done': True})
        # Demo user will be used to run tests
        demo_user = self.env.ref('base.user_demo')
        # Create two Todo tasks to use in tests
        t0 = date.today()
        Todo = self.env['todo.task'].sudo(demo_user)
        self.todo1 = Todo.create({
            'name': 'Todo1',
            'date_deadline': fields.Date.to_string(t0)})
        self.todo2 = Todo.create({
            'name': 'Todo2'})
        # Create Wizard instance to use in tests
        Wizard = self.env['todo.wizard'].sudo(demo_user)
        self.wizard = Wizard.create({})
```

To test our wizard, we want to have exactly two open Todos. So we start by closing any existing Todos, so that they don't get in the way of our tests, and create two new Todos for tests, using the Demo user. We finally create a new instance of our wizard, using the Demo user, and assign it to `self.wizard`, so that is available to the test methods.

Testing exceptions

Sometimes we need our tests to check if an exception was generated. A common case is when testing if some validations are being done properly.

In our example, the `test_count()` method uses a `Warning` exception as a way to give information to the user. To check if an exception is raised, we place the corresponding code inside a `with self.assertRaises()` block.

We need to import the `Warning` exception at the top of the file:

```
from odoo.exceptions import Warning
```

And add to the test class a method with another test case:

```
def test_count(self):
    "Test count button"
    with self.assertRaises(Warning) as e:
        self.wizard.do_count_tasks()
    self.assertIn(' 2 ', str(e.exception))
```

If the `do_count_tasks()` method does not raise an exception, the check will fail. If it does raise that exception, the check succeeds and the exception raised is stored in the `e` variable.

We use that to further inspect it. The exception message contains the number of tasks counted, that we expect to be two. In the final statement we use `assertIn` to check that the exception text contains the `' 2 '` string.

Running tests

The tests are written, it's time to run them. For that we just need to add the `--test-enable` option to the Odoo server start command, while installing or upgrading (`-i` or `-u`) the addon module.

The command would look like this:

```
$ ./odoo-bin -d todo --test-enable -i todo_wizard --stop-after-init
--addons-path="..."
```

Only the modules installed or upgraded will be tested. If some dependencies need to be installed, their tests will run too. If you want to avoid this, you can install the module to test the usual way, and then run the tests while performing an upgrade (`-u`) of the module to test.

About YAML tests

Odoo also supports a second type of tests, described using YAML data files. Originally all tests used YAML, until more recently the `unittest` based tests were introduced. While both are supported, and many core addons still include YAML tests, the official documentation currently does not mention the YAML tests. The last documentation on it is available at `https://doc.odoo.com/v6.0/contribute/15_guidelines/coding_guidelines_testing/`.

Developers with a Python background will probably feel more at home with `unittest`, since it is a standard Python feature, while YAML tests are designed with Odoo-specific conventions. The trend clearly is to prefer `unittest` over YAML, and YAML support can be expected to be dropped in future versions.

For these reasons, we will not do an in-depth coverage of YAML tests. It might still be useful to have some basic understanding on how they work.

YAML tests are data files, similar to CSV and XML. In fact the YAML format was intended to be a more compact data format that can be used in place of XML. Unlike Python tests, where tests must be in a `test/` subdirectory, the YAML test files can be anywhere inside the addon module. But frequently they will be inside a `tests/` or `test/` subdirectory. And while Python tests are automatically discovered, YAML tests must be declared in the `__manifest__.py` manifest file. This is done with the `test` key, similar to the `data` key we already know.

In Odoo 10 YAML tests are not used anymore, but here is an example, from the `02_order_to_invoice.yml` in the `point_of_sale` addon module:

```
-
  I click on the "Make Payment" wizard to pay the PoS order
-
  !record {model: pos.make.payment, id: pos_make_payment_2, context:
'{"active_id": ref("pos_order_pos1"), "active_ids":
[ref("pos_order_pos1")]}' }:
    amount: !eval >
        (450*2 + 300*3*1.05)*0.95
-
  I click on the validate button to register the payment.
-
  !python {model: pos.make.payment}: |
    self.check(cr, uid, [ref('pos_make_payment_2')], context={'active_id':
ref('pos_order_pos1')} )
```

The lines that begin with a `!` are YAML tags, equivalent to the tag elements we find in XML files. In the preceding code we can see a `!record` tag, equivalent to the XML `<record>`, and a `!python` tag, that allows us to run Python code on a model, `pos.make.payment` in the example.

As you can see, YAML tests use a Odoo-specific syntax that needs learning. In comparison, Python tests use the existing `unittest` framework, only adding Odoo-specific wrapper classes like `TransactionCase`.

Development tools

There are a few techniques developer should learn to aid them in their work. In `Chapter 1`, *Getting Started with Odoo Development*, we already introduced the user interface **Developer Mode**. We also have available a server option providing some developer friendly features. We will be describing it in more detail next. After that we will discuss another relevant topic for developers: how to debug server side code.

Server development options

The Odoo server provides the `--dev` option to enable some developer features speeding up our development cycle, such as:

- Enter the debugger when an exception is found in an addon module
- Reload Python code automatically, once a Python file is saved, avoiding a manual server restart
- Read view definitions directly from the XML files, avoiding manual module upgrades

The `--dev` option accepts a comma separated list of options, although the all option will be suitable most of the time. We can also specify the debugger we prefer to use. By default the Python debugger, `pdb`, is used. Some people might prefer to install and use alternative debuggers. Here also supported are `ipdb` and `pudb`.

Before Odoo 10 we had instead the `--debug` option, allowing to open the debugger on an addon module exception.

When working on Python code, the server needs to be restarted every time the code is changed, so that it is reloaded. The `--dev` command line option makes that reloading: when the server detects that a Python file is changed, it automatically repeats the server loading sequence, making the code change immediately effective.

To use it just add the option `--dev=all` to the server command:

```
$ ./odoo-bin -d todo --dev=all
```

For this to work the `watchdog` Python package is required, and it should be installed as shown here:

```
$ pip install watchdog
```

Note that this is useful only for Python code changes and view architectures in XML files. For other changes, such as model data structure, a module upgrade is needed, and the reload is not enough.

Debugging

We all know that a good part of a developer's work is to debug code. To do this we often make use of a code editor that can set breakpoints and run our program step by step.

If you're using Microsoft Windows as your development workstation, setting up an environment capable of running Odoo code from source is a nontrivial task. Also the fact that Odoo is a server that waits for client calls, and only then acts on them, makes it quite different to debug compared to client-side programs.

The Python debugger

While it may look a little intimidating for newcomers, the most pragmatic approach to debug Odoo is to use the Python integrated debugger, `pdb`. We will also introduce extensions to it that provide a richer user interface, similar to what sophisticated IDEs usually provide.

To use the debugger, the best approach is to insert a breakpoint on the code we want to inspect, typically a model method. This is done by inserting the following line in the desired place:

```
import pdb; pdb.set_trace()
```

Now restart the server so that the modified code is loaded. As soon as the program execution reaches that line, a `(pdb)` Python prompt will be shown in the terminal window where the server is running, waiting for our input.

The `--dev` option is not needed to use manually set Python debugger breakpoints.

This prompt works as a Python shell, where you can run any expression or command in the current execution context. This means that the current variables can be inspected and even modified. These are the most important shortcut commands available:

- `h` (help) displays a summary of the pdb commands available
- `p` (print) evaluates and prints an expression
- `pp` (pretty print) is useful to print data structures such as dictionaries or lists
- `l` (list) lists the code around the instruction to be executed next
- `n` (next) steps over to the next instruction
- `s` (step) steps into the current instruction
- `c` (continue) continues execution normally
- `u` (up) move up the execution stack
- `d` (down) move down in the execution stack

The Odoo server also supports the `dev=all` option. If activated, when an exception is raised the server enters a *post mortem* mode at the corresponding line. This is a `pdb` prompt, such as the one described earlier, allowing us to inspect the program state at the moment where the error was found.

While `pdb` has the advantage of being available out-of-the-box, it can be quite terse, and a few more comfortable options exist.

A sample debugging session

Let's see how a simple debugging session looks like. We can start by adding debugger breakpoint in the first line of the `do_populate_tasks` wizard method:

```
def do_populate_tasks(self):
    import pdb; pdb.set_trace()
    self.ensure_one()
    # ...
```

Now restart the server, open a **To-do Tasks Wizard** form, and click on the **Get All** button. This will trigger the `do_populate_tasks` wizard method on the server, and the web client will stay in a **Loading...** state, waiting for the server response. Looking at the terminal window where the server is running, you will see something similar to this:

```
> /home/daniel/odoo-dev/custom-
addons/todo_wizard/models/todo_wizard_model.py(54)do_populate_tasks()
-> self.ensure_one()
(Pdb)
```

This is the `pdb` debugger prompt, and the two first lines give you information about where you are in the Python code execution. The first line informs the file, line number and function name you are in, and the second line is the next line of code to be run.

During a debug session, server log messages can creep in. These won't harm our debugging, but they can disturb us. We can avoid that by reducing the verbosity of the log messages. Most of the time these log messages will be from the `werkzeug` module. We can silence them using the option `--log-handler=werkzeug:CRITICAL`. If this is not enough, we can lower the general log level, using `--log-level=warn`.

If we type `h` now, we will see a quick reference of the commands available. Typing `l` shows the current line of code and the surrounding lines of code.

Typing `n` will run the current line of code and move to the next. If we just press *Enter*, the previous command will be repeated. So do that three times and we should be at the method's return statement.

We can inspect the content on any variable, such as the `open_tasks` used in this method. and typing `p open_tasks` or `print open_tasks` will show the representation of that variable. Any Python expressions are allowed, even variable assignments. For example, to show a friendlier list with the Task names we could use:

```
(pdb) p open_tasks.mapped('name')
```

Running the return line, using `n` once more, we will be shown the returning values of the function. Something like this:

```
--Return--
> /home/daniel/odoo-dev/custom-
addons/todo_wizard/models/todo_wizard_model.py(59)do_populate_tasks()->{'re
s_id': 14, 'res_model': 'todo.wizard', 'target': 'new', 'type':
'ir.actions.act_window', ...}
-> return self._reopen_form()
```

The debugging session will continue on the caller's lines of code, but we can finish it and continue normal execution typing `c`.

Alternative Python debuggers

While `pdb` has the advantage of being available out of the box, it can be quite terse, and a few more comfortable options exist.

The Iron Python debugger, `ipdb`, is popular choice that uses the same commands as `pdb`, but adds improvements such as tab completion and syntax highlighting, for a more comfortable usage. It can be installed with:

```
$ sudo pip install ipdb
```

And a breakpoint is added with the line:

```
import ipdb; ipdb.set_trace()
```

Another alternative debugger is `pudb`. It also supports the same commands as `pdb` and works in text-only terminals, but uses a graphical display similar to what you can find in an IDE debugger. Useful information, such as the variables in the current context and their values, is readily available in the screen in their own windows:

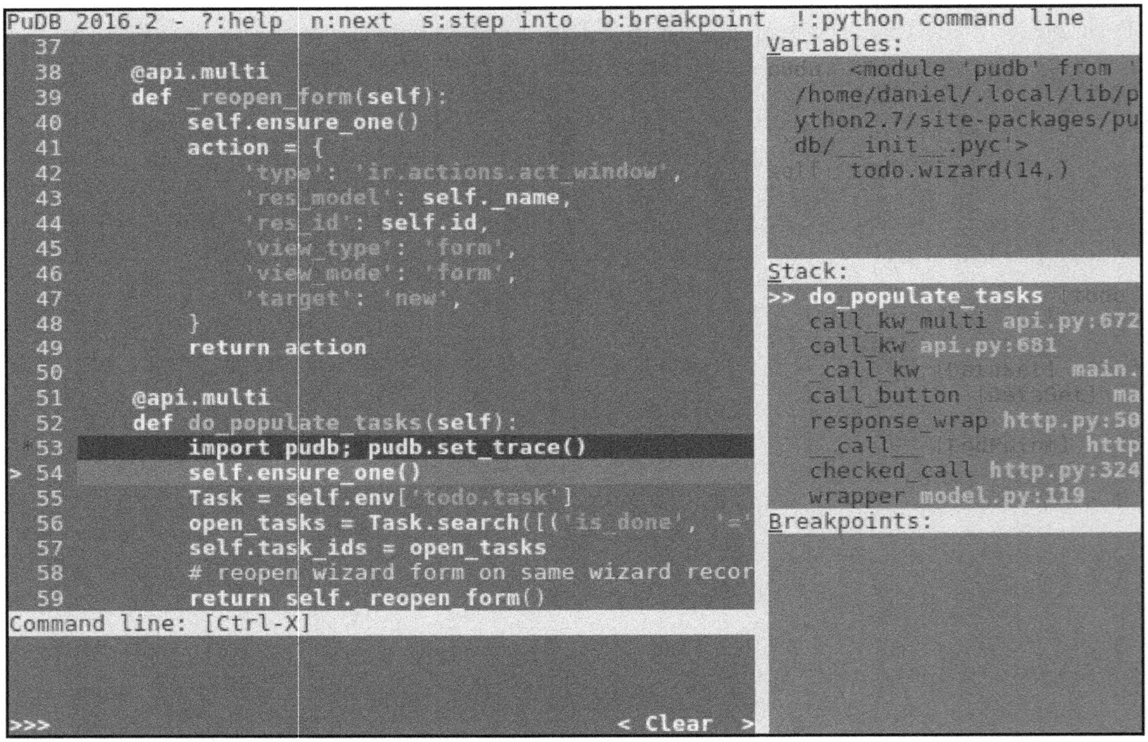

```
PuDB 2016.2 - ?:help  n:next  s:step into  b:breakpoint  !:python command line

    @api.multi
    def _reopen_form(self):
        self.ensure_one()
        action = {
            'type': 'ir.actions.act_window',
            'res_model': self._name,
            'res_id': self.id,
            'view_type': 'form',
            'view_mode': 'form',
            'target': 'new',
        }
        return action

    @api.multi
    def do_populate_tasks(self):
        import pudb; pudb.set_trace()
        self.ensure_one()
        Task = self.env['todo.task']
        open_tasks = Task.search([('is_done', '='
        self.task_ids = open_tasks
        # reopen wizard form on same wizard recor
        return self._reopen_form()
Command line: [Ctrl-X]

>>>                                          < Clear >

Variables:
  <module 'pudb' from '
  /home/daniel/.local/lib/p
  ython2.7/site-packages/pu
  db/__init__.pyc'>
  todo.wizard(14,)

Stack:
>> do_populate_tasks
   call_kw_multi api.py:672
   call_kw api.py:681
   _call_kw                main.
   call_button             ma
   response_wrap http.py:50
   __call__                http
   checked_call http.py:324
   wrapper model.py:119
Breakpoints:
```

It can be installed either through the system package manager or through `pip`, as shown here:

```
$ sudo apt-get install python-pudb  # using OS packages
$ sudo pip install pudb  # using pip, possibly in a virtualenv
```

Adding a `pudb` breakpoint is done just the way you would expect:

```
import pudb; pudb.set_trace()
```

Printing messages and logging

Sometimes we just need to inspect the values of some variables or check if some code blocks are being executed. A Python `print` statement can do the job perfectly without stopping the execution flow. As we are running the server in a terminal window, the printed text will be shown in the standard output. But it won't be stored to the server log if it's being written to a file.

Another option to keep in mind is to set debug level log messages at sensitive points of our code if we feel that we might need them to investigate issues in a deployed instance. It would only be needed to elevate that server logging level to debug and then inspect the log files.

Inspecting running processes

There are also a few tricks that allow us to inspect a running Odoo process.

For that we first need to find the corresponding process ID (PID). To find the PID run another terminal window and type:

```
$ ps ax | grep odoo-bin
```

The first column in the output is the PID for that process. Take a note on the PID for the process to inspect, since we will need it next.

Now we want to send a signal the process. The command used to do that is kill. By default it sends a signal to terminate a process, but it can also send other friendlier signals.

Knowing the PID for our running Odoo server process, we can print the traces of the code currently being executed using:

```
$ kill -3 <PID>
```

If we look at the terminal window or log file where the server output is being written, we will see the information on the several threads being run and detailed stack traces on what line of code they are running.

We can also see a dump of the cache/memory statistics using:

```
$ kill -USR1 <PID>
```

Summary

Automated tests are a valuable practice, both for business applications in general, and for ensuring the code robustness in a dynamic programming language, such as Python.

We learned the basic principles of how to add and run tests for a addon module. We also discussed some techniques to help us debug our code.

In the next chapter, we will go deeper into the views layer, and will discuss the kanban views.

9
QWeb and Kanban Views

QWeb is a template engine used by Odoo. It is XML-based and is used to generate HTML fragments and pages. QWeb was first introduced in version 7.0 to enable richer kanban views and, since version 8.0, is also used for report design and CMS website pages.

Here you will learn about the QWeb syntax and how to use it to create your own kanban views and custom reports. Let's get started by learning more about kanban boards.

About kanban boards

Kanban is a Japanese word used to represent a work queue management method. It takes inspiration from the Toyota Production System and Lean Manufacturing. It has become popular in the software industry with the adoption of Agile methodologies.

The **kanban board** is a tool to visualize the work queue. The board is organized in columns representing the **stages** of the work process. Work items are represented by **cards** placed on the appropriate column of the board. New work items start from the leftmost column and travel through the board until they reach the rightmost column, representing completed work.

The simplicity and visual impact of kanban boards make them excellent to support simple business processes. A basic example of a kanban board can have three columns, as shown in the following image: **To Do**, **Doing**, and **Done**.

It can, of course, be extended to whatever specific process steps we may need:

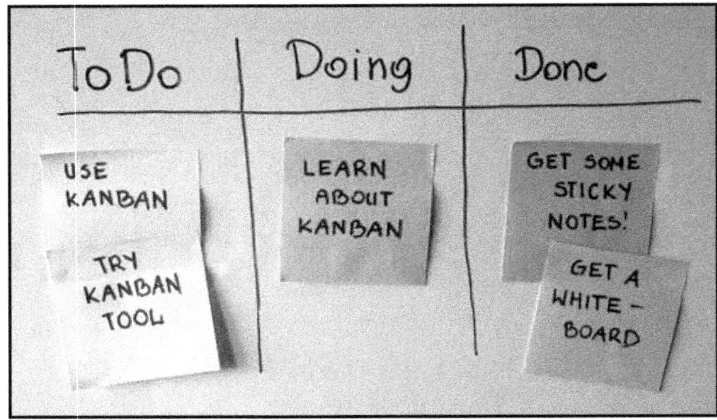

Photo credits: "A Scrum board suggesting to use kanban" by Jeff.lasovski. Courtesy of Wikipedia.

Kanban views

For many business use cases, a kanban board can be a more effective way to manage the corresponding process than the typically heavier workflow engine. Odoo supports kanban board views, along with the classic list and form views. This makes it easy to implement this type of view. Let's learn how to use them.

In form views, we use mostly specific XML elements, such as `<field>` and `<group>`, and few HTML elements, such as `<h1>` or `<div>`. With kanban views, it's quite the opposite; they are HTML-based templates and support only two Odoo-specific elements, `<field>` and `<button>`.

The HTML is dynamically generated using QWeb templates. The QWeb engine processes special XML tags and attributes to produce the final HTML to be presented in the web client. This brings a lot of control over how to render the content but also makes view design more complex.

The kanban view design is quite flexible, so we'll do our best to prescribe a straightforward way for you to quickly build your kanban views. A good approach is to find an existing kanban view similar to what you need, and inspect it to for ideas on how to build yours.

We can see two different ways to use kanban views. One is a card list. It is used in places like contacts, products, employee directories or apps.

Here is how the **Contacts** kanban view looks:

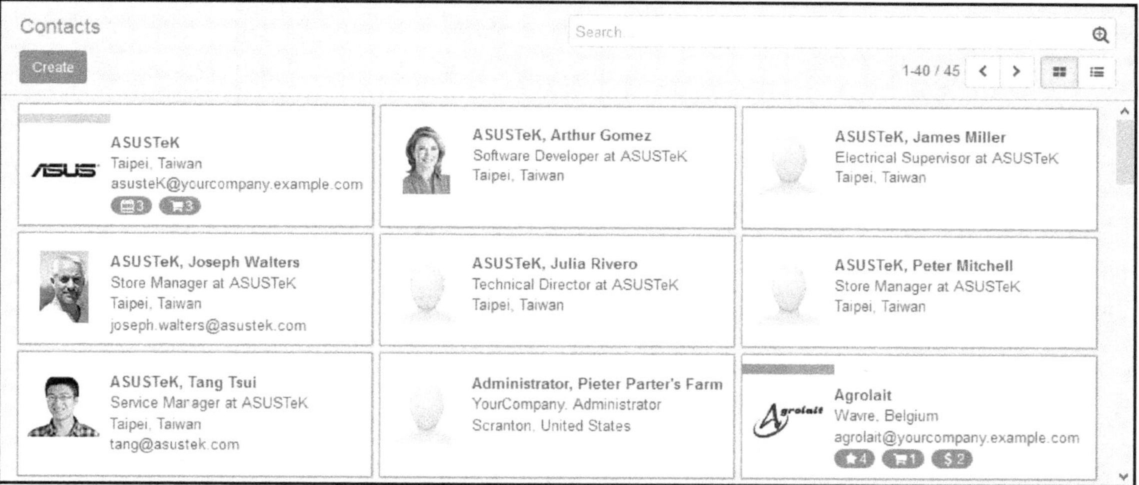

But this is not a true kanban board. A kanban board is expected to have the cards organized in columns, and of course, the kanban view also supports that layout. We can see examples in the **Sales** | **My Pipeline** or in **Project Tasks**.

Here is how the **Sales | My Pipeline** looks:

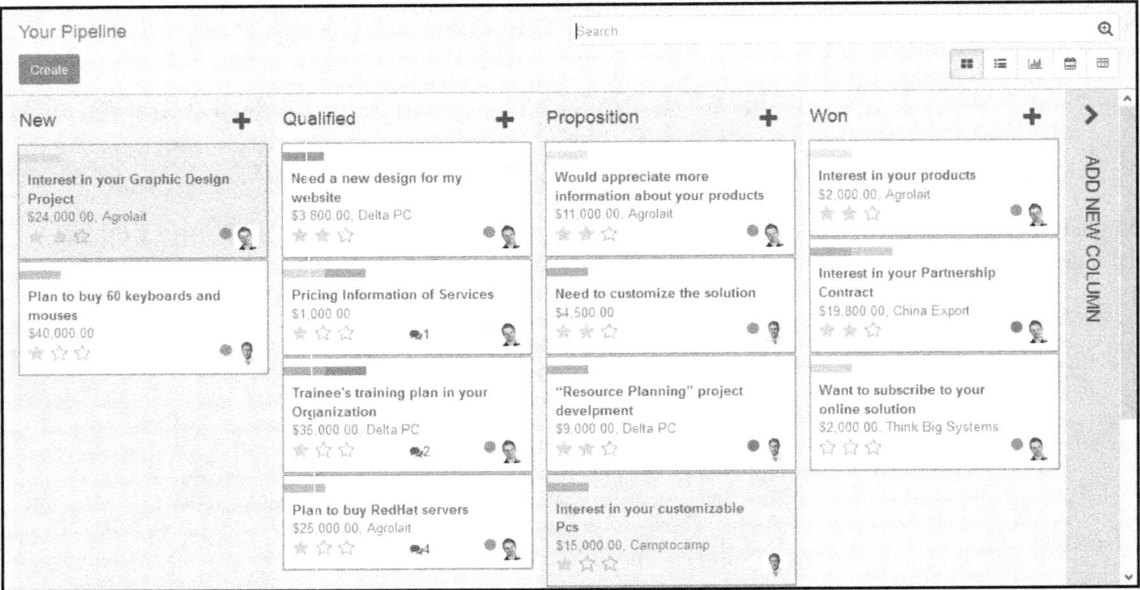

The most striking difference between the two is the kanban board column organization of the cards. This is achieved by the **Group By** feature, similar to what the list views provide. Usually, the grouping is done on a **stage** field. One very useful feature of kanban views is that it supports drag and dropping cards between columns, automatically assigning the corresponding value to the field the view is grouped by.

Looking at the cards in both examples, we can see some differences. In fact, their design is quite flexible, and there is not a single way to design a kanban card. But these two examples can provide a starting point for your designs.

The **Contact** cards basically have an image at the left-hand side, and a bold title in the main area, followed by a list of values. The **My Pipeline** cards have a bit more structure. The main card area also has a title followed by a list of relevant information as well as a footer area, in this case with a priority widget on the left-hand side, and the responsible user at the right-hand side. It is not visible in the image, but the cards also have an options menu at the top-right, shown when hovering the mouse pointer over it. This menu allows, for example, to change the background color of the card.

We will be using this more elaborate structure as a model for the cards on our Todo kanban board.

Designing kanban views

We will be adding the kanban view to the Todo tasks with a new addon module. It would be simpler to add it directly to the `todo_ui` module. However, for a clearer explanation, we will use a new module and avoid too many, possibly confusing, changes in the already created files.

We will name this new addon module as `todo_kanban` and create the usual initial files. Edit the descriptor file `todo_kanban/__manifest__.py` as follows:

```
{'name': 'To-Do Kanban',
 'description': 'Kanban board for to-do tasks.',
 'author': 'Daniel Reis',
 'depends': ['todo_ui'],
 'data': ['views/todo_view.xml'] }
```

Also add an empty `todo_kanban/__init__.py` file, to make the directory Python importable, as required for Odoo addon modules.

Next, create the XML file where our shiny new kanban view will go and set kanban as the default view on the to-do task's window action. This should be in `todo_kanban/views/todo_view.xml`, containing the following code:

```
<?xml version="1.0"?>
<odoo>
  <!-- Add Kanban view mode to the menu Action: -->
  <act_window id="todo_app.action_todo_task" name="To-Do Tasks"
    res_model="todo.task" view_mode="kanban,tree,form,calendar,graph,pivot"
    context="{'search_default_filter_my_tasks': True}" />
  <!-- Add Kanban view -->
  <record id="To-do Task Kanban" model="ir.ui.view">
    <field name="model">todo.task</field>
    <field name="arch" type="xml">
      <kanban>
        <!-- Empty for now, but the Kanban will go here! -->
      </kanban>
    </field>
  </record>
</odoo>
```

Now we have the basic skeleton for our module in place.

Before starting with the kanban views, we need to add a couple of fields to the to-do tasks model.

Priority, kanban state, and color

Other than stages, a few more fields are useful and frequently used in kanban boards.

- `priority` lets users organize their work items, signaling what should be addressed first.
- `kanban_state` signals whether a task is ready to move to the next stage or is blocked for some reason. At the model definition layer, both are selection fields. At the view layer, they have specific widgets for them that can be used on form and kanban views.
- `color` is used to store the color the kanban card should display, and can be set using a color picker menu available on kanban views.

To add these fields to our model, we will add a `models/todo_task_model.py` file.

But first, we will need to make it importable, and edit the `todo_kanban/__init__.py` file to import the `models` subdirectory:

```
from . import models
```

Then create the `models/__init__.py` file with:

```
from . import todo_task
```

Now let's edit the `models/todo_task.py` file:

```
from odoo import models, fields
class TodoTask(models.Model):
    _inherit = 'todo.task'
    color = fields.Integer('Color Index')
    priority = fields.Selection(
        [('0', 'Low'),
         ('1', 'Normal'),
         ('2', 'High')],
        'Priority', default='1')
    kanban_state = fields.Selection(
        [('normal', 'In Progress'),
         ('blocked', 'Blocked'),
         ('done', 'Ready for next stage')],
        'Kanban State', default='normal')
```

Now we can work on the kanban view.

Kanban card elements

The kanban view architecture has a <kanban> top element and the following basic structure:

```
<kanban default_group_by="stage_id" class="o_kanban_small_column" >
  <!-- Fields to use in expressions... -->
  <field name="stage_id" />
  <field name="color" />
  <field name="kanban_state" />
  <field name="priority" />
  <field name="is_done" />
  <field name="message_partner_ids" />
  <!-- (...add other used fields). -->
  <templates>
    <t t-name="kanban-box">
      <!-- HTML QWeb template... -->
    </t>
  </templates>
</kanban>
```

Notice the `default_group_by="stage_id"` attribute used in the <kanban> element. We used it so that, by default, the kanban cards are grouped by stage like kanban boards should. In simple card list kanbans, such as the one in **Contacts**, we don't need this and would instead just use a simple <kanban> opening tag.

The <kanban> top element supports a few interesting attributes:

- `default_group_by` sets the field to use for the default column groups.
- `default_order` sets a default order to use for the kanban items.
- `quick_create="false"` disables the quick create option (the large *plus* sign), available at the top of each column to create new items by providing just a title description. The false value is a JavaScript literal, and must be in lowercase.
- `class` adds a CSS class to the root element of the rendered kanban view. A relevant class is `o_kanban_small_column`, making columns somewhat more compact than the default. Additional classes may be made available by module provided custom CSS.

We then see a list of fields used in templates. To be exact, only fields used exclusively in QWeb expressions need to be declared here, to ensure that their data is fetched from the server.

Next, we have a <templates> element, containing one or more QWeb templates to generate the used HTML fragments. We must have one template named kanban-box, that will render the kanban cards. Additional templates can be also added, usually to define HTML fragments to be reused in the main template.

These templates use standard HTML and the QWeb templating language. QWeb provides special directives, that are processed to dynamically generate the final HTML to be presented.

Odoo uses the Twitter Bootstrap 3 web style library, so those style classes are generally available wherever HTML can be rendered. You can learn more about Bootstrap at https://getbootstrap.com

We will now have a closer look at the QWeb templates to use in the kanban views.

The kanban card layout

The main content area of a kanban card is defined inside the kanban-box template. This content area can also have a footer sub-container.

For a single footer, we would use a <div> element at the bottom of the kanban box, with the oe_kanban_footer CSS class. This class will automatically split its inner elements with flexible spaces, making explicit left- and right- alignment inside it superfluous.

A button opening an action menu may also be featured at the card's top-right corner. As an alternative, the Bootstrap provided classes pull-left and pull-right can be used to add left or right aligned elements anywhere in the card, including in the oe_kanban_footer footer.

Here is our first iteration on the QWeb template for our kanban card:

```
<!-- Define the kanban-box template -->
<t t-name="kanban-box">
  <!-- Set the Kanban Card color: -->
  <div t-attf-class="#{kanban_color(record.color.raw_value)}
    oe_kanban_global_click">
      <div class="o_dropdown_kanban dropdown">
        <!-- Top-right drop down menu here... -->
      </div>
      <div class="oe_kanban_content">
        <div class="oe_kanban_footer">
          <div>
            <!-- Left hand footer... -->
```

```
            </div>
            <div>
              <!-- Right hand footer... -->
            </div>
          </div>
        </div> <!-- oe_kanban_content -->
        <div class="oe_clear"/>
    </div> <!-- kanban color -->
  </t>
```

This lays out the overall structure for the kanban card. You may notice that the `color` field is being used in the top `<div>` element to dynamically set the card's color. We will explain the `t-attf` QWeb directive in more detail in one of the next sections.

Now let's work on the main content area, and choose what to place there:

```
<!-- Content elements and fields go here... -->
 <div>
   <field name="tag_ids" />
 </div>

 <div>
   <strong>
     <a type="open"><field name="name" /></a>
   </strong>
 </div>

 <ul>
   <li><field name="user_id" /></li>
   <li><field name="date_deadline" /></li>
 </ul>
```

Most of this template is regular HTML, but we also see the `<field>` element used to render field values, and the `type` attribute used in regular form view buttons, used here in an `<a>` anchor tag.

On the left-hand footer, we will insert the priority widget:

```
<div>
  <!-- Left hand footer... -->
  <field name="priority" widget="priority"/>
</div>
```

Here we can see the `priority` field added, just like we would do in a form view.

On the right-hand footer we will place the kanban state widget and the avatar for the owner of the to-do task:

```
<div>
  <!-- Right hand footer... -->
  <field name="kanban_state" widget="kanban_state_selection"/>
  <img t-att- t-att-src="kanban_image(
    'res.users', 'image_small', record.user_id.raw_value)"
    width="24" height="24" class="oe_kanban_avatar pull-right" />
</div>
```

The kanban state is added using a `<field>` element, just like in regular form views. The user avatar image is inserted using the HTML `<img>` tag. The image content is dynamically generated using the QWeb `t-att-` directive, that we will explain in a moment.

Sometimes we want to have a small representative image to be shown on the card, like in the **Contacts** example. For reference, this can be done by adding the following as the first content element:

```
<img t-att-src="kanban_image( 'res.partner', 'image_medium',
  record.id.value)" class="o_kanban_image"/>
```

Adding a kanban card option menu

Kanban cards can have an option menu, placed at the top-right. Usual actions are to edit or delete the record, but it's possible to have any action that can be called from a button. We also have a widget to set the card's color available.

The following is a baseline HTML code for the option menu to be added at the top of the `oe_kanban_content` element:

```
<div class="o_dropdown_kanban dropdown">
  <!-- Top-right drop down menu here... -->
  <a class="dropdown-toggle btn" data-toggle="dropdown" href="#">
    <span class="fa fa-bars fa-lg"/>
  </a>
  <ul class="dropdown-menu" role="menu" aria-labelledby="dLabel">
    <!-- Edit and Delete actions, if available: -->
    <t t-if="widget.editable">
      <li><a type="edit">Edit</a></li>
    </t>
    <t t-if="widget.deletable">
      <li><a type="delete">Delete</a></li>
    </t>
    <!-- Call a server-side Model method: -->
```

```
        <t t-if="!record.is_done.value">
          <li><a name="do_toggle_done" type="object">Set as Done</a>
          </li>
        </t>
        <!-- Color picker option: -->
        <li>
          <ul class="oe_kanban_colorpicker" data-field="color"/>
        </li>
      </ul>
    </div>
```

Notice that the above won't work unless we have `<field name="is_done" />` somewhere in the view, because it is used in one of the expressions. If we don't need to use it inside the template, we can declare it before the `<templates>` element, as we did when defining the `<kanban>` view.

The drop-down menu is basically an HTML list of the `<a>` elements. Some options, such as **Edit** and **Delete**, are made available only if certain conditions are met. This is done with the `t-if` QWeb directive. Later in this chapter, we explain this and other QWeb directives in more detail.

The `widget` global variable represents the current `KanbanRecord()` JavaScript object responsible for the rendering of the current kanban card. Two particularly useful properties are `widget.editable` and `widget.deletable` to inspect if the actions are available.

We can also see how to show or hide an option depending on the record field values. The **Set as Done** option will only be displayed if the `is_done` field is not set.

The last option adds the color picker special widget using the `color` data field to select and change the card's background color.

Actions in kanban views

In QWeb templates, the `<a>` tag for links can have a `type` attribute. It sets the type of action the link will perform so that links can act just like the buttons in regular forms. So in addition to the `<button>` elements, the `<a>` tags can also be used to run Odoo actions.

As in form views, the action type can be `action` or `object`, and it should be accompanied by a `name` attribute, identifying the specific action to execute. Additionally, the following action types are also available:

- `open` opens the corresponding form view
- `edit` opens the corresponding form view directly in edit mode
- `delete` deletes the record and removes the item from the kanban view

The QWeb templating language

The QWeb parser looks for special directives in the templates and replaces them with dynamically generated HTML. These directives are XML element attributes, and can be used in any valid tag or element, such as `<div>`, `<span>`, or `<field>`.

Sometimes we want to use a QWeb directive but don't want to place it in any of the XML elements in our template. For those cases, we have a `<t>` special element that can have QWeb directives, such as a `t-if` or a `t-foreach`, but is silent and won't have any output on the final XML/HTML produced.

The QWeb directives will frequently make use of evaluated expressions to produce different results depending on the current record values. There are two different QWeb implementations: client-side JavaScript, and server-side Python.

The reports and website pages use the server-side Python implementation. On the other hand, kanban views use the client-side JavaScript implementation. This means that the QWeb expression used in kanban views should be written using the JavaScript syntax, not Python.

When displaying a kanban view, the internal steps are roughly as follows:

1. Get the XML for the templates to render.
2. Call the server `read()` method to get the data for the fields in the templates.
3. Locate the `kanban-box` template and parse it using QWeb to output the final HTML fragments.
4. Inject the HTML in the browser's display (the DOM).

This is not meant to be technically exact. It is just a mind map that can be useful to understand how things work in kanban views.

Next, we will learn about QWeb expressions evaluation and explore the available QWeb directives, using examples that enhance our to-do task kanban card.

The QWeb JavaScript evaluation context

Many of the QWeb directives use expressions that are evaluated to produce some result. When used from the client-side, as is the case for kanban views, these expressions are written in JavaScript. They are evaluated in a context that has a few useful variables available.

A `record` object is available, representing the record being rendered, with the fields requested from the server. The field values can be accessed using either the `raw_value` or the `value` attributes:

- `raw_value` is the value returned by the `read()` server method, so it's more suitable to use in condition expressions.
- `value` is formatted according to the user settings, and is meant to be used for display in the user interface. This is typically relevant for date/datetime and float/monetary fields.

The QWeb evaluation context also has references available for the JavaScript web client instance. To make use of them, a good understanding of the web client architecture is needed, but we won't be able to go into that in detail. For reference purposes, the following identifiers are available in QWeb expression evaluation:

- `widget` is a reference to the current `KanbanRecord()` widget object, responsible for the rendering of the current record into a kanban card. It exposes some useful helper functions we can use.
- `record` is a shortcut for `widget.records` and provides access to the fields available, using dot notation.
- `read_only_mode` indicates if the current view is in read mode (and not in edit mode). It is a shortcut for `widget.view.options.read_only_mode`.
- `instance` is a reference to the full web client instance.

It is also noteworthy that some characters are not allowed inside expressions. The lower than sign (<) is such a case. This is because of the XML standard, where such characters have special meaning and shouldn't be used on the XML content. A negated >= is a valid alternative, but the common practice is to use the following alternative symbols that are available for inequality operations:

- `lt` is for less than
- `lte` is for less than or equal to
- `gt` is for greater than
- `gte` is for greater than or equal to

Using t-attf for attributes string substitution

Our kanban card is using the `t-attf` QWeb directive to dynamically set a class on the top `<div>` element so that the card is colored depending on the `color` field value. For this, the `t-attf-` QWeb directive was used.

The `t-attf-` directive dynamically generates tag attributes using string substitution. This allows for parts of larger strings generated dynamically, such as a URL address or CSS class names.

The directive looks for expression blocks that will be evaluated and replaced by the result. These are delimited either by `{{` and `}}` or by `#{` and `}`. The content of the blocks can be any valid JavaScript expression and can use any of the variables available for QWeb expressions, such as `record` and `widget`.

In our case, we also used the `kanban_color()` JavaScript function, specially provided to map color index numbers into the CSS class color names.

As a more elaborate example, we can use this directive to dynamically change the color of the **Deadline Date**, so that overdue dates are shown in red.

For this, replace `<field name="date_deadline"/>` in our kanban card with this:

```
<li t-attf-class="oe_kanban_text_{{
  record.date_deadline.raw_value and
  !(record.date_deadline.raw_value > (new Date()))
  ? 'red' : 'black' }}">
  <field name="date_deadline"/>
</li>
```

This results in either `class="oe_kanban_text_red"` or `class="oe_kanban_text_black"`, depending on the deadline date. Please note that, while the `oe_kanban_text_red` CSS class is available in kanban views, the `oe_kanban_text_black` CSS class does not exist and was used to better explain the point.

The lower than sign, <, is not allowed in the expressions, and we chose to work around this by using a negated greater than comparison. Another possibility would be to use the `<` (lower than) escape symbol instead.

Using t-att for dynamic attributes

The `t-att-` QWeb directive dynamically generates an attribute value by evaluating an expression. Our kanban card uses it to dynamically set some attributes on the `<img>` tag.

The `title` element is dynamically rendered using:

```
t-att-
```

The field `.value` returns its value representation as it should be shown on the screen, for many-to-one fields, this is usually the related record's `name` value. For users, this is the username. As a result, when hovering the mouse pointer over the image, you will see the corresponding username.

The `src` tag is also dynamically generated, to provide the image corresponding to the responsible user. The image data is provided by the helper JavaScript function, `kanban_image()`:

```
t-att-src="kanban_image('res.users', 'image_small',
  record.user_id.raw_value)"
```

The function parameters are: the model to read the image from, the field name to read, and the ID of the record. Here we used `.raw_value`, to get the user's database ID instead of its representation text.

It doesn't stop there, and `t-att-NAME` and `t-attf-NAME` can be made to render any attribute, as the name of the generated attribute is taken from the `NAME` suffix used.

Using t-foreach for loops

A block of HTML can be repeated by iterating through a loop. We can use it to add the avatars of the task followers to the task's kanban card.

Let's start by rendering just the Partner IDs of the task, as follows:

```
<t t-foreach="record.message_partner_ids.raw_value" t-as="rec">
  <t t-esc="rec" />;
</t>
```

The `t-foreach` directive accepts a JavaScript expression evaluating to a collection to iterate. In most cases, this will be just the name of a *to-many* relation field. It is used with a `t-as` directive to set the name to be used to refer to each item in the iteration.

The `t-esc` directive used next evaluates the provided expression, just the `rec` variable name in this case, and renders it as safely escaped HTML.

In the previous example, we loop through the task followers, stored in the `message_parter_ids` field. Since there is limited space on the kanban card, we could have used the `slice()` JavaScript function to limit the number of followers to display, as shown in the following:

```
t-foreach="record.message_partner_ids.raw_value.slice(0, 3)"
```

The `rec` variable holds each iteration's value, a Partner ID in this case. With this, we can rewrite the follower's loop as follows:

```
<t t-foreach="record.message_parter_ids.raw_value.slice(0, 3)"
  t-as="rec">
  <img t-att-src="kanban_image('res.partner', 'image_small', rec)"
    class="oe_avatar" width="24" height="24" />
</t>
```

For example, this could be added next to the responsible user image, in the right-hand footer.

A few helper variables are also available. Their name has as prefix the variable name defined in `t-as`. In our example, we used `rec`, so the helper variables available are as follows:

- `rec_index` is the iteration index, starting from zero
- `rec_size` is the number of elements of the collection
- `rec_first` is true on the first element of the iteration
- `rec_last` is true on the last element of the iteration
- `rec_even` is true on even indexes
- `rec_odd` is true on odd indexes
- `rec_parity` is either `odd` or `even`, depending on the current index
- `rec_all` represents the object being iterated over
- `rec_value` when iterating through a dictionary, `{key: value}`, holds the value (`rec` holds the key name)

For example, we could make use of the following to avoid a trailing comma on our ID list:

```
<t t-foreach="record.message_parter_ids.raw_value.slice(0, 3)"
  t-as="rec">
  <t t-esc="rec" />
  <t t-if="!rec_last">;</t>
</t>
```

Using t-if for conditional rendering

Our kanban view used the `t-if` directive in the card option menu to make some options available depending on some conditions. The `t-if` directive expects an expression to be evaluated in JavaScript when rendering kanban views in the client-side. The tag and its content will be rendered only if the condition evaluates to true.

As another example, to display the task effort estimate in the card kanban, only if it has a value, add the following after the `date_deadline` field:

```
<t t-if="record.effort_estimate.raw_value gt 0">
  <li>Estimate <field name="effort_estimate"/></li>
</t>
```

We used a `<t t-if="...">` element so that if the condition is false, the element produces no output. If it is true, only the contained `<li>` element is rendered to the output. Notice that the condition expression used the `gt` symbol instead of >, to represent the *greater than* operator.

Using t-esc and t-raw to render values

We used the `<field>` element to render the field content. But field values can also be presented directly without a `<field>` tag.

The `t-esc` directive evaluates an expression and renders it as an HTML-escaped value, as shown in the following:

```
<t t-esc="record.message_parter_ids.raw_value" />
```

In some cases, and if the source data is ensured to be safe, `t-raw` can be used to render the field raw value without any escaping, as shown in the following example:

```
<t t-raw="record.message_parter_ids.raw_value" />
```

For security reasons, it is important to avoid using `t-raw` as much as possible. Its usage should be strictly reserved for outputting HTML data that was specifically prepared without any user data in it, or where any user data was escaped explicitly for HTML special characters.

Using t-set to set values on variables

For more complex logic, we can store the result of an expression into a variable to use it later in the template. This is to be done using the `t-set` directive, naming the variable to set followed by the `t-value` directive with the expression calculating the value to assign.

As an example, the following code renders missed deadlines in red, just as in the previous section, but uses a `red_or_black` variable for the CSS class to use, as shown in the following:

```
<t t-set="red_or_black" t-value=" record.date_deadline.raw_value and
  record.date_deadline.raw_value lte (new Date())
  ? 'oe_kanban_text_red' : ''" />
<li t-att-class="red_or_black">
  <field name="date_deadline" />
</li>
```

Variables can also be assigned HTML content to a variable, as in the following example:

```
<t t-set="calendar_sign">
  <span class="oe_e">&#128197;  </span>
</t>
<t t-raw="calendar_sign" />
```

The `oe_e` CSS class uses the Entypo pictogram font. The HTML representation of the calendar sign is stored in a variable that can then be used when needed in the template. The **Font Awesome** icon set is also available out of the box, and could have been used.

Using t-call to insert other templates

QWeb templates can be reusable HTML snippet, that can be inserted in other templates. Instead of repeating the same HTML blocks over and over again, we can design building blocks to compose more complex user interface views.

Reusable templates are defined inside the `<templates>` tag and identified by a top element with a `t-name` other than `kanban-box`. These other templates can then be included using the `t-call` directive. This is true for the templates declared alongside in the same kanban view, somewhere else in the same addon module, or in a different addon.

The follower avatar list is something that could be isolated in a reusable snippet. Let's rework it to use a sub-template. We should start by adding another template to our XML file, inside the `<templates>` element, after the `<t t-name="kanban-box">` node, as shown in the following:

```
<t t-name="follower_avatars">
  <div>
    <t t-foreach="record.message_parter_ids.raw_value.slice(0, 3)"
      t-as="rec">
      <img t-att-src="kanban_image('res.partner', 'image_small', rec)"
        class="oe_avatar" width="24" height="24" />
    </t>
  </div>
</t>
```

Calling it from the `kanban-box` main template is quite straightforward. Instead of the `<div>` element containing the `for each` directive, we should use the following:

```
<t t-call="follower_avatars" />
```

To call templates defined in other addon modules, we need to use the `module.name` full identifier, as we do with the other views. For instance, this snippet can be referred using the full identifier `todo_kanban.follower_avatars`.

The called template runs in the same context as the caller, so any variable names available in the caller are also available when processing the called template.

A more elegant alternative is to pass arguments to the called template. This is done by setting variables inside the `t-call` tag. These will be evaluated and made available in the sub-template context only, and won't exist in the caller's context.

We could use this to have the maximum number of follower avatars set by the caller instead of being hard-coded in the sub-template. First, we need to replace the fixed value, 3 with a variable, `arg_max` for example:

```
<t t-name="follower_avatars">
  <div>
    <t t-foreach="record.message_parter_ids.raw_value.slice(0, arg_max)"
      t-as="rec">
      <img t-att-src="kanban_image('res.partner', 'image_small', rec)"
        class="oe_avatar" width="24" height="24" />
    </t>
  </div>
</t>
```

Then, define that variable's value when performing the sub-template call as follows:

```
<t t-call="follower_avatars">
  <t t-set="arg_max" t-value="3" />
</t>
```

The entire content inside the `t-call` element is also available to the sub-template through the magic variable `0`. Instead of argument variables, we can define an HTML code fragment that can be used in the sub-template with `<t t-raw="0" />`.

More ways to use t-attf

We have gone through the most important QWeb directives, but there are a few more we should be aware of. We'll do a short explanation of them.

We have seen the `t-att-NAME` and `t-attf-NAME` style dynamic tag attributes. Additionally, the fixed `t-att` directive can be used. It accepts either a key-value dictionary mapping or a pair (a two-element list).

Use the following mapping:

```
<p t-att="{'class': 'oe_bold', 'name': 'test1'}" />
```

This results in the following:

```
<p class="oe_bold" name="test1" />
```

Use the following pair:

```
<p t-att="['class', 'oe_bold']" />
```

This results in the following:

```
<p class="oe_bold" />
```

Inheritance on kanban views

The templates used in kanban views and reports are extended using the regular techniques used for other views, for example using XPath expressions. See `Chapter 3`, *Inheritance – Extending Existing Applications*, for more details.

A common case is to use the `<field>` elements as selector, to then add other elements before or after them. In the case of kanban views, the same field can be declared more than once, for example, once before the templates, and again inside the templates. Here the selector will match the first field element and won't add our modification inside the template, as intended.

To work around this, we need to use XPath expressions to make sure that the field inside the template is the one matched. For example:

```
<record id="res_partner_kanban_inherit" model="ir.ui.view">
  <field name="name">Contact Kanban modification</field>
  <field name="model">res.partner</field>
  <field name="inherit_id" ref="base.res_partner_kanban_view" />
  <field name="arch" type="xml">
    <xpath expr="//t[@t-name='kanban- box']//field[@name='display_name']"
      position="before">
      <span>Name:</span>
    </xpath>
  </field>
</record>
```

In the above example, the XPath looks for a `<field name="display_name">` element inside a `<t tname="kanban-box">` element. This rules out the same field element outside of the `<templates>` section.

For these, more complex, XPath expressions, we can explore the correct syntax using some command-line tools. The `xmllint` command-line utility is probably already available on your Linux system, and has an `--xpath` option to perform queries on XML files.

Another option, providing nicer outputs, is the `xpath` command from the `libxml-xpath-perl` Debian/Ubuntu package:

```
$ sudo apt-get install libxml-xpath-perl
$ xpath -e "//record[@id='res_partner_kanban_view']" -e
```

```
"//field[@name='display_name']]" /path/to/*.xml
```

Custom CSS and JavaScript assets

As we have seen, kanban views are mostly HTML and make heavy use of CSS classes. We have been introducing some frequently used CSS classes provided by the standard product. But for best results, modules can also add their own CSS.

We won't go into detail here on how to write CSS code, but it's relevant to explain how a module can add its own CSS (and JavaScript) web assets. Odoo assets for the backend are declared in the `assets_backend` template. To add our module assets, we should extend that template. The XML file for this is usually placed inside a `views/` module subdirectory.

The following is a sample XML file to add a CSS and a JavaScript file to the `todo_kanban` module, and it could be at `todo_kanban/views/todo_kanban_assets.xml`:

```
<?xml version="1.0" encoding="utf-8"?>
<odoo>
  <template id="assets_backend" inherit_id="web.assets_backend"
    name="Todo Kanban Assets" >
    <xpath expr="." position="inside">
      <link rel="stylesheet"
        href="/todo_kanban/static/src/css/todo_kanban.css"/>
      <script type="text/javascript"
       src="/todo_kanban/static/src/js/todo_kanban.js">
      </script>
    </xpath>
  </template>
</odoo>
```

As usual, it should be referenced in the `__manifest__.py` descriptor file. Notice that the assets are located inside a `/static/src` subdirectory. While this is not required, it is a generally used convention.

Summary

You learned about kanban boards and how to build kanban views to implement them. We also introduced QWeb templating and how it can be used to design kanban cards. QWeb is also the rendering engine powering the website CMS, so it's growing in importance in the Odoo toolset. In the next chapter, we will keep using QWeb, but on the server side, to create our custom reports.

10
Creating QWeb Reports

Reports are an invaluable feature for business apps. The built-in QWeb reports engine, available since version 8.0, is the default report engine. Reports are designed using QWeb templates to produce HTML documents that can then be converted to PDF form.

The Odoo built-in report engines have undergone significant changes. Before version 7.0 reports were based on the ReportLab library and used a specific markup syntax, RML. In version 7.0, the Webkit report engine was included in the core, allowing for reports to be designed using regular HTML instead. Finally, in version 8.0 this concept was taken a little further, and the QWeb templates became the main concept behind the built-in reporting engine.

This means we can conveniently leverage what we have learned about QWeb and apply it to create business reports. In this chapter, we will be adding a report to our **To Do** app, and will review the most important techniques to use with QWeb reports , including report computations, such as totals, translation and print paper formats.

But before we start, we must make sure that we have installed the recommended version of the utility used to convert HTML into PDF documents.

Installing wkhtmltopdf

To correctly generate reports, the recommended version of the `wkhtmltopdf` library needs to be installed. Its name stands for **Webkit HTML to PDF**. Odoo uses it to convert a rendered HTML page into a PDF document.

Older versions of the `wkhtmltopdf` library are known to have issues, such as not printing page headers and footers, so we need to be picky about the version to use. For version 9.0, at the time of writing the recommended version is 0.12.1. Unfortunately, the odds are that the packaged version provided for your host system, Debian/Ubuntu or other, is not adequate. So we should download and install the package recommended for our OS and CPU architecture. The download links can be found at `http://wkhtmltopdf.org or http://download.gna.org/wkhtmltopdf`.

We should first make sure that we don't have an incorrect version already installed in our system:

```
$ wkhtmltopdf --version
```

If the above reports a version other than the one we want, we should uninstall it. On a Debian/Ubuntu system we can use:

```
$ sudo apt-get remove --purge wkhtmltopdf
```

Next we need to download the appropriate package for our system and install it. Check the correct file name at `http://download.gna.org/wkhtmltopdf/0.12/0.12.1`. For Ubuntu 14.04 LTS (Trusty) 64 bits, the download command would be like this:

```
$ wget
http://download.gna.org/wkhtmltopdf/0.12/0.12.1/wkhtmltox-0.12.1_linux-trus
ty-amd64.deb -O /tmp/wkhtml.deb
```

Next we should install it. Installing a local `deb` file does not automatically install dependencies, so a second step will be needed to do that and complete the installation:

```
$ sudo dpkg -i wkhtml.deb
$ sudo apt-get -f install
```

Now we can check if `wkhtmltopdf` library is correctly installed, and confirm it's version number is the one we want:

```
$ wkhtmltopdf --version
wkhtmltopdf 0.12.1 (with patched qt)
```

After this, the Odoo server start sequence won't display the **You need Wkhtmltopdf to print a pdf version of the report's** info message.

Creating business reports

Usually we would implement the report in our To Do app addon module. But for learning purposes, we will create a new addon module just for our report.

Our report will look like this:

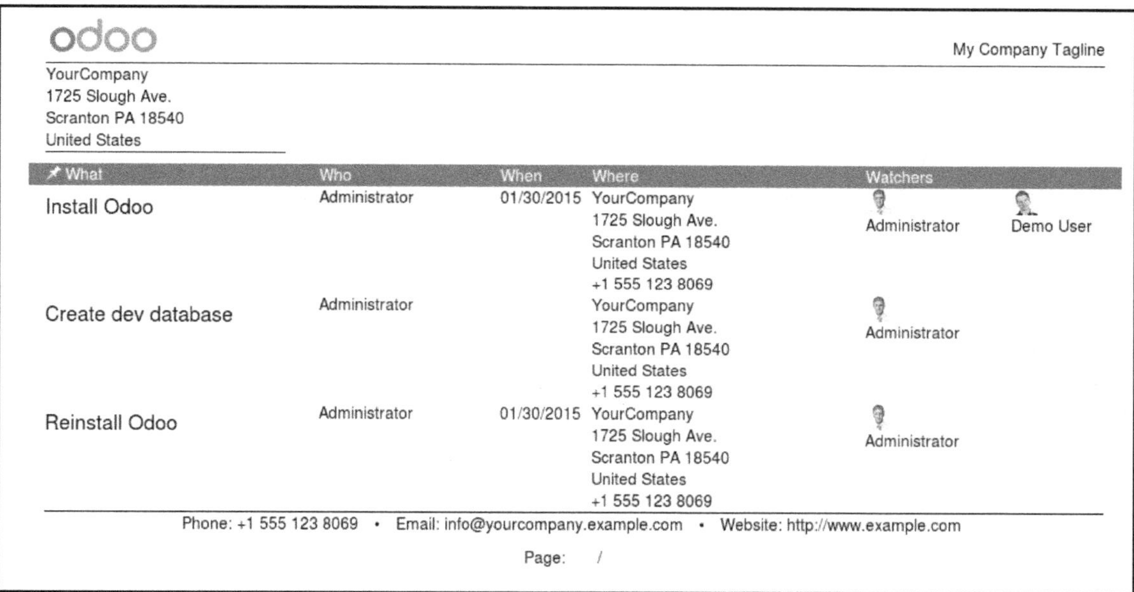

odoo

My Company Tagline

YourCompany
1725 Slough Ave.
Scranton PA 18540
United States

What	Who	When	Where	Watchers	
Install Odoo	Administrator	01/30/2015	YourCompany 1725 Slough Ave. Scranton PA 18540 United States +1 555 123 8069	Administrator	Demo User
Create dev database	Administrator		YourCompany 1725 Slough Ave. Scranton PA 18540 United States +1 555 123 8069	Administrator	
Reinstall Odoo	Administrator	01/30/2015	YourCompany 1725 Slough Ave. Scranton PA 18540 United States +1 555 123 8069	Administrator	

Phone: +1 555 123 8069 • Email: info@yourcompany.example.com • Website: http://www.example.com

Page: /

We will name this new addon module `todo_report`. The first thing to do is to create an empty `__init__.py` file and the `__manifest__.py` manifest file:

```
{
  'name': 'To-Do Report',
  'description': 'Report for To-Do tasks.',
  'author': 'Daniel Reis',
  'depends': ['todo_kanban'],
  'data': ['reports/todo_report.xml'] }
```

The `reports/todo_report.xml` file can start by declaring the new report as follows:

```
<?xml version="1.0"?>
<odoo>
  <report id="action_todo_task_report"
    string="To-do Tasks"
    model="todo.task"
    report_type="qweb-pdf"
```

```
    name="todo_report.report_todo_task_template"
  />
</odoo>
```

The <report> tag is a shortcut to write data to the ir.actions.report.xml model, which is a particular type of client action. Its data is available in the **Settings** | **Technical** | **Reports** menu option.

During the design of the report, you might prefer to leave report_type="qweb-html", and change it back to qweb-pdf file once finished. This will make it quicker to generate and easier to inspect the HTML result from the OWeb template.

After installing this, the to-do task form view will display a **Print** button at the top, to the left of the **More** button, containing this option to run the report.

It won't work right now, since we haven't defined the report yet. This will be a QWeb report, so it will use a QWeb template. The name attribute identifies the template to be used. Unlike other identifier references, the module prefix in the name attribute is required. We must use the full reference <module_name>.<identifier_name>.

QWeb report templates

The reports will usually follow a basic skeleton, as shown in the following. This can be added to the reports/todo_report.xml file, just after the <report> element.

```
<template id="report_todo_task_template">
  <t t-call="report.html_container">
    <t t-call="report.external_layout">
      <div class="page">
        <!-- Report page content -->
      </div>
    </t>
  </t>
</template>
```

The most important elements here are the t-call directives using standard report structures. The report.html_container template does the basic setup to support an HTML document. The report.external_layout template handles the report header and footer, using the corresponding setup from the appropriate company. As an alternative, we can use report.internal_layout template instead, which uses only a basic header.

Now we have in place, the basic skeleton for our module and report view. Notice that, since reports are just QWeb templates, inheritance can be applied, just like in the other views. QWeb templates used in reports can be extended using the regular inherited views with **XPATH** expressions.

Presenting data in reports

Unlike Kanban views, the QWeb templates in reports are rendered server side, and use a Python QWeb implementation. We can see this as two implementations of the same specification, and there are some differences that we need to be aware of.

To start with, QWeb expressions are evaluated using Python syntax, not JavaScript. For the simplest expressions, there may be little or no difference, but more complex operations will probably be different.

The way expressions are evaluated is also different. For reports, we have the following variables available:

- `docs` is an iterable collection with the records to print
- `doc_ids` is a list of the IDs of the records to print
- `doc_model` identifies the model of the records, `todo.task` for example
- `time` is is a reference to Python's time library
- `user` is the record for the user running the report
- `res_company` is the record for the current user's company

The report content is written in HTML, field values can be referenced using the `t-field` attribute, and it can be complemented with the `t-field-options` attribute to use a specific widget to render the field content.

Now we can start designing the page content for our report:

```
<!-- Report page content
<div class="row bg-primary">
  <div class="col-xs-3">
    <span class="glyphicon glyphicon-pushpin" />
      What
  </div>
  <div class="col-xs-2">Who</div>
  <div class="col-xs-1">When</div>
  <div class="col-xs-3">Where</div>
  <div class="col-xs-3">Watchers</div>
</div>
```

```
<t t-foreach="docs" t-as="o">
  <div class="row">
    <!-- Data Row Content -->
  </div>
</t>
```

The layout of the content can use the Twitter Bootstrap HTML grid system. In a nutshell, Bootstrap has a grid layout with 12 columns. A new row can be added using `<div class="row">`. Inside a row, we have cells, each spanning though a certain number of columns, that should take up the 12 columns. Each cell can be defined with row `<div class="col-xs-N">`, where N is the number of columns it spans.

A complete reference for Bootstrap, describing these and other style elements, can be found at `http://getbootstrap.com`.

Here we are adding a header row with titles, and then we have a `t-foreach` loop, iterating through each record, and rendering a row for each one.

Since the rendering is done server-side, records are objects and we can use dot notation to access fields from related data records. This makes it easy to follow through relational fields to access their data. Notice that this is not possible in client-side rendered Qweb,views, such as the web client kanban views.

This is the XML for the content of the record rows:

```
<div class="col-xs-3">
  <h4><span t-field="o.name" /></h4>
</div>
<div class="col-xs-2">
  <span t-field="o.user_id" />
</div>
<div class="col-xs-1">
  <span t-field="o.date_deadline" />
    <span t-field="o.amount_cost"
      t-field-options='{
        "widget": "monetary",
        "display_currency": "o.currency_id"}'/>
</div>
<div class="col-xs-3">
  <div t-field="res_company.partner_id"
    t-field-options='{
      "widget": "contact",
      "fields": ["address", "name", "phone", "fax"],
                "no_marker": true}' />
```

```
</div>
<div class="col-xs-3">
  <!-- Render followers -->
</div>
```

As we can see, fields can be used with additional options. These are very similar to the `options` attribute used on form views, as seen in `Chapter 6`, *Views – Designing the User Interface*, used with an additional `widget` to set the widget to use to render the field.

An example is the monetary widget, used above, next to the deadline date.

A more sophisticated example is the `contact` widget, used to format addresses. We used the company address, `res_company.partner_id`, since it has some default data and we can immediately see the rendered address. But it would make more sense to use the assigned user's address, `o.user_id.partner_id`. By default the `contact` widget displays addresses with some pictograms, such as a phone icon. The `no_marker="true"` option we used disables them.

Rendering images

The last column of our report will feature the list of followers, with the avatars. We will use the `media-list` Bootstrap component and a loop through the followers to render each one of them:

```
<!-- Render followers -->
<ul class="media-list">
  <t t-foreach="o.message_follower_ids" t-as="f">
    <li t-if="f.partner_id.image_small"
      class="media-left">
      <img class="media-object"
        t-att-src="'data:image/png;base64,%s' %
          f.partner_id.image_small"
        style="max-height: 24px;" />
      <span class="media-body"
        t-field="f.partner_id.name" />
    </li>
  </t>
</ul>
```

The content of binary fields is provided in a base64 representation. The <img> element can directly accept this type of data for the src attribute. Thus we can use the t-att-src QWeb directive to dynamically generate each of the images.

Summary totals and running totals

A common need in reports is to provide totals. This can be done using Python expressions to compute those totals.

After the closing tag of the <t t-foreach>,we will add a final row with the totals:

```
<!-- Totals -->
<div class="row">
  <div class="col-xs-3">
    Count: <t t-esc="len(docs)" />
  </div>
  <div class="col-xs-2" />
  <div class="col-xs-1">
    Total:
   <t t-esc="sum([o.amount_cost for o in docs])" />
  </div>
  <div class="col-xs-3" />
  <div class="col-xs-3" />
</div>
```

The len() Python statement is used to count the number of elements in a collection. Totals can be computed using sum() value over a list of values. In the example preceding, we use a list comprehension to produce a list of values out of the docs recordset. You can think of list comprehensions like an embedded for loop.

Sometimes we want to perform some computations as we go along with the report. For example, a running total, with the total up to the current record. This can be implemented with t-set to define an accumulating variable, and then update it on each row.

To illustrate this, we can compute the accumulated number of followers. We should start by initializing the variable, just before the t-foreach loop on the docs recordset, using:

```
<t t-set="follower_count" t-value="0" />
```

And then, inside the loop, add the record's number of followers to the variable. We will choose to do this right after presenting the list of followers, and will also print out the current total on every line:

```
<!-- Running total-->
  <t t-set="follower_count"
    t-value="follower_count + len(o.message_follower_ids)" />
  Accumulated # <t t-esc="follower_count" />
```

Defining paper formats

At this point our report looks good in HTML, but it doesn't print out nicely on a PDF page. We might get some better results using a landscape page. So we need to add this paper format.

At the top of the XML file, add this record:

```
<record id="paperformat_euro_landscape"
        model="report.paperformat">
  <field name="name">European A4 Landscape</field>
  <field name="default" eval="True" />
  <field name="format">A4</field>
  <field name="page_height">0</field>
  <field name="page_width">0</field>
  <field name="orientation">Landscape</field>
  <field name="margin_top">40</field>
  <field name="margin_bottom">23</field>
  <field name="margin_left">7</field>
  <field name="margin_right">7</field>
  <field name="header_line" eval="False" />
  <field name="header_spacing">35</field>
  <field name="dpi">90</field>
</record>
```

It is a copy of the European A4 format, defined in `addons/report/data`, `report_paperformat.xml` file, but changing the orientation from Portrait to Landscape. The defined paper formats can be seen from the web client through the menu **Settings** | **Technical** | **Reports** | **Paper Format**.

Now we can use it in our report. The default paper format is defined in the company setup, but we can also specify the paper format to be used by a specific report. That is done using a `paperfomat` attribute in the report action.

Let's edit the action used to open our report, to add this attribute:

```
<report id="action_todo_task_report"
  string="To-do Tasks"
  model="todo.task"
  report_type="qweb-pdf"
  name="todo_report.report_todo_task_template"
  paperformat="paperformat_euro_landscape"
/>
```

The `paperformat` attribute on the `<report>` tag was added in version 9.0. For 8.0 we need to use a `<record>` element to add a report action with a `paperformat` value.

Enabling language translation in reports

To enable translations for a report, it needs to be called from a template, using a `<t t-call>` element with a `t-lang` attribute.

The `t-lang` attribute should evaluate to a language code, such as `es` or `en_US`. It needs the name of the field where the language to use can be found. This will frequently be the language of the Partner the document is to be sent to, stored at `partner_id.lang` field. In our case, we don't have a Partner field, but we can use the responsible user, and the corresponding language preference is in `user_id.lang`.

The function expects a template name, and will render and translate it. This means that we need to define the page content of our report in a separate template, as shown in the following:

```
<report id="action_todo_task_report_translated"
  string="Translated To-do Tasks"
  model="todo.task"
  report_type="qweb-pdf"
  name="todo_report.report_todo_task_translated"
  paperformat="paperformat_euro_landscape"
/>

<template id="report_todo_task_translated">
  <t t-call="todo_report.report_todo_task_template"
    t-lang="user.lang" >
    <t t-set="docs"
      t-value="docs" />
    </t>
```

```
    </t>
  </template>
```

Reports based on custom SQL

The report we built was based on a regular recordset. But in some cases we need to transform or aggregate data in ways that are not easy when processing data on the fly, such as while rendering the report.

One approach for this is to write a SQL query to build the dataset we need, expose those results through a special Model, and have our report work based on a recordset.

For this, we will create a `reports/todo_task_report.py` file with this code:

```
# -*- coding: utf-8 -*-
from odoo import models, fields

class TodoReport(models.Model):
    _name = 'todo.task.report'
    _description = 'To-do Report'
    _sql = """
           CREATE OR REPLACE VIEW todo_task_report AS
           SELECT *
           FROM todo_task
           WHERE active = True
           """
    name = fields.Char('Description')
    is_done = fields.Boolean('Done?')
    active = fields.Boolean('Active?')
    user_id = fields.Many2one('res.users', 'Responsible')
    date_deadline = fields.Date('Deadline')
```

For this file to be loaded we need to add a `from . import reports` line to the top `__init__.py` file, and `from . import todo_task_report` to the `reports/__init__.py` file.

The `sql` attribute is used to override the database table automatic creation, providing an SQL for that. We want it to create a database view to provide the data needed for the report. Our SQL query is quite simple, but the point is that we could use any valid SQL query for our view.

We also mapped the fields we need with ORM field types, so that they are available on recordsets generated on this model.

Next we can add a new report based on this model, `reports/todo_model_report.xml`:

```
<odoo>

<report id="action_todo_model_report"
  string="To-do Special Report"
  model="todo.task"
  report_type="qweb-html"
  name="todo_report.report_todo_task_special"
/>

<template id="report_todo_task_special">
  <t t-call="report.html_container">
    <t t-call="report.external_layout">
      <div class="page">

        <!-- Report page content -->
        <table class="table table-striped">
          <tr>
            <th>Title</th>
            <th>Owner</th>
            <th>Deadline</th>
          </tr>
          <t t-foreach="docs" t-as="o">
            <tr>
              <td class="col-xs-6">
                <span t-field="o.name" />
              </td>
              <td class="col-xs-3">
                <span t-field="o.user_id" />
              </td>
              <td class="col-xs-3">
                <span t-field="o.date_deadline" />
              </td>
            </tr>
          </t>
        </table>

      </div>
```

```
        </t>
      </t>
    </template>

    </odoo>
```

For even more complex cases, we can use a different solution: a wizard. For this we should create a transient model with related lines, where the header includes report parameters, introduced by the user, and the lines will have the generated data to be used by the report. These lines are generated by a model method that can contain whatever logic we may need. It is strongly recommended to get inspiration from an existing similar report.

Summary

In the previous chapter we learned about QWeb, and how to use it to design a Kanban view. In this chapter we learned about the QWeb report engine, and the most important techniques to build reports with the QWeb templating language.

In the next chapter, we will keep working with QWeb, this time to build website pages. We will also learn to write web controllers, providing richer features to our web pages.

11
Creating Website Frontend Features

Odoo began as a backend system, but the need for a frontend interface was soon felt. The early portal features, based on the same interface as the backend, were not very flexible nor mobile device-friendly.

To solve this gap, version 8 introduced new website features, adding a **Content Management System** (**CMS**) to the product. This would allow us to build beautiful and effective frontends without the need to integrate a third-party CMS.

Here we will learn how to develop our own frontend oriented addon modules, leveraging the website feature provided by Odoo.

Roadmap

We will create a website page listing our To-do Tasks, allowing us to navigate to a detailed page for each existing task. We also want to be able to propose new To-do Tasks through a web form.

With this, we will be able to cover the essential techniques for website development: creating dynamic pages, passing parameters to another page, creating forms and handling their validation, and computation logic.

But first, we will introduce the basic website concepts with a very simple **Hello World** web page.

Our first web page

We will create an addon module for our website features. We can call it `todo_website`. To introduce the basics of Odoo web development, we will implement a simple **Hello World** web page. Imaginative, right?

As usual, we will start creating it's manifest file. Create the `todo_website/__manifest__.py` file with:

```
{
  'name': 'To-Do Website',
  'description': 'To-Do Tasks Website',
  'author': 'Daniel Reis',
  'depends': ['todo_kanban']}
```

We are building on top of the `todo_kanban` addon module, so that we have all the features available added to the To-do Tasks model throughout the book.

Notice that right now we are not depending on the `website` addon module. While `website` provides a useful framework to build full featured websites, the basic web capabilities are built into the core framework. Let's explore them.

Hello World!

To provide our first web page, we will add a controller object. We can begin by having its file imported with the module:

First add a `todo_website/__init__.py` file with following line:

```
from . import controllers
```

And then add a `todo_website/controllers/__init__.py` file with following line:

```
from . import main
```

Now add the actual file for the controller, `todo_website/controllers/main.py`, with the following code:

```
# -*- coding: utf-8 -*-
from odoo import http

class Todo(http.Controller):

    @http.route('/helloworld', auth='public')
    def hello_world(self):
        return('<h1>Hello World!</h1>')
```

The `odoo.http` module provides the Odoo web-related features. Our controllers, responsible for page rendering, should be objects inheriting from the `odoo.http.Controller` class. The actual name used for the class is not important; here we chose to use `Main`.

Inside the controller class we have methods, that match routes, does some processing, and then returns a result; the page to be shown to the user.

The `odoo.http.route` decorator is what binds a method to a URL route. Our example uses the `/hello` route. Navigate to `http://localhost:8069/hello` and you will be greeted with a **Hello World** message. In this example the processing performed by the method is quite trivial: it just returns a text string with the HTML markup for the **Hello World** message.

You probably noticed that we added the `auth='public'` argument to the route. This is needed for the page to be available to non-authenticated users. If we remove it, only authenticated users can see the page. If no session is active, the login screen will be shown instead.

Hello World! with a Qweb template

Using Python strings to build HTML will get boring very fast. QWeb templates do a much better job at that. So let's improve our **Hello World** web page to use a template instead.

QWeb templates are added through XML data files, and technically they are a type of view, alongside form or tree views. They are actually stored in the same model, `ir.ui.view`.

As usual, data files to be loaded must be declared in the manifest file, so edit the `todo_website/__manifest__.py` file to add the key:

```
'data': ['views/todo_templates.xml'],
```

And then add the actual data file, `views/todo_web.xml`, with the following content:

```
<odoo>
  <template id="hello" name="Hello Template">
    <h1>Hello World !</h1>
  </template>
</odoo>
```

The `<template>` element is actually a shortcut for declaring a `<record>` for the `ir.ui.view` model, using `type="qweb"`, and a `<t>` template inside it.

Now we need to have our controller method use this template:

```
from odoo.http import request
# ...
@http.route('/hello', auth='public')
def hello(self, **kwargs):
    return request.render('todo_website.hello')
```

Template rendering is provided by `request`, through its `render()` function.

Notice that we added `**kwargs` to the method arguments. With this if any additional parameters provided by the HTTP request, such as query string or `POST` parameters, can be captured by the `kwargs` dictionary. This makes our method more robust, since providing unexpected parameters will not cause it to error.

Extending web features

Extensibility is something we expect in all features of Odoo, and the web features are no exception. And indeed we can extend existing controllers and templates. As an example, we will extend our **Hello World** web page so that it takes a parameter with the name to greet: using the URL `/hello?name=John` would return a **Hello John!** greeting.

Extending is usually done from a different addon module, but it works as well inside the same addon. To keep things concise and simple, we'll do it without creating a new addon module.

Let's add a new `todo_website/controllers/extend.py` file with the following code:

```
# -*- coding: utf-8 -*-
from odoo import http
from odoo.addons.todo_website.controllers.main import Todo

class TodoExtended(Todo):
    @http.route()
    def hello(self, name=None, **kwargs):
        response = super(TodoExtended, self).hello()
        response.qcontext['name'] = name
        return response
```

Here we can see what we need to do to extend a controller.

First we use a Python `import` to get a reference to the controller class we want to extend. Compared with models, they have a central registry, provided by the `env` object, where a reference to any model class can be obtained, without the need to know the module and file implementing them. With controllers we don't have that, and need to know the module and file implementing the controller we want to extend.

Next we need to (re)define the method from the controller being extended. It needs to be decorated with at least the simple `@http.route()` for its route to be kept active. Optionally, we can provide parameters to `route()`, and then we will be replacing and redefining its routes.

The extended `hello()` method now has a `name` parameter. The parameters can get their values from segments of the route URL, from query string parameters, or from `POST` parameters. In this case, the route has no extractable variable (we'll show that in a moment), and since we are handling `GET` requests, not `POST`, the value for the name parameter will be extracted from the URL query string. A test URL could be `http://localhost:8069/hello?name=John`.

Inside the `hello()` method we run the inherited method to get its response, and then get to modify it according to our needs. The common pattern for controller methods is for them to end with a statement to render a template. In our case:

```
return request.render('todo_website.hello')
```

This generates a `http.Response` object, but the actual rendering is delayed until the end of the dispatching.

This means that the inheriting method can still change the QWeb template and context to use for the rendering. We could change the template modifying `response.template`, but we won't need that. We rather want to modify `response.qcontext` to add the `name` key to the rendering context.

Don't forget to add the new Python file to `todo_website/controllers/__init__.py`:

```
from . import main
from . import extend
```

Now we need to modify the QWeb template, so that it makes use of this additional piece of information. Add a `todo/website/views/todo_extend.xml`:

```
<odoo>
  <template id="hello_extended"
    name="Extended Hello World"
    inherit_id="todo_website.hello">
    <xpath expr="//h1" position="replace">
      <h1>
        Hello <t t-esc="name or 'Someone'" />!
      </h1>
    </xpath>
  </template>
</odoo>
```

Web page templates are XML documents, just like the other Odoo view types, and we can use `xpath` to locate elements and then manipulate them, just like we could with the other view types. The inherited template is identified in the `<template>` element by the `inherited_id` attribute.

We ought not forget to declare this additional data file in our addon manifest, `todo_website/__manifest__.py`:

```
'data': [
  'views/todo_web.xml',
  'views/todo_extend.xml'],
```

After this, accessing `http://localhost:8069/hello?name=John` should show us a **Hello John!** message.

We can also provide parameters through URL segments. For example, we could get the exact same result from the `http://localhost:8069/hello/John` URL using this alternative implementation:

```
class TodoExtended(Todo):
    @http.route(['/hello', '/hello/<name>])
    def hello(self, name=None, **kwargs):
        response = super(TodoExtended, self).hello()
        response.qcontext['name'] = name
        return response
```

As you can see, routes can contain **placeholders** corresponding to parameters to be extracted, and then passed on to the method. Placeholders can also specify a converter to implement a specific type mapping. For example, `<int:user_id>` would extract the `user_id` parameter as an integer value.

Converters are a feature provided by the `werkzeug` library, used by Odoo, and most of the ones available can be found in `werkzeug` library's documentation, at `http://werkzeug.pocoo.org/docs/routing/`.

Odoo adds a specific and particularly helpful converter: extracting a model record. For example `@http.route('/hello/<model("res.users"):user>)` extracts the user parameter as a record object on for the `res.users` model.

HelloCMS!

Let's make this even more interesting, and create our own simple CMS. For this we can have the route expect a template name (a page) in the URL and then just render it. We could then dynamically create web pages and have them served by our CMS.

It turns out that this is quite easy to do:

```
@http.route('/hellocms/<page>', auth='public')
def hello(self, page, **kwargs):
    return http.request.render(page)
```

Now, open `http://localhost:8069/hellocms/todo_website.hello` in your web browser and you will see our **Hello World** web page!

In fact, the built-in website provides CMS features including a more robust implementation of the above, at the /page endpoint route.

In werkzeug jargon the endpoint is an alias of the route, and represented by its static part (without the placeholders). For our simple CMS example, the endpoint was /hellocms.

Most of the time we want our pages to be integrated into the Odoo website. So for the remainder of this chapter our examples we will be working with the website addon.

Building websites

The pages given by the previous examples are not integrated into the Odoo website: we have no page footer, menu, and so on. The Odoo website addon module conveniently provides all these features so that we don't have to worry about them ourselves.

To use it, we should start by installing the website addon module in our work instance, and then add it as a dependency to our module. The __manifest__.py key depends should look like this:

```
'depends': ['todo_kanban', 'website'],
```

To use the website, we also need to modify the controller and the template.

The controller needs an additional website=True argument on the route:

```
@http.route('/hello', auth='public', website=True)
def hello(self, **kwargs):
    return request.render('todo_website.hello')
```

And the template needs to be inserted inside the website general layout:

```
<template id="hello" name="Hello World">
  <t t-call="website.layout">
    <h1>Hello World!</h1>
  </t>
</template>
```

With this, the **Hello World!** example we used before should now be shown inside an Odoo website page.

Adding CSS and JavaScript assets

Our website pages might need some additional CSS or JavaScript assets. This aspect of the web pages is managed by the website, so we need a way to tell it to also use our files.

We will add some CSS to add a simple strikeout effect for the done tasks. For that, create the `todo_website/static/src/css/index.css` file with this content:

```
.todo-app-done {
    text-decoration: line-through;
}
```

Next we need to have it included in the website pages. This is done by adding them in the `website.assets_frontend` template responsible for loading website-specific assets. Edit the `todo_website/views/todo_templates.xml` data file, to extend that template:

```
<odoo>
  <template id="assets_frontend"
    name="todo_website_assets"
    inherit_id="website.assets_frontend">
    <xpath expr="." position="inside">
      <link rel="stylesheet" type="text/css"
        href="/todo_website/static/src/css/index.css"/>
    </xpath>
  </template>
</odoo>
```

We will soon be using this new `todo-app-done` style class. Of course, JavaScript assets can also be added using a similar approach.

The to-do list controller

Now that we went through the basics, let's work on our Todo Task list. We will have a `/todo` URL showing us a web page with a list of Todo Tasks.

For that, we need a controller method, preparing the data to present, and a QWeb template to present that list to the user.

Edit the `todo_website/controllers/main.py` file, to add this method:

```
#class Main(http.Controller):
    @http.route('/todo', auth='user' , website=True)
    def index(self, **kwargs):
        TodoTask = request.env['todo.task']
        tasks =  TodoTask.search([])
        return request.render(
            'todo_website.index', {'tasks': tasks})
```

The controller retrieves the data to be used and makes it available to the rendered template. In this case the controller requires an authenticated session, since the route has the `auth='user'` attribute. Even if that is the default value, it's a good practice to explicitly state that a user session is required.

With this, the Todo Task `search()` statement will run with the current session user.

The data accessible to public users is very limited, when using that type of route, we often need to use `sudo()` to elevate access and make the page data available that otherwise would not be accessible.

This can also be a security risk, so be careful on the validation of the input parameters and on the actions made. Also keep the `sudo()` recordset usage limited to the minimum operations possible.

The `request.render()` method expects the identifier of the QWeb template to render, and a dictionary with the context available for the template evaluation.

The to-do list template

The QWeb template should be added by a data file, and we can add it to the existing `todo_website/views/todo_templates.xml` data file:

```
<template id="index" name="Todo List">
  <t t-call="website.layout">
    <div id="wrap" class="container">
      <h1>Todo Tasks</h1>

      <!-- List of Tasks -->
      <t t-foreach="tasks" t-as="task">
        <div class="row">
          <input type="checkbox" disabled="True"
            t-att-checked=" 'checked' if task.is_done else {}" />
          <a t-attf-href="/todo/{{slug(task)}}">
            <span t-field="task.name"
```

```
                t-att-class="'todo-app-done' if task.is_done
                  else ''" />
            </a>
          </div>
        </t>

        <!-- Add a new Task -->
        <div class="row">
          <a href="/todo/add" class="btn btn-primary btn-lg">
              Add
          </a>
        </div>

      </div>
    </t>
  </template>
```

The preceding code uses the `t-foreach` directive to render a list of tasks. The `t-att` directive used on the input checkbox allows us to add, or not, a `checked` attribute depending on the `is_done` value.

We have a checkbox input, and want it to be checked if the task is done. In HTML, a checkbox is checked depending on it having or not a `checked` attribute. For this we use the `t-att-NAME` directive to dynamically render the `checked` attribute depending on an expression. In this case, the expression evaluates to `None`, QWeb will omit the attribute, which is convenient for this case.

When rendering the task name, the `t-attf` directive is used to dynamically create the URL to open the detail form for each specific task. We used the special function `slug()` to generate a human-readable URL for each record. The link won't work for now, since we are still to create the corresponding controller.

On each task we also use the `t-att` directive to set the `todo-app-done` style only for the tasks that are done.

Finally, we have an **Add** button to open a page with a form to create a new Todo Task. We will use it to introduce web form handling next.

The To-do Task detail page

Each item in the Todo list is a link to a detail page. We should implement a controller for those links, and a QWeb template for their presentation. At this point, this should be a straightforward exercise.

In the `todo_website/controllers/main.py` file add the method:

```
#class Main(http.Controller):

    @http.route('/todo/<model("todo.task"):task>', website=True)
    def index(self, task, **kwargs):
        return http.request.render(
            'todo_website.detail',
            {'task': task})
```

Notice that the route is using a placeholder with the `model("todo.task")` converter, mapping to the task variable. It captures a Task identifier from the URL, either a simple ID number or a slug representation, and converts it into the corresponding browse record object.

And for the QWeb template add following code to the `todo_website/views/todo_web.xml` data file:

```
<template id="detail" name="Todo Task Detail">
<t t-call="website.layout">
  <div id="wrap" class="container">
    <h1 t-field="task.name" />
    <p>Responsible: <span t-field="task.user_id" /></p>
    <p>Deadline: <span t-field="task.date_deadline" /></p>
  </div>
</t>
</template>
```

Noteworthy here is the usage of the `<t t-field>` element. It handles the proper representation of the field value, just like in the backend. It correctly presents date values and many-to-one values, for example.

Website forms

Forms are a common feature found on websites. We already have all the tools needed to implement one: a QWeb template can provide the HTML for the form, the corresponding submit action can be an URL, processed by a controller that can run all the validation logic, and finally store the data in the proper model.

But for non-trivial forms this can be a demanding task. It's not that simple to perform all the needed validations and provide feedback to the user about what is wrong.

Since this is a common need, a `website_form` addon is available to aid us with this. Let's see how to use it.

Looking back at the **Add** button in the Todo Task list, we can see that it opens the `/todo/add` URL. This will present a form to submit a new Todo Task, and the fields available will be the task name, a person (user) responsible for the task, and a file attachment.

We should start by adding the `website_form` dependency to our addon module. We can replace `website`, since keeping it explicitly would be redundant. On the `todo_website/__manifest__.py` edit the `depends` keyword to:

```
'depends': ['todo_kanban', 'website_form'],
```

Now we will add the page with the form.

The form page

We can start by implementing the controller method to support the form rendering, in the `todo_website/controllers/main.py` file:

```
@http.route('/todo/add', website=True)
def add(self, **kwargs):
    users = request.env['res.users'].search([])
    return request.render(
        'todo_website.add', {'users': users})
```

This is a simple controller, rendering the `todo_website.add` template, and providing it with a list of users, so that it can be used to build a selection box.

Now for the corresponding QWeb template. We can add it into the `todo_website/views/todo_web.xml` data file:

```
<template id="add" name="Add Todo Task">
  <t t-call="website.layout">
    <t t-set="additional_title">Add Todo</t>
    <div id="wrap" class="container">
      <div class="row">
        <section id="forms">

          <form method="post"
            class="s_website_form
              container-fluid form-horizontal"
            action="/website_form/"
            data-model_name="todo.task"
            data-success_page="/todo"
            enctype="multipart/form-data" >

          <!-- Form fields will go here! -->

            <!-- Submit button -->
            <div class="form-group">
              <div class="col-md-offset-3 col-md-7
                col-sm-offset-4 col-sm-8">
                <a class="o_website_form_send
                  btn btn-primary btn-lg">
                  Save
                </a>
                <span id="o_website_form_result"></span>
              </div>
            </div>
          </form>
        </section>
      </div> <!-- rows -->
    </div> <!-- container -->
  </t> <!-- website.layout -->
</template>
```

As expected, we can find the Odoo-specific `<t t-call="website.layout">` element, responsible for inserting the template inside the website layout, and the `<t t-set="additional_title">` that sets an additional title, expected by the website layout.

For the content, most of what we can see in this template can be found on a typical Bootstrap CSS form. But we also have a few attributes and CSS classes that are specific to the website forms. We marked them in bold in the code, so that it's easier for you to identify them.

The CSS classes are needed for the JavaScript code to be able to correctly perform its form handling logic. And then we have a few specific attributes on the `<form>` element:

- `action` is a standard form attribute, but must have the `"/website_form/"` value. The trailing slash is required.
- `data-model_name` identifies the model to write to, and will be passed to the `/website_form` controller.
- `data-success_page` is the URL to redirect to after a successful form submission. In this case we will be sent back to the `/todo` list.

We won't need to provide our own controller method to handle the form submission. The `/website_form` route will do that for us. It takes all information it needs from the form, including the specific attributes just described, and then performs essential validations on the input data, and creates a new record on the target model.

For advanced use cases, we can force a custom controller method to be used. For that we should add a `data-force_action` attribute to the `<form>` element, with the keyword for the target controller to use. For example, `data-force_action="todo-custom"` would have the form submission to call the `/website_form/todo-custom` URL. We should then provide a controller method attached to that route. However, doing this will be out of our scope here.

We still need to finish our form, adding the fields to get inputs from the user. Inside the `<form>` element add:

```
<!-- Description text field, required -->
<div class="form-group form-field">
  <div class="col-md-3 col-sm-4 text-right">
    <label class="control-label" for="name">To do*</label>
  </div>
  <div class="col-md-7 col-sm-8">
    <input name="name" type="text" required="True"
      class="o_website_from_input form-control" />
  </div>
</div>

<!-- Add an attachment field -->
<div class="form-group form-field">
  <div class="col-md-3 col-sm-4 text-right">
    <label class="control-label" for="file_upload">
      Attach file
    </label>
  </div>
  <div class="col-md-7 col-sm-8">
```

```
        <input name="file_upload" type="file"
          class="o_website_from_input form-control" />
      </div>
    </div>
```

Here we are adding two fields, a regular text field for the description and a file field, to upload an attachment. All the markup can be found in regular Bootstrap forms, except for the `o_website_from_input` class, needed for the website form logic to prepare the data to submit.

The user selection list is not much different except that it needs to use a `t-foreach` QWeb directive to render the list of selectable users. We can do this because the controller retrieves that recordset and makes it available to the template under the name `users`:

```
<!-- Select User -->
<div class="form-group form-field">
  <div class="col-md-3 col-sm-4 text-right">
    <label class="control-label" for="user_id">
      For Person
    </label>
  </div>
  <div class="col-md-7 col-sm-8">
    <select name="user_id"
      class="o_website_from_input form-control" >
      <t t-foreach="users" t-as="user">
        <option t-att-value="user.id">
          <t t-esc="user.name" />
        </option>
      </t>
    </select>
  </div>
</div>
```

However, our form still won't work until we do some access security setup.

Access security and menu item

Since this generic form handling is quite open, and relies on untrusted data sent by the client, for security reasons it needs some server-side set up on what the client is allowed to do. In particular, the model fields that can be written based on form data should be whitelisted.

To add fields to this whitelist, a helper function is provided and we can use it from an XML data file. We should create the `todo_website/data/config_data.xml` file with:

```
<?xml version="1.0" encoding="utf-8"?>
<odoo>
  <data>

    <record id="todo_app.model_todo_task" model="ir.model">
      <field name="website_form_access">True</field>
    </record>

    <function model="ir.model.fields"
      name="formbuilder_whitelist">
      <value>todo.task</value>
      <value eval="['name', 'user_id', 'date_deadline']"/>
    </function>

  </data>
</odoo>
```

For a model to be able to be used by forms, we must do two things: enable a flag on the model, and whitelist the field that can be used. These are the two actions being done in the preceding data file.

Don't forget that, for our addon module to know about this data file, it needs to be added to the `data` key of the manifest file.

It would also be nice for our Todo page to be available from the website menu. Let's add that using this same data file. Add another `<data>` element like this:

```
<data noupdate="1">
  <record id="menu_todo" model="website.menu">
    <field name="name">Todo</field>
    <field name="url">/todo</field>
    <field name="parent_id" ref="website.main_menu"/>
    <field name="sequence" type="int">50</field>
  </record>
</data>
```

As you can see, to add a website menu item we just need to create a record in the `website.menu` model, with a name, URL, and the identifier of the parent menu item. The top level of this menu has as parent; the `website.main_menu` item.

Adding custom logic

Website forms allow us to plug in our own validations and computations to the form processing. This is done by implementing a `website_form_input_filter()` method with the logic on the target model. It accepts a `values` dictionary, validates and makes changes to it, and then returns the possibly modified `values` dictionary.

We will use it to implement two features: remove any leading and trailing spaces from the task title, and enforce that the task title must be at least three characters long.

Add the `todo_website/models/todo_task.py` file containing the following code:

```
# -*- coding: utf-8 -*-
from odoo import api, models
from odoo.exceptions import ValidationError

class TodoTask(models.Model):
    _inherit = 'todo.task'

    @api.model
    def website_form_input_filter(self, request, values):
        if 'name' in values:
            values['name'] = values['name'].strip()
            if len(values.['name']) < 3:
                raise ValidationError(
                    'Text must be at least 3 characters long')
        return values
```

The `website_form_input_filter` method actually expects two parameters: the `request` object and the `values` dictionary. Errors preventing form submission should raise a `ValidationError` exception.

Most of the time this extension point for forms should allow us to avoid custom form submission handlers.

As usual, we must make this new file Python imported, by adding `from .import models` in the `todo_website/__init__.py` file, and adding the `todo_website/models/__init__.py` file with a `from . import todo_task` line.

Summary

You should now have a good understanding about the essentials of the website features. We have seen how to use web controllers and QWeb templates to render dynamic web pages. We then learned how to use the website addon and create our own pages for it. Finally, we introduced the website forms addon that helped us create a web form. These should provide us the core skills needed to create website features.

Next, we will learn how to have external applications interact with our Odoo apps.

12
External API – Integrating with Other Systems

The Odoo server also provides an external API, which is used by its web client and is also available for other client applications.

In this chapter, we will learn how to use the Odoo external API from our own client programs. Any programming language can be used, as long as it has support for XML-RPC or JSON-RPC protocols. As an example, the official documentation provides code samples for four popular programming languages: Python, PHP, Ruby, and Java.

To avoid introducing additional languages the reader might not be familiar with, here we will focus on Python-based clients, although the techniques to handle the RPC calls also apply to other programming languages.

We will describe how to use the Odoo RPC calls, and then use that to build a simple To-Do desktop app using Python.

Finally, we will introduce the ERPPeek client. It is a Odoo client library, that can be used as a convenient abstraction layer for the Odoo RPC calls, and is also a command-line client for Odoo, allowing to remotely manage Odoo instances.

Setting up a Python client

The Odoo API can be accessed externally using two different protocols: XML-RPC and JSON-RPC. Any external program capable of implementing a client for one of these protocols will be able to interact with an Odoo server. To avoid introducing additional programming languages, we will keep using Python to explore the external API.

Until now, we have been running Python code only on the server. This time, we will use Python on the client side, so it's possible you might need to do some additional set up on your workstation.

To follow the examples in this chapter, you will need to be able to run Python files on your work computer. The Odoo server requires Python 2, but our RPC client can be in any language, so Python 3 will be just fine. However, since some readers may be running the server on the same machine they are working on (hello Ubuntu users!), it will be simpler for everyone to follow if we stick to Python 2.

If you are using Ubuntu or a Mac, Python is probably already installed. Open a terminal console, type `python`, and you should be greeted with something like the following:

```
Python 2.7.12 (default, Jul  1 2016, 15:12:24)
[GCC 5.4.0 20160609] on linux2
Type "help", "copyright",", "credits" or "license" for more information.
>>>
```

Windows users can find an installer for Python and also quickly get up to speed. The official installation packages can be found at `https://www.python.org/downloads/`.

If you are a Windows user and have Odoo installed in your machine, you might be wondering why you don't already have a Python interpreter, and additional installation is needed. The short answer is that the Odoo installation has an embedded Python interpreter that is not easily used outside.

Calling the Odoo API using XML-RPC

The simplest method to access the server is using XML-RPC. We can use the `xmlrpclib` library from Python's standard library for this. Remember that we are programming a client in order to connect to a server, so we need an Odoo server instance running to connect to. In our examples, we will assume that an Odoo server instance is running on the same machine (`localhost`), but you can use any reachable IP address or server name, if the server is running in a different machine.

Opening an XML-RPC connection

Let's have a first contact with the Odoo external API. Start a Python console and type in the following:

```
>>> import xmlrpclib
>>> srv = 'http://localhost:8069'
>>> common = xmlrpclib.ServerProxy('%s/xmlrpc/2/common' % srv)
>>> common.version()
{'server_version_info': [10, 0, 0, 'final', 0, ''], 'server_serie': '10.0',
'server_version': '10.0', 'protocol_version': 1}
```

Here, we import the `xmlrpclib` library and then set up a variable with the information for the server address and listening port. Feel free to adapt these to your specific set up.

Next, we set up access to the server's public services (not requiring a login), exposed at the `/xmlrpc/2/common` endpoint. One of the methods that is available is `version()`, which inspects the server version. We use it to confirm that we can communicate with the server.

Another public method is `authenticate()`. In fact, this does not create a session, as you might be led to believe. This method just confirms that the username and password are accepted and returns the user ID that should be used in requests instead of the username, as shown here:

```
>>> db = 'todo'
>>> user, pwd = 'admin', 'admin'
>>> uid = common.authenticate(db, user, pwd, {})
>>> print uid
```

If the login credentials are not correct, a `False` value is returned, instead of a user ID.

Reading data from the server

With XML-RPC, no session is maintained and the authentication credentials are sent with every request. This adds some overhead to the protocol, but makes it simpler to use.

Next, we set up access to the server methods that need a login to be accessed. These are exposed at the `/xmlrpc/2/object` endpoint, as shown in the following:

```
>>> api = xmlrpclib.ServerProxy('%s/xmlrpc/2/object' % srv)
>>> api.execute_kw(db, uid, pwd, 'res.partner', 'search_count'[[]])
40
```

Here, we are doing our first access to the server API, performing a count on the **Partner** records. Methods are called using the `execute_kw()` method that takes the following arguments:

- The name of the database to connect to
- The connection user ID
- The user password
- The target model identifier name
- The method to call
- A list of positional arguments
- An optional dictionary with keyword arguments

The preceding example calls the `search_count` method of the `res.partner` model with one positional argument, `[]`, and no keyword arguments. The positional argument is a search domain; since we are providing an empty list, it counts all the Partners.

Frequent actions are `search` and `read`. When called from the RPC, the `search` method returns a list of IDs matching a domain. The `browse` method is not available from the RPC, and `read` should be used in its place to give a list of record IDs and retrieve their data, as shown in the following code:

```
>>> api.execute_kw(db, uid, pwd, 'res.partner', 'search', [[('country_id',
'=', 'be'), ('parent_id', '!=', False)]])
[18, 33, 23, 22]
>>> api.execute_kw(db, uid, pwd, 'res.partner', 'read',  [[18]],
{'fields': ['id', 'name', 'parent_id']})
[{'parent_id': [8, 'Agrolait'], 'id': 18, 'name': 'Edward Foster'}]
```

Note that for the `read` method, we are using one positional argument for the list of IDs, `[18]`, and one keyword argument, `fields`. We can also notice that many-to-one relational fields are retrieved as a pair, with the related record's ID and display name. That's something to keep in mind when processing the data in your code.

The `search` and `read` combination is so frequent that a `search_read` method is provided to perform both operations in a single step. The same result as the previous two steps can be obtained with the following:

```
>>> api.execute_kw(db, uid, pwd, 'res.partner', 'search_read',
[[('country_id', '=', 'be'), ('parent_id', '!=', False)]],  {'fields':
['id', 'name', 'parent_id']})
```

The `search_read` method behaves like `read`, but expects a domain as a first positional argument instead of a list of IDs. It's worth mentioning that the `field` argument on `read` and `search_read` is not mandatory. If not provided, all fields will be retrieved. This may cause expensive computations of function fields and a large amount data to be retrieved , but probably never used, so it is generally recommended to provide an explicit list of fields.

Calling other methods

All other model methods are exposed through RPC, except for the ones prefixed with an underscore, that are considered private. This means that we can use `create`, `write`, and `unlink` to modify data on the server as follows:

```
>>> api.execute_kw(db, uid, pwd, 'res.partner', 'create', [{'name': 'Packt
Pub'}])
45
>>> api.execute_kw(db, uid, pwd, 'res.partner', 'write', [[45], {'name':
'Packt Publishing'}])
True
>>> api.execute_kw(db, uid, pwd, 'res.partner', 'read', [[45], ['id',
'name']])
[{'id': 45, 'name': 'Packt Publishing'}]
>>> api.execute_kw(db, uid, pwd, 'res.partner', 'unlink', [[45]])
True
```

One limitation of the XML-RPC protocol is that it does not support `None` values. The implication is that methods that don't return anything won't be usable through XML-RPC, since they are implicitly returning `None`. This is why methods should always finish with at least a `return True` statement.

It is worth repeating that the Odoo external API can be used by most programming languages. In the official documentation we can find practical examples for Ruby, PHP, and Java. It is available at `https://www.odoo.com/documentation/10.0/api_integration.html`.

Writing a Notes desktop application

Let's do something interesting with the RPC API. Odoo provides a simple app for notes. What if users could manage their personal notes directly from their computer's desktop? Let's write a simple Python application to do just that, as shown in the following screenshot:

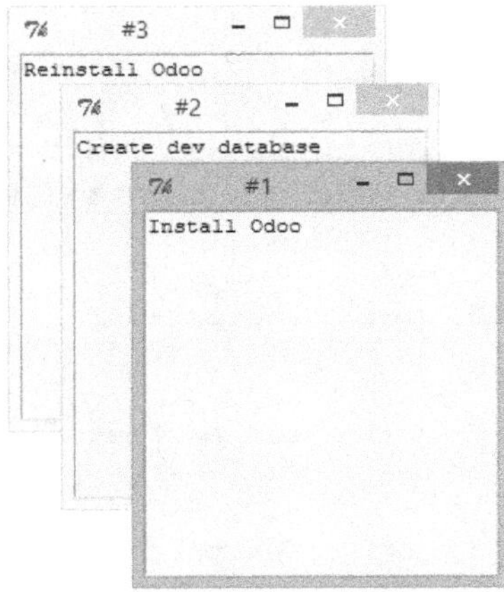

For clarity, we will split it into two files: one dealing with interactions with the server backend, `note_api.py`, and another with the graphical user interface, `note_gui.py`.

Communication layer with Odoo

We will create a class to set up the connection and store its information. It should expose two methods: `get()` to retrieve task data and `set()` to create or update tasks.

Select a directory to host the application files and create the `note_api.py` file. We can start by adding the class constructor, as follows:

```
import xmlrpclib
class NoteAPI():
    def __init__(self, srv, db, user, pwd):
        common = xmlrpclib.ServerProxy(
            '%s/xmlrpc/2/common' % srv)
        self.api = xmlrpclib.ServerProxy(
            '%s/xmlrpc/2/object' % srv)
        self.uid = common.authenticate(db, user, pwd, {})
        self.pwd = pwd
        self.db = db
        self.model = 'note.note'
```

Here we store all the information needed in the created object to execute calls on a model: the API reference, `uid`, password, database name, and the model to use.

Next, we will define a helper method to execute the calls. It takes advantage of the object stored data to provide a smaller function signature, as shown next:

```
def execute(self, method, arg_list, kwarg_dict=None):
    return self.api.execute_kw(
        self.db, self.uid, self.pwd, self.model,
        method, arg_list, kwarg_dict or {})
```

Now we can use it to implement the higher level `get()` and `set()` methods.

The `get()` method will accept an optional list of IDs to retrieve. If none are listed, all records will be returned:

```
def get(self, ids=None):
    domain = [('id',' in', ids)] if ids else []
    fields = ['id', 'name']
    return self.execute('search_read', [domain, fields])
```

The `set()` method will have the task text to write, and an optional ID as arguments. If ID is not provided, a new record will be created. It returns the ID of the record written or created, as shown here:

```
def set(self, text, id=None):
    if id:
        self.execute('write', [[id], {'name': text}])
    else:
        vals = {'name': text, 'user_id': self.uid}
        id = self.execute('create', [vals])
    return id
```

Let's end the file with a small piece of test code that will be executed if we run the Python file:

```
if __name__ == '__main__':
    srv, db = 'http://localhost:8069', 'todo'
    user, pwd = 'admin', 'admin'
    api = NoteAPI(srv, db, user, pwd)
    from pprint import pprint
    pprint(api.get())
```

If we run the Python script, we should see the content of our to-do tasks printed out. Now that we have a simple wrapper around our Odoo backend, let's deal with the desktop user interface.

Creating the GUI

Our goal here was to learn to write the interface between an external application and the Odoo server, and this was done in the previous section. But it would be a shame not to go the extra step and actually make it available to the end user.

To keep the setup as simple as possible, we will use Tkinter to implement the graphical user interface. Since it is part of the standard library, it does not require any additional installation. It is not our goal to explain how Tkinter works, so we will be short on an explanation of it.

Each **task** should have a small yellow window on the desktop. These windows will have a single **text** widget. Pressing *Ctrl* + *N* will open a new note, and pressing *Ctrl* + *S* will write the content of the current note to the Odoo server.

Now, alongside the `note_api.py` file, create a new `note_gui.py` file. It will first import the Tkinter modules and widgets we will use, and then the `NoteAPI` class, as shown in the following:

```
from Tkinter import Text, Tk
import tkMessageBox
from note_api import NoteAPI
```

If the preceding code errors with `ImportError: No module named _tkinter, please install the python-tk package`, that means additional libraries are needed on your system. On Ubuntu you would need to run the following command:

```
$ sudo apt-get install python-tk
```

Next we create our own Text widget derived from the Tkinter one. When creating an instance, it will expect an API reference, to use for the `save` action, and also the task's text and ID, as shown in the following:

```
class NoteText(Text):
    def __init__(self, api, text='', id=None):
        self.master = Tk()
        self.id = id
        self.api = api
        Text.__init__(self, self.master, bg='#f9f3a9',
                      wrap='word', undo=True)
        self.bind('<Control-n>', self.create)
        self.bind('<Control-s>', self.save)
        if id:
            self.master.title('#%d' % id)
        self.delete('1.0', 'end')
        self.insert('1.0', text)
        self.master.geometry('220x235')
        self.pack(fill='both', expand=1)
```

The `Tk()` constructor creates a new UI window and the text widget places itself inside it, so that creating a new `NoteText` instance automatically opens a desktop window.

Next, we will implement the `create` and `save` actions. The `create` action opens a new empty window, but it will be stored in the server only when a `save` action performed. Here is the corresponding code:

```
def create(self, event=None):
    NoteText(self.api, '')

def save(self, event=None):
    text = self.get('1.0', 'end')
    self.id = self.api.set(text, self.id)
    tkMessageBox.showinfo('Info', 'Note %d Saved.' % self.id)
```

The `save` action can be performed either on existing or on new tasks, but there is no need to worry about that here since those cases are already handled by the `set()` method of `NoteAPI`.

Finally, we will add the code that retrieves and creates all note windows when the program is started, as shown in the following code:

```
if __name__ == '__main__':
    srv, db = 'http://localhost:8069', 'todo'
    user, pwd = 'admin', 'admin'
    api = NoteAPI(srv, db, user, pwd)
    for note in api.get():
        x = NoteText(api, note['name'], note['id'])
    x.master.mainloop()
```

The last command runs `mainloop()` on the last note window created, to start waiting for window events.

This is a very basic application, but the point here is to make an example of interesting ways to leverage the Odoo RPC API.

Introducing the ERPpeek client

ERPpeek is a versatile tool that can be used both as an interactive **Command-line Interface** (**CLI**) and as a **Python library**, with a more convenient API than the one provided by `xmlrpclib`. It is available from the PyPi index and can be installed with the following:

```
$ pip install -U erppeek
```

On a Unix system, if you are installing it system wide, you might need to prepend `sudo` to the command.

The ERPpeek API

The `ERPpeek` library provides a programming interface, wrapping around `xmlrpclib`, which is similar to the programming interface we have for the server-side code.

Our point here is to provide a glimpse of what the `ERPpeek` library has to offer, and not to provide a full explanation of all its features.

We can start by reproducing our first steps with `xmlrpclib` using the `erppeek` as follows:

```
>>> import erppeek
>>> api = erppeek.Client('http://localhost:8069', 'todo','admin', 'admin')
>>> api.common.version()
>>> api.count('res.partner', [])
>>> api.search('res.partner', [('country_id', '=', 'be'),
('parent_id', '!=', False)])
>>> api.read('res.partner', [44], ['id', 'name', 'parent_id'])
```

As you can see, the API calls use fewer arguments and are similar to the server-side counterparts.

But `ERPpeek` doesn't stops here, and also provides a representation for models. We have the following two alternative ways to get an instance for a model, either using the `model()` method or accessing it as a camel case attribute name:

```
>>> m = api.model('res.partner')
>>> m = api.ResPartner
```

Now we can perform actions on that model as follows:

```
>>> m.count([('name', 'like', 'Packt%')])
1
>>> m.search([('name', 'like', 'Packt%')])
[44]
```

It also provides client-side object representation for records as follows:

```
>>> recs = m.browse([('name', 'like', 'Packt%')])
>>> recs
<RecordList 'res.partner,[44]'>
>>> recs.name
['Packt Publishing']
```

As you can see, `erppeek` library goes a long way from plain `xmlrpclib`, and makes it possible to write code that can be reused server side with little or no modification.

The ERPpeek CLI

Not only can `erppeek` library be used as a Python library, it is also a CLI that can be used to perform administrative actions on the server. Where the `odoo shell` command provided a local interactive session on the host server, `erppeek` library provides a remote interactive session on a client across the network.

Opening a command line, we can have a peek at the options available, as shown in the following:

```
$ erppeek --help
```

Let's see a sample session as follows:

```
$ erppeek --server='http://localhost:8069' -d todo -u admin
Usage (some commands):
    models(name)                    # List models matching pattern
    model(name)                     # Return a Model instance
(...)
Password for 'admin':
Logged in as 'admin'
todo >>> model('res.users').count()
3
todo >>> rec = model('res.partner').browse(43)
todo >>> rec.name
'Packt Publishing'
```

As you can see, a connection was made to the server, and the execution context provided a reference to the `model()` method to get model instances and perform actions on them.

The `erppeek.Client` instance used for the connection is also available through the `client` variable.

Notably, it provides an alternative to the web client to manage the add-on modules installed:

- `client.modules()`: lists modules available or installed
- `client.install()`: performs module installation
- `client.upgrade()`: performs module upgrades
- `client.uninstall()`: uninstalls modules

So, `erppeek` can also provide good service as a remote administration tool for Odoo servers.

Summary

Our goal for this chapter was to learn how the external API works and what it is capable of. We started exploring it using a simple Python XML-RPC client, but the external API can be used from any programming language. In fact, the official docs provide code examples for Java, PHP, and Ruby.

There are a number of libraries to handle XML-RPC or JSON-RPC, some generic and some specific for use with Odoo. We tried not to point out any libraries in particular, except for `erppeek`, since it is not only a proven wrapper for the Odoo/OpenERP XML-RPC but because it is also an invaluable tool for remote server management and inspection.

Until now, we used our Odoo server instances for development and tests. But to have a production grade server, there are additional security and optimization configurations that need to be done. In the next chapter, we will focus on them.

13
Deployment Checklist – Going Live

In this chapter, you will learn how to prepare your Odoo server for use in a production environment.

There are many possible strategies and tools that can be used to deploy and manage an Odoo production server. We will guide you through one way of doing it.

This is the server set up checklist that we will follow:

- Install dependencies and a dedicated user to run the server
- Install Odoo from the source
- Set up the Odoo configuration file
- Set up multiprocessing workers
- Set up the Odoo system service
- Set up a reverse proxy with SSL support

Let's get started.

Available prebuilt packages

Odoo has a Debian/Ubuntu package available for installation. Using it, you get a working server process that automatically starts on system boot. This installation process is straightforward, and you can find all you need at `https://nightly.odoo.com`. You can also find the `rpm` builds for CentOS and the `.exe` installers there.

While this is an easy and convenient way to install Odoo, most integrators prefer to deploy and run version-controlled source code. This provides better control over what is deployed and makes it easier to manage changes and fixes once in production.

Installing dependencies

When using a Debian distribution, by default your login is `root` with administrator powers, and your command prompt shows `#`. When using Ubuntu, logging with the `root` account is disabled, and the initial user configured during the installation process is a *sudoer*, meaning that it is allowed to use the `sudo` command to run commands with root privileges.

First, we should update the package index, and then perform an upgrade to make sure all installed programs are up to date:

```
$ sudo apt-get update
$ sudo apt-get upgrade -y
```

Next, we will install the PostgreSQL database, and make our user a database superuser:

```
$ sudo apt-get install postgresql -y
$ sudo su -c "createuser -s $(whoami)" postgres
```

We will be running Odoo from source, but before that we need to install the required dependencies. These are the Debian packages required:

```
$ sudo apt-get install git python-pip python2.7-dev -y
$ sudo apt-get install libxml2-dev libxslt1-dev libevent-dev \
libsasl2-dev libldap2-dev libpq-dev libpng12-dev libjpeg-dev \
poppler-utils node-less node-clean-css -y
```

We should not forget to install `wkhtmltox`, which is needed to print reports:

```
$ wget
http://nightly.odoo.com/extra/wkhtmltox-0.12.1.2_linux-jessie-amd64.deb
$ sudo dpkg -i wkhtmltox-0.12.1.2_linux-jessie-amd64.deb
$ sudo apt-get -fy install
```

The installation instructions will report a missing dependencies error, but the last command forces the installation of those dependencies and correctly finishes the installation.

Now we are only missing the Python packages required by Odoo. Many of them also have Debian/Ubuntu system packages. The official Debian installation package uses them, and you can find the package names in the Odoo source code, in the `debian/control` file.

However, these Python dependencies can be also installed directly from the **Python Package Index** (**PyPI**). This is friendlier for those who prefer to install Odoo in `virtualenv`. The required package list is in the Odoo's `requirements.txt` file, as is usual for Python-based projects. We can install them with these commands:

```
$ sudo -H pip install --upgrade pip  # Ensure pip latest version
$ wget https://raw.githubusercontent.com/odoo/odoo/10.0/requirements.txt
$ sudo -H pip install -r requirements.txt
```

Now that we have all dependencies installed, database server, system packages, and Python packages, we can install Odoo.

Preparing a dedicated system user

A good security practice is to run Odoo using a dedicated user, with no special privileges on the system.

We need to create the system and database users for that. We can name them `odoo-prod`, for example:

```
$ sudo adduser --disabled-password --gecos "Odoo" odoo
$ sudo su -c "createuser odoo" postgres
$ createdb --owner=odoo odoo-prod
```

Here, `odoo` is the username and `odoo-prod` is the name of the database supporting our Odoo instance.

Note that these are regular users without any administration privileges. A home directory is automatically created for the new system user. In this example, it is `/home/odoo`, and the user can refer to its own home directory with the ~ shortcut symbol. We will use it for that user's Odoo specific configurations and files.

We can open a session as this user using the following command:

```
$ sudo su odoo
```

The `exit` command terminates that session and returns to our original user.

Installing from the source code

Sooner or later, your server will need upgrades and patches. A version controlled repository can be of great help when the time comes. We use `git` to get our code from a repository, just like we did to install the development environment.

Next, we will impersonate the `odoo` user and download the code into its home directory:

```
$ sudo su odoo
$ git clone https://github.com/odoo/odoo.git /home/odoo/odoo-10.0 -b 10.0
--depth=1
```

The `-b` option makes sure that we get the right branch, and the `--depth=1` option ignores the change history and retrieves only the latest code revision, making the download much smaller and faster.

Git will surely be an invaluable tool to manage the versions of your Odoo deployments. We just scratched the surface of what can be done to manage code versions. If you're not already familiar with Git, it's worth learning more about it. A good starting point is `http://git-scm.com/doc`.

By now we should have everything needed to run Odoo from source. We can check that it starts correctly and then exit from the dedicated user's session:

```
$ /home/odoo/odoo-10.0/odoo-bin --help
$ exit
```

Next, we will set up some system-level files and directories to be used by the system service.

Setting up the configuration file

Adding the `--save` option when starting an Odoo server saves the configuration used to the `~/.odoorc` file. We can use the file as a starting point for our server configuration, which will be stored at `/etc/odoo`, as shown in the following code:

```
$ sudo su -c "~/odoo-10.0/odoo-bin -d odoo-prod --save --stop-after-init"
odoo
```

This will have the configuration parameters to be used by our server instance.

The former `.openerp_serverrc` config file is still supported, and used if found. This can cause some confusion when setting up Odoo 10 in a machine that was also used to run previous Odoo versions. On this case the `--save` option might be updating the `.openerp_serverrc` file instead of `.odoorc`.

Next, we need to place the config file in the expected location:

```
$ sudo mkdir /etc/odoo
$ sudo cp /home/odoo/.odoorc /etc/odoo/odoo.conf
$ sudo chown -R odoo /etc/odoo
```

We should also create the directory where the Odoo service will store its log files. This is expected to be somewhere inside `/var/log`:

```
$ sudo mkdir /var/log/odoo
$ sudo chown odoo /var/log/odoo
```

Now we should make sure that a few important parameters are configured. Here are suggested values for the most important ones:

```
[options]
addons_path = /home/odoo/odoo-10.0/odoo/addons, /home/odoo/odoo-10.0/addons
admin_passwd = False
db_user = odoo-prod
dbfilter = ^odoo-prod$
logfile = /var/log/odoo/odoo-prod.log
proxy_mode = True
without_demo = True
workers = 3
xmlrpc_port = 8069
```

Let's explain them:

- `addons_path` is a comma-separated list of the paths where add-on modules will be looked up. It is read from left to right, with the leftmost directories having a higher priority.
- `admin_passwd` is the master password to access the web client database management functions. It's critical to set this with a strong password or, even better, to set it to `False` to deactivate the function.
- `db_user` the database instance to initialize during the server startup sequence.

- `dbfilter` is a filter for the databases to be made accessible. It is a Python-interpreted regex expression. For the user to not be prompted to select a database, and for unauthenticated URLs to work properly, it should be set with `^dbname$`, for example, `dbfilter=^odoo-prod$`. It supports the `%h` and `%d` placeholders, that are replaced by the HTTP request hostname and subdomain name.
- `logfile` is where the server log should be written. For system services the expected location is somewhere inside `/var/log`. If left empty, or set to `False`, the log print to standard output instead.
- `proxy_mode` should be set to `True` when Odoo is accessed behind a reverse proxy, as we will do.
- `without_demo` should be set to `True` in production environments so that new databases do not have demo data on them.
- `workers` with a value of two or more enables multiprocessing mode. We will discuss this in more detail in a moment.
- `xmlrpc_port` is the port number at which the server will listen. By default, port `8069` is used.

The following parameters can also be helpful:

- `data_dir` is the path where session data and attachment files are stored. Remember to have backups on it
- `xmlrpc-interface` sets the addresses that will be listened to. By default, it listens to all `0.0.0.0`, but when using a reverse proxy, it can be set to `127.0.0.1` in order to respond only to local requests

We can check the effect of the settings made by running the server with the `-c` or `--config` option as follows:

```
$ sudo su -c "~/odoo-10.0/odoo-bin -c /etc/odoo/odoo.conf" odoo
```

Running Odoo with the above settings won't display any output to the console, since it is being written to the log file defined in the configuration file. To follow what is going on with the server we need to open another terminal window, and run there:

```
$ sudo tail -f /var/log/odoo/odoo-prod.log
```

If is also possible to use the configuration file and still force the log output to be printed to the console, by adding the `--logfile=False` option, like this:

```
$ sudo su -c "~/odoo-10.0/odoo-bin -c /etc/odoo/odoo.conf --logfile=False"
odoo
```

Multiprocessing workers

A production instance is expected to handle a significant workload. By default, the server runs one process and can use only one CPU core for processing, because of the Python language GIL. However, a multiprocess mode is available so that concurrent requests can be handled. The option `workers=N` sets the number of worker processes to use. As a guideline, you can try setting it to `1+2*P`, where `P` is the number of processors. The best setting to use needs to be tuned for each case, since it depends on the server load and what other load intensive services are running on the server, such as PostgreSQL.

It is better to set workers too high for the load than too low. The minimum should be 6 due to the parallel connections used by most browsers, and the maximum is generally be limited by the amount of RAM on the machine.

There a few `limit-*` config parameters to tune the workers. Workers are recycled when they reach these limits—the corresponding process is stopped, a new one is started. This protects the server from memory leaks and from particular processes overloading the server resources.

The official documentation already provides good advice on the tuning of the worker parameters, and you may refer to it for more details, at `https://www.odoo.com/documentation/10.0/setup/deploy.html`.

Setting up as a system service

Next, we will want to set up Odoo as a system service and have it started automatically when the system boots.

In Ubuntu/Debian, the `init` system is responsible, to start services. Historically, Debian (and derived operating systems) has used `sysvinit` and Ubuntu has used a compatible system called `Upstart`. Recently, this has changed, and the `init` system used in the latest version is now `systemd`.

This means that there are two different ways to install a system service, and you need to pick the correct one depending on the version of your operating system.

On the last Ubuntu stable version, 16.04, we should be using `systemd`. But older versions such as 14.04 are still used in many cloud providers, so there is a good chance that you might need to use it.

To check if `systemd` is used in your system try this command:

```
$ man init
```

This opens the documentation for the currently used `init` system, and you will be able to check what is being used.

Creating a systemd service

If the operating system you are using is recent, such as Debian 8 or Ubuntu 16.04, you should be using `systemd` for `init` system.

To add a new service to the system, we just need to create a file describing it. Create a `/lib/systemd/system/odoo.service` file with the following content:

```
[Unit]
Description=Odoo
After=postgresql.service

[Service]
Type=simple
User=odoo
Group=odoo
ExecStart=/home/odoo/odoo-10.0/odoo-bin -c /etc/odoo/odoo.conf

[Install]
WantedBy=multi-user.target
```

Next, we need to register the new service:

```
$ sudo systemctl enable odoo.service
```

To start this new service use following command:

```
$ sudo systemctl odoo start
```

And to check its status run this:

```
$ sudo systemctl odoo status
```

Finally, if you want to stop it, use this command:

```
$ sudo systemctl odoo stop
```

Creating an Upstart/sysvinit service

If you are using an older operating system, such as Debian 7, Ubuntu 15.04, or even 14.04, chances are that your system is `sysvinit` on `Upstart`. For this purpose, both should behave the same way. Many cloud VPS services are still based on Ubuntu 14.04 images, so this might be a scenario you may encounter when deploying your Odoo server.

Many cloud VPS services are still based on Ubuntu 14.04 images, so this might be a scenario you may encounter when deploying your Odoo server.

The Odoo source code includes an `init` script used for the Debian packaged distribution. We can use it as our service `init` script with minor modifications, as follows:

```
$ sudo cp /home/odoo/odoo-10.0/debian/init /etc/init.d/odoo
$ sudo chmod +x /etc/init.d/odoo
```

At this point, you might want to check the content of the `init` script. The key parameters are assigned to variables at the top of the file. A sample is as follows:

```
PATH=/sbin:/bin:/usr/sbin:/usr/bin:/usr/local/bin
DAEMON=/usr/bin/odoo
NAME=odoo
DESC=odoo
CONFIG=/etc/odoo/odoo.conf
LOGFILE=/var/log/odoo/odoo-server.log
PIDFILE=/var/run/${NAME}.pid
USER=odoo
```

These variables should be adequate and we will prepare the rest of the set up with their default values in mind. But of course, you can change them to better suit your needs.

The `USER` variable is the system user under which the server will run. We have already created the expected `odoo` user.

The `DAEMON` variable is the path to the server executable. Our actual executable to start Odoo is in a different location, but we can create a symbolic link to it:

```
$ sudo ln -s /home/odoo/odoo-10.0/odoo-bin /usr/bin/odoo
$ sudo chown -h odoo /usr/bin/odoo
```

The `CONFIG` variable is the configuration file to use. In a previous section, we created a configuration file in the default expected location: `/etc/odoo/odoo.conf`.

Finally, the `LOGFILE` variable is the directory where log files should be stored. The expected directory is `/var/log/odoo` that we created when we were defining the configuration file.

Now we should be able to start and stop our Odoo service as follows:

```
$ sudo /etc/init.d/odoo start
Starting odoo: ok
```

Stopping the service is done in a similar way, as shown in the following:

```
$ sudo /etc/init.d/odoo stop
Stopping odoo: ok
```

In Ubuntu, the `service` command can also be used:

```
$ sudo service odoo start
$ sudo service odoo status
$ sudo service odoo config
```

We now only need to make this service start automatically on system boot:

```
$ sudo update-rc.d odoo defaults
```

After this, when we reboot our server, the Odoo service should be started automatically and with no errors. It's a good time to check that all is working as expected.

Checking the Odoo service from the command line

At this point, we could confirm if our Odoo instance is up and responding to requests.

If Odoo is running properly, we should now be able to get a response from it and see no errors in the log file. We can check inside the server if Odoo is responding to HTTP requests using the following command:

```
$ curl http://localhost:8069
<html><head><script>window.location = '/web' +
location.hash;</script></head></html>
```

And to see what is in the log file we can use the following:

$ sudo less /var/log/odoo/odoo-server.log In case you are just starting with Linux, you will like to know that you can follow what is going on in the log file using tail -f:

```
$ sudo tail -f /var/log/odoo/odoo-server.log
```

Using a reverse proxy

While Odoo itself can serve web pages, it is strongly recommended to have a reverse proxy in front of it. A reverse proxy acts as an intermediary managing the traffic between the clients sending requests and the Odoo servers responding to them. Using a reverse proxy has several benefits.

On the security side, it can do the following:

- Handle (and enforce) HTTPS protocols to encrypt traffic
- Hide the internal network characteristics
- Act as an *application firewall* limiting the URLs accepted for processing

And on the performance side, it can provide significant improvements:

- Cache static content, thus reducing the load on the Odoo servers
- Compress content to speed up loading times
- Act as a load balancer, distributing load between several servers

Apache is a popular option to use as a reverse proxy. Nginx is a recent alternative with good technical arguments. Here, we will choose to use Nginx as a reverse proxy and show how it can be used to perform the security and performance side functions mentioned here.

Setting up Nginx for reverse proxy

First, we should install Nginx. We want it to listen on the default HTTP ports, so we should make sure they are not already taken by some other service. Performing this command should result in an error, as follows:

```
$ curl http://localhost
curl: (7) Failed to connect to localhost port 80: Connection refused
```

If not, you should disable or remove that service to allow Nginx to use those ports. For example, to stop an existing Apache server you should use this command:

```
$ sudo service apache2 stop
```

Or better yet, you should consider removing it from your system, or reconfigure it to listen on another port, so the HTTP and HTTPS ports (`80` and `443`) are free to be used by Nginx.

Now we can install Nginx, which is done in the expected way:

```
$ sudo apt-get install nginx
```

To confirm that it is working correctly, we should see a **Welcome to nginx** page when visiting the server address with a browser or using `curl http://localhost` inside our server.

Nginx configuration files follow the same approach as Apache: they are stored in `/etc/nginx/available-sites/` and activated by adding a symbolic link in `/etc/nginx/enabled-sites/`. We should also disable the default configuration provided by the Nginx installation, as follows:

```
$ sudo rm /etc/nginx/sites-enabled/default
$ sudo touch /etc/nginx/sites-available/odoo
$ sudo ln -s  /etc/nginx/sites-available/odoo /etc/nginx/sites-enabled/odoo
```

Using an editor, such as `nano` or `vi`, we should edit our Nginx configuration file as follows:

```
$ sudo nano /etc/nginx/sites-available/odoo
```

First, we add the upstreams, and the backend servers Nginx will redirect traffic to the Odoo server in our case, which is listening on port `8069`, as follows:

```
upstream backend-odoo {
  server 127.0.0.1:8069;
}
server {
  location / {
    proxy_pass http://backend-odoo;
  }
}
```

To test if the edited configuration is correct, use the following command:

```
$ sudo nginx -t
```

If you find errors, confirm the configuration file is correctly typed. Also, a common problem is for the default HTTP to be taken by another service, such as Apache or the default Nginx website. Double-check the instructions given before to make sure that this is not the case, then restart Nginx. After this, we can have Nginx to reload the new configuration as follows:

```
$ sudo /etc/init.d/nginx reload
```

We can now confirm that Nginx is redirecting traffic to the backend Odoo server:

```
$ curl http://localhost
<html><head><script>window.location = '/web' +
location.hash;</script></head></html>
```

Enforcing HTTPS

Next, we should install a certificate to be able to use SSL. To create a self-signed certificate, follow the following steps:

```
$ sudo mkdir /etc/nginx/ssl && cd /etc/nginx/ssl
$ sudo openssl req -x509  -newkey rsa:2048 -keyout key.pem -out cert.pem -
days 365 -nodes
$ sudo chmod a-wx *            # make files read only
$ sudo chown www-data:root *   # access only to www-data group
```

This creates an `ssl/` directory inside the `/etc/nginx/` directory and creates a passwordless self-signed SSL certificate. When running the `openssl` command, some additional information will be asked, and a certificate and key files are generated. Finally, the ownership of these files is given to the user `www-data` used to run the web server.

Using a self-signed certificate can pose some security risks, such as man-in-the-middle attacks, and may even not be allowed by some browsers. For a robust solution, you should use a certificate signed by a recognized certificate authority. This is particularly important if you are running a commercial or e-commerce website.

Now that we have an SSL certificate, we are ready to configure Nginx to use it.

To enforce HTTPS, we will redirect all HTTP traffic to it. Replace the `server` directive we defined previously with the following:

```
server {
  listen 80;
  add_header Strict-Transport-Security max-age=2592000;
  rewrite ^/.*$ https://$host$request_uri? permanent;
}
```

If we reload the Nginx configuration now and access the server with a web browser, we will see that the `http://` address will be converted into an `https://` address.

But it won't return any content before we configure the HTTPS service properly, by adding the following server configuration:

```
server {
  listen 443 default;
  # ssl settings
  ssl on;
  ssl_certificate     /etc/nginx/ssl/cert.pem;
  ssl_certificate_key /etc/nginx/ssl/key.pem;
  keepalive_timeout 60;
```

```
      # proxy header and settings
      proxy_set_header Host $host;
      proxy_set_header X-Real-IP $remote_addr;
      proxy_set_header X-Forwarded-For $proxy_add_x_forwarded_for;
      proxy_set_header X-Forwarded-Proto $scheme;
      proxy_redirect off;
      location / {
        proxy_pass http://backend-odoo;
      }
    }
```

This will listen to the HTTPS port and use the `/etc/nginx/ssl/` certificate files to encrypt the traffic. We also add some information to the request header to let the Odoo backend service know it's being proxied.

For security reasons, it's important for Odoo to make sure the `proxy_mode` parameter is set to `True`. The reason for this is that, when Nginx acts as a proxy, all request will appear to come from the server itself instead of the remote IP address. Setting the `X-Forwarded-For` header in the proxy and enabling `--proxy-mode` solves that. But enabling `--proxy-mode` without forcing this header at the proxy level would allow anyone to spoof their remote address.

At the end, the `location` directive defines that all request are passed to the `backend-odoo` upstream.

Reload the configuration, and we should have our Odoo service working through HTTPS, as shown in the following commands:

```
$ sudo nginx -t
nginx: the configuration file /etc/nginx/nginx.conf syntax is ok
nginx: configuration file /etc/nginx/nginx.conf test is successful
$ sudo service nginx reload
* Reloading nginx configuration nginx
...done.
$ curl -k https://localhost
<html><head><script>window.location = '/web' +
location.hash;</script></head></html>
```

The last output confirms that the Odoo web client is being served over HTTPS.

For the particular case where an Odoo POSBox is being used, we need to add an exception for the `/pos/` URL to be able to access it in HTTP mode. The POSBox is located in the local network but does not have SSL enabled. If the POS interface is loaded in HTTPS it won't be able to contact the POSBox at all.

Nginx optimizations

Now, it is time for some fine-tuning of the Nginx settings. They are recommended to enable response buffering and data compression that should improve the speed of the website. We also set a specific location for the logs.

The following configurations should be added inside the server listening on port `443`, for example, just after the proxy definitions:

```
# odoo log files
access_log /var/log/nginx/odoo-access.log;
error_log  /var/log/nginx/odoo-error.log;
# increase proxy buffer size
proxy_buffers 16 64k;
proxy_buffer_size 128k;
# force timeouts if the backend dies
proxy_next_upstream error timeout invalid_header http_500  http_502
http_503;
# enable data compression
gzip on;
gzip_min_length 1100;
gzip_buffers 4 32k;
gzip_types text/plain text/xml text/css text/less application/x-javascript
application/xml application/json application/javascript;
gzip_vary on;
```

We can also activate static content caching for faster responses to the types of requests mentioned in the preceding code example and to avoid their load on the Odoo server. After the `location /` section, add the following second location section:

```
location ~* /web/static/ {
  # cache static data
  proxy_cache_valid 200 60m;
  proxy_buffering on;
  expires 864000;
  proxy_pass http://backend-odoo;
}
```

With this, the static data is cached for 60 minutes. Further requests on those requests in that interval will be responded to directly by Nginx from the cache.

Long polling

Long polling is used to support the instant messaging app, and when using multiprocessing workers, it is handled on a separate port, which is `8072` by default.

For our reverse proxy, this means that the long polling requests should be passed to this port. To support this, we need to add a new upstream to our Nginx configuration, as shown in the following code:

```
upstream backend-odoo-im { server 127.0.0.1:8072; }
```

Next, we should add another location to the server handling the HTTPS requests, as shown in the following code:

```
location /longpolling { proxy_pass http://backend-odoo-im;}
```

With these settings, Nginx should pass these requests to the proper Odoo server port.

Server and module updates

Once the Odoo server is ready and running, there will come a time when you need to install updates on Odoo. This involves two steps: first, to get the new versions of the source code (server or modules), and second, to install them.

If you have followed the approach described in the *Installing from the source code* section, we can fetch and test the new versions in the staging repository. It is strongly advised that you make a copy of the production database and test the upgrade on it. If `odoo-prod` is your production database, this could be done with the following commands:

```
$ dropdb odoo-stage; createdb odoo-stage
$ pg_dump odoo-prod | psql -d odoo-stage
$ sudo su odoo
$ cd ~/.local/share/Odoo/filestore/
$ cp -al odoo-prod odoo-stage
$ ~/odoo-10.0/odoo-bin -d odoo-stage --xmlrpc-port=8080 -c
/etc/odoo/odoo.conf
$ exit
```

If everything goes OK, it should be safe to perform the upgrade on the production service. Remember to make a note of the current version Git reference in order to be able to roll back by checking out this version again. Keeping a backup of the database before performing the upgrade is also highly advised.

The database copy can be made in much faster way, using the following `createdb` command:

```
$ createdb --template odoo-prod odoo-stage
```

The caveat here is that for it to run there can't be any open connections to the odoo-prod database, so the Odoo server needs to be stopped to perform the copy.

After this, we can pull the new versions to the production repository using Git and complete the upgrade, as shown here:

```
$ sudo su odoo
$ cd ~/odoo-10.0
$ git pull
$ exit
$ sudo service odoo restart
```

Regarding the Odoo release policy, no minor versions are released anymore. GitHub branches are expected to represent the latest stable version. The nightly builds are considered the latest official stable release.

On the update frequency, there is no point in updating too frequently, but also not to wait one year between updates. Performing an update every few months should be fine. And usually a server restart will be enough to enable to code updates, and module upgrades shouldn't be necessary.

Of course, if you need a specific bug fix, an earlier update should probably be made. Also remember to watch out for security bugs disclosures on the public channels—GitHub Issues or the Community mailing list. As part of the service, enterprise contract customers can expect early email notifications of this type of issues.

Summary

In this chapter, you learned about the additional steps to set up and run Odoo in a Debian-based production server. The most important settings in the configuration file were visited, and you learned how to take advantage of the multiprocessing mode.

For improved security and scalability, you also learned how to use Nginx as a reverse proxy in front of our Odoo server processes.

This should cover the essentials of what is needed to run an Odoo server and provide a stable and secure service to your users.

To learn more about Odoo you should also look at the official documentation, at `https://www.odoo.com/documentation`. Some topics are covered in more detail there, and you will also find topics not covered in this book.

There are also other published books on Odoo you might also find useful. Pack Publishing has a few in its catalog, and in particular the *Odoo Development Cookbook* provides more advanced material, covering more topics not discussed here.

And finally, Odoo is an open source product with a vibrant community. Getting involved, asking questions and contributing is a great way not only to learn but also to build a business network. On this we can't help mentioning the **Odoo Community Association** (**OCA**), promoting collaboration and quality open source code. You can learn more about it at `odoo-comunity.org`.

Index

D

N

O

P

Q

R

U

V

W

X

Y

www.ingramcontent.com/pod-product-compliance
Lightning Source LLC
LaVergne TN
LVHW081336050326
832903LV00024B/1172
* 9 7 8 1 7 8 5 8 8 4 8 8 7 *